Criminal Justice and Mental Health

Jada Hector • David Khey

Criminal Justice and Mental Health

An Overview for Students

 Springer

Jada Hector
New Orleans, LA, USA

David Khey
University of Louisiana
Lafayette, LA, USA

ISBN 978-3-319-76441-2   ISBN 978-3-319-76442-9   (eBook)
https://doi.org/10.1007/978-3-319-76442-9

Library of Congress Control Number: 2018934430

Printed on acid-free paper

This Springer imprint is published by the registered company Springer International Publishing AG part of Springer Nature.
The registered company address is: Gewerbestrasse 11, 6330 Cham, Switzerland

Contents

About the Authors

Jada Hector is an accomplished mental health clinician with an array of experience from treating severe mental illness, trauma, substance use and abuse, to everyday mental health struggles shared by Americans and their loved ones. These days, Ms. Hector lends those experiences to help local and state governments remedy gaps in mental health surveillance, treatment, and recovery options, create better policy, and heal communities. She is a graduate of the Louisiana State University with a master's degree in counseling and is a Licensed Professional Counselor in the state of Louisiana. She also attended B.I. Moody III College of Business Administration at the University of Louisiana at Lafayette where she earned an undergraduate degree in business with a concentration in marketing.

David Khey has focused his research on a few areas in criminology, criminal justice, and forensic science. In particular, he is currently investigating mental health policy, drug policy, control, toxicology, chemistry, and addiction, as well as the changing evidentiary power of forensic science technologies. Born and raised in South Florida during the late 1970s and early 1980s, drug policy and enforcement quickly piqued his interest. In this topical area, Dr. Khey has presented research on drug and alcohol use/abuse and provided policy analysis to local and state officials in Florida. A highlight of this work includes an invitation to address the Governor's Office Drug Policy Advisory Council in 2007. Soon after moving to Louisiana at a time when divestments in mental health services were at its modern day peak, mental health policy quickly became one of his key areas of focus and remains that way to this day. Dr. Khey holds an advanced degree in pharmacy and pharmaceutical sciences with a concentration in forensic drug chemistry and doctorate in criminology, law, and society from the University of Florida.

Chapter 1
Mental Illness, Then and Now

Of all the calamities to which humanity is subject, none is so dreadful as insanity.... All experience shows that insanity seasonably treated is as certainly curable as a cold or a fever.—Dorothea Dix

Mental illness impacts millions of people as well as their loved ones. It can take many forms; it can ebb and flow throughout the life course; it can be the root of a life of suffering; yet, in most cases, it does not have to be a life sentence of misery. The intersection of *crime* and *mental health* has been a long-standing issue spanning across many decades, even centuries. In more recent times, professionals in the United States have begun to detail the "cracks" within the criminal justice system with better precision, especially in relation to inmates with mental health concerns. Unfortunately, despite the recognition of these cracks and their potential "fixes," the implementation of change continues to be a struggle. The federal system, state system, and local county/parish jail system each have their own obstacles to overcome. Furthermore, these systems do not always work together for the common cause of public health for various reasons. Even further, integrating the mental health system into the criminal justice system at these levels can at times seem impossible; yet, the capacity for coordinated change has never been more possible. This text serves to educate students and professionals not only on the system of interconnected cracks, but also on the recommendations and innovations set forth by different interests at varying levels of the said system. All of the answers may not have been discovered yet, but the impetus for change is on the horizon for those with mental illness in the criminal justice system. The hopes of change begin with discussion on the problems, particularly in a historical context. This text seeks to be that vehicle for change in the future to ensure the care and safety of justice-involved individuals with mental illness.

© Springer International Publishing AG, part of Springer Nature 2018
J. Hector, D. Khey, *Criminal Justice and Mental Health*,
https://doi.org/10.1007/978-3-319-76442-9_1

1.1   A Brief History

Most detailed histories of American mental health care begin with a discussion of the vast abuses and subhuman conditions endured by those with mental illnesses in the pre-Civil War era. The plight of this vulnerable class came to light in the mid-nineteenth century primarily due to the tenacity of a woman named Dorothea Dix. In fact, it is her words that first underscore the issues of the "idiots" and the "insane," which were the most productive terms for people with mental illness available in the mid-1800s. Muckenhoupt's (2004) biography of Dix aptly describes how she "single-handedly created most of the 19th-century public institutions east of the Mississippi River that served people with mental illness" by being "unyielding and effective, a symbol of women's good works" (p. 7). In an era when the vast majority of women spent their time homemaking and serving a family, Dix never fit that mold; this, in part, allowed her to be an effective advocate for change.

1.1.1   The First Impetus for Change: Dorothea Dix

A brief explanation of Dix's life begins with a child born into a complicated family. The Dix family ascended into Bostonian wealth beginning with her grandfather, Elijah. Her father, Joseph, was the misfit of a rich family—a Harvard dropout and alcoholic with a temper who ended up marrying a woman from a less well-to-do family. This meant that Dorothea's branch of the family tree was considered a stain and an embarrassment—in other words, "the black sheep" of the family. After Elijah Dix died, he left his son Joseph with nothing while leaving Dorothea an annuity that would provide an income for her until she married (Muckenhoupt, 2004). It was this source of funds that would allow for her to run away from her parents and seek help from her grandmother, Dorothy. Madame Dix would eventually arrange for Dorothea to live with one of her well-to-do cousins. She would live there as a very independent teenager, and when she came of age, Dorothea would become an educator and operated her own schoolhouse. Ironically, she never had attended a single school in her life. She would also go on to write successfully, bringing additional income to support her independent lifestyle. Yet, it seemed Dorothea always wanted something more, just not a husband or a traditional female role. She would end up traveling Europe, turning her mind on to social justice, and bringing that passion back to America (Fig. 1.1).

The quintessential "spark" for Dix's advocacy for mental illness occurred by happenstance in the Spring of 1841. Back in Boston, Dix was offered a position to take over a Sunday school class at a local jail, the Middlesex County House of Correction (Muckenhoupt, 2004). It was here where Dix saw the suffering of "public drunks, poor men paying their debts by making shoes, and people who were mentally ill" (p. 42). She observed all of these men cramped in cold rooms without access to heat or fire. Dix first reported this issue to the warden who refused to build

Fig. 1.1 Portrait of Dorothea Dix. Courtesy of the US National Library of Medicine (2017)

a fire as it would be dangerous. Besides, he claimed, it did not seem necessary. Dix would then go to court on this matter. At the time, there was a state law requiring "a suitable and convenient apartment or receptacle for idiots and lunatic or insane persons, not furiously mad," (p. 42) which Dix would cite in her arguments for more humane treatment of inmates at the jail. The courts sided with Dix and ordered the warden to heat the cells. Quickly, she single-handedly created change, and this changed her life; this gave her a spark of inspiration and a taste for and reward of successful advocacy. Over the next few years, Dix would travel across the state visiting jails and prisons, cataloging what she witnessed. This culminated in a defining moment as an advocate for social justice for those with mental illness, *Memorial to the Legislature of Massachusetts,* delivered on January 19, 1843:

> About two years since leisure afforded opportunity and duty prompted me to visit several prisons and almshouses in the vicinity of this metropolis. I found, near Boston, in the jails and asylums for the poor, a numerous class brought into unsuitable connection with criminals and the general mass of paupers. I refer to idiots and insane persons, dwelling in circumstances not only adverse to their own physical and moral improvement, but productive of extreme disadvantages to all other persons brought into association with them....I shall be obliged to speak with great plainness, and to reveal many things revolting to the taste, and from which my woman's nature shrinks with peculiar sensitiveness.... *I tell what I have seen* - painful and shocking as the details often are - that from them you may feel more deeply the imperative obligation which lies upon you to prevent the possibility of a repetition or continuance of such outrages upon humanity.
>
> I proceed, gentlemen, briefly to call your attention to the *present* state of insane persons confined within this Commonwealth, in *cages, closets, cellars, stalls, pens! Chained, naked, beaten with rods,* and *lashed into obedience.*
>
> ...[F]ound the mistress, and was conducted to the place, which was called *"the home"* of the *forlorn* maniac, a young woman, exhibiting a condition of neglect and misery

blotting out the faintest idea of the comfort, and outraging every sentiment of decency. She had been, I learnt, "a respectable person, industrious and worthy. Disappointments and trials shook her mind, and, finally, laid prostrate reason and self-control. She became a maniac for life. She had been at Worcester Hospital for a considerable time, and had been returned as incurable." ...[T]here she stood with naked arms and disheveled hair; the unwashed frame invested with fragments of unclean garments, the air so extremely offensive, though ventilation was afforded on all sides save one, that it was possible to remain beyond a few moments without retreating for recovery to the outward air. Irritation of body, produced by utter filth and exposure, incited her to the horrid process of tearing off her skin by inches; her face, neck, and person, were thus disfigured to hideousness; she held up a fragment just rent off; to my exclamation of horror, the mistress replied, "oh, we can't help it; half the skin is off sometimes; we can do nothing with her; and it makes no difference what she eats, for she consumes her own filth as readily as food which is brought to her."

These words would soon culminate in the increased capacity of the Massachusetts state insane asylum in Worcester (Worcester State Hospital) as authorized through state legislation, with broad support by the state legislators. Importantly, the new laws shifted the care of the idiots, lunatics, and insane persons, not furiously mad, from local "caretakers" to state specialists with the hopes that this would lead to "moral treatment" and humane conditions. Dix would continue on to petition other state governments: New Jersey would open an asylum as ordered by the legislature in 1845, Illinois—its first—ordered in 1847, and North Carolina ordered in 1849. All of this eventually surmounted into the Bill for the Benefit of the Indigent Insane, a Federal bill that would earmark over 12 million acres of Federal land and resources to address the "newly" identified problem. US Congress would passionately shepherd it through the legislation process, only to have then President Franklin Pierce veto the bill, demanding this issue be relegated to individual states. Dix would end up traveling abroad after this defeat, continuing her efforts in other countries.

1.1.2 Moral Treatment Thrives and Declines

Yet, the momentum spearheaded by Dix was beyond reproach. Even in her absence, broad reform continued to develop. Dedicated institutions for individuals with mental illness blossomed in the post-Dix era, particularly those that offered forms of "moral treatment," an early progressive treatment modality developed in the Enlightenment in Europe. The American concept of *moral treatment* was championed by Benjamin Rush, a prominent medical doctor in Philadelphia (Trent, 2017). Rush's thought was that the root of mental illness was chaos of a modern life that, theoretically, could be treated in a hospital setting mainly by withdrawing someone from all of life's stressors under supervised medical care. While Rush used some provocative procedures—blood-letting and prolonged restraint in a "tranquilizer chair" (that he invented) being two of the more controversial—moral treatment was grounded in medical interventions seeking to soothe a patient in a comfortable setting, engage in exercise and conversation, and explore the individual needs of each individual under care (Fig. 1.2).

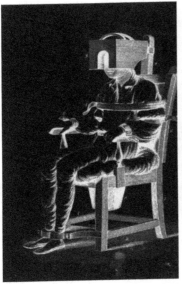

Fig. 1.2 A negative of Benjamin Rush's tranquilizer chair (left) and an image of Benjamin Rush (right), courtesy of the National Library of Medicine. A note from the NLM catalog regarding the tranquilizer chair: "A patent sitting in a chair; his body is immobilized by straps at the shoulders, arms, waist, and feet; a box-like apparatus is used to confine the head. There is a bucket attached beneath the seat"

Even with this progressive modality—which would eventually become a mainstay in the mental health care of the rich and powerful as it became perfected—the sciences of psychiatry and psychology were far too nascent to offer substantial care for this population. Outcomes were abysmal, breakthroughs were few and far between, and the growing body of mental health research reinforced a sense of pessimism. While this may not be surprising, it helps to consider that medical science figured out that surgical complications and deaths can be drastically reduced by sterilizing operator's hands in 1846 (Ignaz Semmelweis), the American Medical Association was established in 1847, crude medicines like morphine began to show marked medical utility in the mid-1850s, and the first modern American medical school (Johns Hopkins University School of Medicine) opened its doors in 1893 (Carter & Carter, 1994; Haller, 1981; Packard, 1901). But, while medicine continued to progress and grow rapidly, treatment for mental illness was stymied.

Muckenhoupt (2004) suggests that the progress Dix helped to influence hit a turning point when Pliny Earle published his research on the lack of success of mental health treatment, only affirming what most medical professionals of the era already had suspected. Nothing was working. Earle discovered that patients who were discharged and formally cleared as "sane" were consistently readmitted, casting doubt on the true number of "recoveries." This is one reason states began to divest in mental hospitals, layered with the consistent underlying and persistent stigma and lack of understanding of mental illness. Asylums gradually became overcrowded, dilapidated, and disorderly. Working in these state institutions never gained the prestige as did being a professional in the other medical sciences—*any* other medical science. Thus, the administrators of these facilities were not typically the best and brightest.

One can easily argue that this is the point where America has come full circle in the manner it treats the idiots and lunatics or insane persons and that policy simply changed the setting in which "treatment" was given—from jails and prisons to prison-like asylums. Further, these prison-like asylums, or "hospitals," concentrated stigma and rapidly became a place for a "new" class of people. It would not be a stretch of the imagination to conceive that this concentration of the problem of the mentally ill in these ghastly institutions only helped the eugenic movement of the early twentieth century to target this class of people for sterilization or complete elimination from the gene pool. Thankfully, this is not the path history takes us.

1.1.3   The Miracle Drugs

Finally, over a 100 years into this American story, a breakthrough occurred; research on chlorpromazine, known for its trade name Thorazine®, began to surface in the 1950s (see Fig. 1.3). The drug launched quickly from laboratory, to trial use, to widespread use, all during that same decade. Physicians quickly knew Thorazine® as a wonder drug for its abilities to breakthrough psychotic symptoms, so much that when they saw marked improvements in their patients, mental hospital doctors

Fig. 1.3 Thorazine® advertisement in the *Journal of American Psychiatry* in 1980. Courtesy of GSK. Reproduced with permission

would release them in droves—even without knowing the long-term efficacy or potential pitfall of these decisions. Just think, Thorazine® was first produced in a laboratory in 1950, showed significant promise in animal studies in early 1951, was released to physicians as a research drug in the late spring of 1951, and was documented to produce dramatic improvement in psychotic symptoms by the end of the year (Healy, 2009). By late 1957, psychiatrists Kris and Carmichael (1957) observed that "modern drug therapy has brought about a considerable increase in the number of patients returning to the community" in their follow-up study of 160 patients released from the New York metro area hospitals.

This New York study, as many others like it, vetted the viability of using drug therapy to treat diagnoses such as schizophrenia, "manic-depressive" or "manic disorders," alcohol psychosis, and "involutional psychosis." The prognosis seemed positive with the following caveats: (1) patients must be reevaluated by professionals often "not only in order to avoid unpleasant complications, but also to vary the dosage according to individual needs, taking into account increased stress situations which (sic) have to be faced by these patients outside the hospital," (2) patients with "enduring" conditions (e.g., chronic and severe mental illness) must receive maintenance dosages of Thorazine® to prevent recurrence of symptoms once the drug is discontinued, (3) physicians must ensure compliance with doctor's orders (particularly with taking the correct dose at the recommended intervals), and (4) physicians must evaluate the social situations that may trigger a return to the hospital. The last point they make is interesting regarding the social situations that may trigger relapse; Kris and Carmichael go on to suggest that Thorazine® may be the most potent and valuable "weapon" against mental illness, yet they want to make clear that when it fails to treat someone effectively, social factors should be to blame, not the drug.

Drugs like Thorazine® thrived in this scientific environment so eager for a breakthrough after decades of slow progress toward finding effective treatments for diseases that we were only beginning to understand. In fact, the drug revolution brought a renaissance of psychiatric treatment of mental illness, helping to vastly expand our knowledge of the topic at a quickened pace. In his history of therapeutic medicines, Healy noted, "the 1955 meeting of the American Psychiatric Association (APA) should have been dominated by Thorazine®. But while Thorazine® was on stage, the whispers in the wings were of an even newer drug, Miltown® (meprobamate) which was launched in the second half of 1955....By any reckoning, therefore, while Miltown® might never have made a splash elsewhere (outside of the United States), Thorazine's time at the center stage in American psychiatry should have been short. The fact that it survived the inroads of Miltown® and remained at the center of the scientific stage is compelling testimony to the recognition that chlorpromazine truly was a different drug" (98–99). He goes on to describe the amazement some experts had with Thorazine®; for example, one professional was so impressed that he took equity out of his house to buy stock in the pharmaceutical company manufacturing the drug.

Thus, Thorazine® exploded onto therapeutic use in the United States, and American practitioners were more eager than their European counterparts to push the limits of the drug, increase dosage, and begin pursuing advancing outpatient care in the community now that severe symptoms were being significantly allayed.

And while there were many success stories, it truly took science over 40 years to understand the psychopharmacology of what would be known as a broader class of drugs—the antipsychotics 1.3.

1.1.4 Deinstitutionalization

Thorazine® and the first-generation antipsychotic family of drugs—called the phenothiazines—thus sparked the *deinstitutionalization* movement. Plainly, deinstitutionalization refers to the shift of caring for individuals with severe mental illness in state mental hospitals to community centers and outpatient services from the 1950s arguably through the date of this writing. Torrey (1997) calls this shift "one of the largest social experiments in American history" as he opines over the sheer magnitude of this change as demonstrated by the numbers of patients residing in state mental hospitals from the 1950s. Torrey cites that in 1955, state hospitals had a population of 558,239 persons; yet, by 1994, this population was reduced to 71,619 nationwide. The exact numbers often vary in the literature; however, three key sources have reliably documented the dramatic changes over this period—the National Institute of Mental Health, the Center for Mental Health Services, and individual states. A summary of CMHS data can be found in Fig. 1.4.

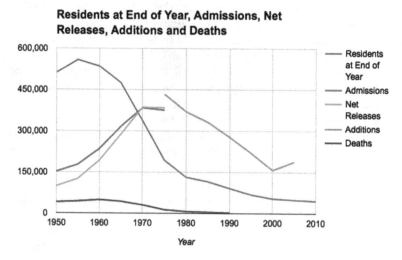

Fig. 1.4 Number of hospital residents, admissions, net releases, additions, and deaths, using CMHS data presented in a national report entitled, "Funding and Characteristics of State Mental Health Agencies, 2007" (SAMHSA, 2007) with year 2010 added from "Behavioral Health United States, 2012 (SAMHSA, 2013)

Further, psychiatry had progressed as a science enough to broadly define the types of diseases facing this population: roughly half had a diagnosis of schizophrenia, about 10–15% were diagnosed with manic depression (now, bipolar disorder) or "severe" depression, another 10–15% had mental health issues due to organic brain disease, and the remainder had diagnoses such as mental retardation with psychosis, childhood disorders, and brain disease in conjunction with an addiction (Torrey, 1997). Was it possible to effectively treat these issues outside of a hospital setting? For over 100 years, establishing effective treatments for these diagnoses eluded mental health professionals. Real change was finally happening, but was it positive change?

As these questions were being wrangled with, political pressure from various sources was pushing states to decrease the size of state mental hospitals. It was certainly easier to acquiesce to these pressures with the broader adoption of the phenothiazines; however, the combination of the Community Mental Health Centers Act of 1963 with the enactment of Medicaid and Medicare (via Title XVIII and XIX of the Social Security Act, signed into law by Lyndon B. Johnson) cemented the trend of treating mental illness outside of hospital settings (Torrey, 1997; SAMHSA, 2007). In particular, the Community Mental Health Centers Act was put in place to develop a network of community mental health centers at the local level, reversing the trend that Dorothea Dix promoted. Medicaid and Medicare helped to cover the cost of using these centers for patients. This shift may have led to positive results if, in fact, the nationwide mental health network could prove successful. This would mean that the system ensures that people with mental illness receive medication, rehabilitation services, and aftercare to ensure ongoing treatment compliance, yielding the best chances for personal success with treatment. Unfortunately, this great experiment is absent of success stories. In later decades, the narrative of mental health would become entangled in another failing policy shift of the twentieth century—American criminal justice reform, including its war on drugs.

1.1.5   The Media Coverage of Hospital Conditions and Homelessness and Social Awareness

As the Federal government pushed forward with policies favoring treatment of mental illness in local communities over state-run institutions, additional forces added to the momentum—or, at minimum, aided to continue to reduce the size and scope of state mental hospitals. The most potent of these forces is the effect of mass media coverage of the hospitals, which have become dilapidated and chaotic messes as their resources continued to dwindle in these years. For example, Life Magazine published Albert Q. Maisel's (1946) photo essay on the horrors of state-run mental hospitals, "Bedlam 1946: Most U.S. Mental Hospitals Are a Shame and a Disgrace." The impact of visualizing the suffering in photographs was certainly palpable, with the captions reading "NEGLECT. In Cleveland Hospital's bare wards a patient lies unnoticed and unattended on stone floor," "RESTRAINT. This woman wears a camisole with sleeves tied behind her. Ulcers on leg are bandaged," "USELESS WORK. At Massillon Ohio State Hospital barefoot patients polish splintered wooden floor in 1890 building - a poor substitute for occupational therapy," and so on with explicit photographs depicting "NAKEDNESS... OVERCROWDING... FORCED LABOR... IDLENESS... [and] DESPAIR." The 13-page spread dedicated to the issue began to raise awareness on a growing problem, a problem that seemed intractable, until pharmaceutical and policy intervention. This copyrighted work—including its shocking visceral images—is available online at the time of this writing, easily searchable by the article's title.

This was certainly not the only instance of mass media's contribution to the conversation. One of the most iconic exposés of this era that brought these issues into the public spotlight was Geraldo Rivera's work on Willowbrook State School in Staten Island, New York, called "The Last Great Disgrace 1972."

> When Dr. Wilkins slid back the heavy door of B Ward, building No 6, the horrible smell of the place staggered me. It was so wretched that my first thought was that the air was poisonous and would kill me. I looked down to steady myself and I saw a freak: a grotesque caricature of a person, lying under the sink on an incredibly filthy floor in an incredibly filthy bathroom. It was wearing trousers, but they were pulled down around the ankles. It was shinny. It was twisted. It was lying in its own feces. And it wasn't alone. Sitting next to this thing was another freak. In a parody of human emotion they were holding hands. They were making a noise. It was a wailing sound that I still hear and that I will never forget. I said out loud, but to nobody in particular, "My God, they're children." Wilkens looked at me and said, "Welcome to Willowbrook." (Rivera, 2017)

There are some very notable contrasts and similarities of Rivera's words to Dix. First, the stark contrast each observer's characterization of the mentally ill is staggering: Dix refers to the vulnerable people she witnessed as idiots and lunatics, acceptable early medical labels for the mentally ill in that era, while Rivera uses the stigmatic word *freak*. Yet, the message was essentially the same. How was it possible for the government, at any level, to treat the vulnerable in such an inhumane way? In today's terms, the exposé would go viral. One cannot underestimate the impact of photojournalism and documentary-style exposes in their potential to elicit a grassroots and/or policy response; at minimum, the ongoing and visceral reporting on the issue of mental illness reinforced the political sentiment of the era to increase resources for mental health services in communities while divesting in state-run institutions, and many would argue with convincing evidence that this sets the stage to defund almost all state mental hospitals by the end of the twentieth century.

At this point in history, the issue becomes much more complex, and the following forces are at play: the mass media, professional medical organizations, the pharmaceutical industry, policymakers and political figures, and a growing socially aware populace with broader access to political influence. Deinstitutionalization has triggered the process of reintroducing a sizeable population of individuals with severe mental illness to the public, whereas in the past, this group was kept vastly segregated and out of sight. This was done largely without a scientific assurance that individuals with mental illness could live successfully, with minimal symptoms, in the mental health networks created for their treatment. While the available treatment would, in fact, work well for some people, it would end up leaving many vulnerable, without access, and untreated. These individuals would soon become documented in a growing scientific literature on the failures of deinstitutionalization, namely, for ending up in the swelling numbers of the homeless or criminally institutionalized in the nation's jails and prisons.

Yet, as deinstitutionalization would quietly criminalize untreated mental illness, American mass media would instead become focused on homelessness. Buck and Toro (2004) point to several reasons why this occurred in the 1980s. First, Ronald Reagan's administration led the initiative of making substantial cuts to social programs in light of a recession. In response, Reagan's political opponents aligned with homelessness activists to begin a media campaign on the issue in sharp rebuke of the administration with hopes of political fallout. Second, many aging urban centers were redeveloping and becoming gentrified, leading to fewer affordable housing options. The combination was proved to be excellent kindling for a crisis with a political environment to keep this story in the news. The previous issue of vagrancy, an often-stigmatized term with a lengthy negative history, would become homelessness. Tramps and hobos would become the homeless.

In their 2004 study, Buck, Toro, and Ramos evaluated these trends in print coverage from 1972 (well before media interest began on the issue) to 2001 (well after the issue attracted front covers) in four leading newspapers: *The New York Times*, *The Washington Post*, *The Los Angeles Times*, and *The Chicago Tribune*. These researchers took 500 randomly selected articles and identified four distinct time periods, labeled pre-interest (1972–1980), rise and peak (1981–1987), decline (1988–1993), and plateau (1994–2001). They argued that the rise and peak time period seemed to be "the most revealing." It is during these years that the media departed from their previous view of the homeless and would, generally, cast a more sympathetic light on these individuals. But, while the media reported on mental health as a contributing factor and tied deinstitutionalization and related structural issues to the broader homelessness problem, Buck and Toro found that most of the coverage failed to talk about services or long-term programs to address homelessness, noting that few services or programs existed during that time. In the decline years, negative reporting returned in greater frequency, often bringing back stereotypes of skid row alcoholics and drug addicts, with the addition of the mentally ill and dangerous stigma. It is not that the media completely turned their backs to the plight of the homeless; instead, Buck, Toro, and Ramos argue that the American public grew to understand that homelessness is complex and the media coverage of the time reflects that by its broad coverage of the issue.

Instead of a broad compassionate policy response as seen in previous eras, mental illness was on a collision course with criminal justice reform. For many with mental illness, deinstitutionalization increased the risk of substance use and abuse (called co-occurring disorders—more on this later) and illegal behaviors (some may be contributed directly to the illness). Many were left vulnerable and without a safety net as the community mental health networks never became comprehensive enough to effectively treat the population previously served by state-run mental hospitals. The war on drugs began with Richard Nixon's administration; but it was the Reagan administration and the 98th (1983–1985) and 99th (1985–1987) US Congress that initiated the criminal justice reforms that would rapidly accelerate the growth of the rate Americans incarcerate their citizens. This trend would continue into the administrations of George H.W. Bush and Bill Clinton with the full support of Congress. With a fragmented mental health treatment network as the only option for many vulnerable people, their fate amounted to a different iteration of the incarceration faced by those in state-run mental hospitals. Except, this time, their experiences would be much worse as American jails and prisons were hardly prepared to care for this population.

1.1.6   The Impact of the War on Crime and the Incarceration State

The primary drivers of moving individuals with mental illness in the community into jails and prisons are substance use and abuse and untreated or undertreated symptoms. Just as Kris and Carmichael may have predicted, untreated or undertreated symptoms would produce a return to the state hospital—except that these hospitals had shuttered, with remaining facilities having vastly reduced capacities and a bare-bones operation that would only serve the most severe cases. Further, the struggles facing this vulnerable population do not occur in isolation; in other words, poverty, homelessness, substance use and abuse and self-medication, violence and victimization, and frayed social support, to name a few, can all influence each other and influence one's mental health to deteriorate or symptoms to appear—again, a theme that was foreshadowed by Kris and Carmichael's Thorazine® study. Figure 1.5 lists the policies, the timing of the policies, and their effects on mental health and criminal justice.

The "Tough on Crime" movement has led to dramatic changes. Foremost, jails and prison populations have increased exponentially. While *total* numbers are difficult to come by for this entire time period, the Bureau of Justice Statistics (BJS)—an agency within the Department of Justice tasked with collecting data on the operation of justice systems among all levels of government—maintains a dataset called the National Prisoner Statistics Program that has followed the State and Federal prison population since 1925 (Bureau of Justice Statistics, 1982). While it excludes data on local (jail) inmates, the dataset clearly shows stability of the prison population around 100 per 100,000 persons in the United States until the mid-1970s (Fig. 1.6). By all accounts, this figure trended aggressively upward through the 1980s, 1990s, and into the new millennium—exceeding 500 per 100,000 persons. Yet, to truly understand the impact of deinstitutionalization apart from the "Tough on Crime" movement, one would also need to observe changes in all segments of the *justice-involved population*. Justice involved is a broad term that refers to individuals in State and Federal prisons, in community corrections (e.g., State and

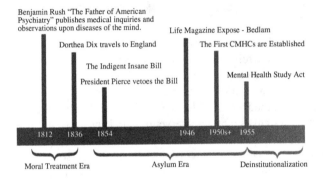

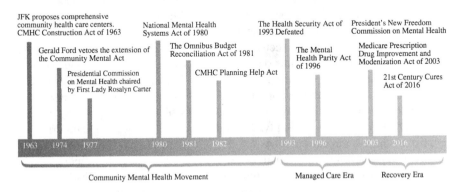

Fig. 1.5 Mental health policies over time

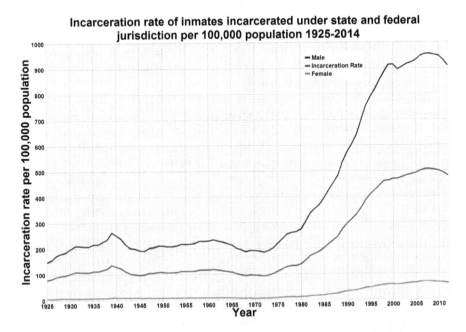

Fig. 1.6 Data from the National Prisoner Statistics Program, Bureau of Justice Statistics

Federal probation and parole), and in local jails either awaiting trial or serving time. Unfortunately, since consistent and reliable data on all segments of the justice-involved population only began to be collected in the late 1970s, it is truly difficult to follow the impact of deinstitutionalization on justice involvement.

The newly available data from the Bureau of Justice Statistics certainly suggests the use of the criminal justice system as a broad intervention tool for substance use and abuse and "criminality." Starkly, the reach of the criminal justice system peaked in 2008 at 2405 per 100,000 adult Americans involved in the system in some way, up from 800 per 100,000 in 1980 (Bureau of Justice Statistics, 2017a, b). Put another way, that amounts to just over two per every 100 adults in the United States were in prison or jail or on probation or parole, in 2008. Many of these individuals were swept up into the system for nonviolent drug offenses as a direct result of the "Tough on Crime" movement, which focused so much of its efforts on drug policy. As Jonathan Rothwell (2015) points out, while 1 in 5 state prisoners are incarcerated for drug offenses on average, there were three million admissions (just above 30% of all admissions) to both state and Federal prisons for this type of offense from 1993 to 2011, far more than any other type (e.g., violent crimes, property crimes, and all other crimes). Quite simply, drug crimes continue to be the main driver of imprisonment, even in current times.

Yet, many questions still remain—how many of those adults are mentally ill? What was the true impact of deinstitutionalization? If deinstitutionalization trends began in 1955, how can one effectively explain why prison populations did not trend upward until the mid-1970s? The capacity to answer how many justice-involved persons have mental illness is growing, and the true impact of deinstitutionalization mostly relies on anecdotal conjecture as consistent and reliable data identifying justice-involved individuals with mental illness only has recently become routine. After all, a scenario may exist that the proportion of mentally-ill, justice-involved persons has stayed consistent, with just the total population ballooning; yet, all available evidence does not bear this out.

Many observers, such as Lamb and Weinberger (2005), have argued that mental illness has effectively become criminalized over this time period. The exact numbers are still elusive to this date; however, there are a few ways to estimate the number of individuals with mental illness in the *current* justice-involved population. One way, Lamb and Weinberger suggest, is to take the estimation of the percentage of individuals in jails and prisons who could be diagnosed with serious debilitating mental illness (e.g., major depression, schizophrenia, bipolar disorders, and various other psychotic disorders) as published in current scientific literature, which at the time, ranged from 16% to 24%. Using a conservative approach, Lamb and Weinberger use the 16% for the year 2000 and estimated 113 per 100,000 individuals in jails and prisons to be severely mentally ill. "Severely mentally ill individuals who formerly would have been psychiatrically hospitalized when there were a sufficient number of psychiatric inpatient beds are now entering the criminal justice system for a variety of reasons. Those most commonly cited are: (1) deinstitutionalization in the terms of limited availability of psychiatric hospital beds; (2) the lack of access to adequate treatment for mentally ill persons in the community;

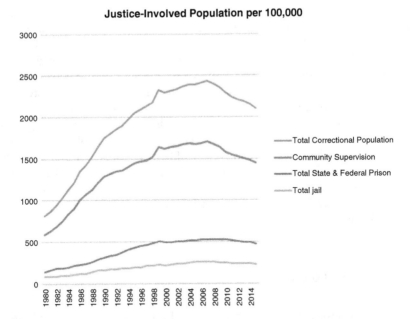

Fig. 1.7   Data from the Bureau of Justice Statistics, Key Statistic: Total Correctional Population

(3) the interactions between severely mentally ill persons and law enforcement personnel; and (4) more formal and rigid criteria for civil commitment (Fig. 1.7)."

Taking a more liberal approach, two BJS statisticians—James and Glaze (2006)—analyzed personal interviews with prisoners and local jail inmates in two surveys performed just a few years prior in a special report. In their analysis, James and Glaze were able to decipher individuals with mental health problems by one of two ways to gain better insight into this population: (1) recent history (within the last 12 months) of a clinical diagnosis and/or treatment by a mental health professional and (2) exhibiting symptoms of a mental health disorder as determined by targeted questions on the two surveys. The results were staggering: 705,600 (56%) state prisoners, 78,800 (45%) Federal prisoners, and 479,900 (64%) local jail inmates met criteria for having a mental health problem, amounting to just over *half* of the total population. These figures differ considerably from the first comprehensive accounting of mentally ill subpopulation by the BJS performed only a few years prior in 1999. At that time, BJS statistician Paula Ditton had access to survey questions asking participants directly if they suffer from a mental illness or if they had stayed overnight in a mental hospital. This line of questioning resulted in estimates of 283,800 individuals with mental illness in jails and prisons, with 16% of state inmates, 7% of Federal inmates, and 16% of local jail inmates self-reporting mental illness in this manner. The differences between these two undertakings are essentially underscoring the potential undiagnosed mental health problems endemic to this justice-involved population. More on this in later chapters.

The updated report also included a more comprehensive description of mentally ill, justice-involved individuals, giving supporting evidence to the anecdotal descriptions of this population in the literature at the time: state prisoners and jail inmates with mental health problems are more likely to report being incarcerated three or more times relative to those who do not report mental health problems; female inmates reported mental health problems more than male inmates; about three quarters of the individuals reporting mental health problems also met criteria for substance use disorder or abuse; nearly two-thirds of these individuals used drugs in the month prior to their arrest; and state prisoners with a mental health problem were twice as likely to be homeless and twice as likely to be injured in a fight since admission relative to individuals who did not (James & Glaze, 2006). There is little doubt that a sizeable portion of the people who need mental health services have, at minimum, a higher likelihood of contact with the criminal justice system since deinstitutionalization.

1.2   Current Policy

While the prognosis may appear grim, policy efforts to address the fallout from the "Tough on Crime" movement are ongoing. Further, a functional network of community-based mental health services is possible; in fact, these networks are already in place for those who have access through private health insurance. Much of the innovation for the vulnerable populations discussed above—the homeless, individuals with mental illness, and/or those with addiction—stems from the Second Chance Act of 2007 and Justice Reinvestment Initiative legislation. Briefly, the Second Chance Act was a bipartisan law easily passed under the George W. Bush administration that earmarked funding to invest in programs to reduce recidivism while ensuring public safety. To date, over $475 million has been invested in promising programs via grants, marking a formal start to the "Reentry" movement. A primary caveat to receive these funds at the local or state level is to initiate programs or services that are *evidence based*. Two Second Chance Act programs are specifically relevant here—Targeting Adults with Co-occurring Substance Abuse and Mental Health Disorders and the Statewide Adult Recidivism Reduction Strategic Planning Program. The first of the two has further refined our knowledge of what works to help individuals with mental illness return to the community and reduce their chances of being re-incarcerated, while the latter has enabled states to develop the policy initiatives to help drive this sort of change for state prisoners and local jail inmates alike.

The Justice Reinvestment Initiatives are currently a collaborative project with states and localities and the Pew Charitable Trusts, with funds authorized by Congress in 2010 via the Bureau of Justice Assistance. These initiatives require broad participation by stakeholders in each location to participate in a comprehensive analysis of their criminal justice system in order to define which evidence-based strategies could be put in place to reduce recidivism and cost while maintaining

Table 1.1 Participants served by Second Chance Act programs, 2009–2015

SCA programming	Number served
Co-occurring	9048
Family-based	8375
Mentoring	25,573
Technology careers	6632
Reentry demonstration	61,105
Reentry court	2595
Overall	113,328

Courtesy of the Bureau of Justice Assistance

public safety. Generally, these initiatives tend not to put direct focus on mental health issues; however, many initiatives have better defined the problems facing justice-involved individuals with mental illness and have generated plans to mitigate these problems (Table 1.1).

The key of both of these strategies is to promulgate evidence-based practices and services that are proven to reduce recidivism while further vetting promising practices and services that may lead to beneficial results. For justice-involved individuals with mental illness, this means provision of adequate care in *all* settings—jails, prisons, and upon return to the community. This means that a comprehensive review of these settings is beginning to take shape or has been completed since 2002. Progress is beginning to take shape across the United States, and never has American justice and mental health policy been closer to the ideal of providing mental health services in the *least restrictive* manner (Atkinson & Garner, 2002; World Health Organization, 1996)—that is, fewer locked doors, less incarceration or commitment, fewer shackles, chains, restraints, and so on.

It also should be noted that both strategies placed substantial focus on overall cost reduction of criminal justice as overall expenditures were getting out of hand, particularly during times of recession. This emphasis on "smart" cost savings has enabled broad support for policies that are affecting change since the beginning of the century. While change has been slow to come, its momentum continues to expand the array of services available to the very same vulnerable population cast aside since the days of Dorothea Dix. One recent example was the passage of the Twenty-First Century Cures Act—a bipartisan effort signed into law by Barack Obama at the end of his last term. Within the legislation, the 114th Congress embedded previous iterations of the Helping Families in Mental Health Crisis Act as Division B of the Cures Act. This section is dedicated to completely revision mental health services in the United States. Key provisions of the Act include creating an assistant secretary for Mental Health and Substance Abuse and an assistant secretary of Planning and Evaluation within the Substance Abuse and Mental Health Services Administration; creating a biennial report to tabulate progress and developing a strategic plan—all to bolster leadership and accountability of mental health services; encouraging the development of evidence-based programs and services and other innovation via grants, prioritizing development of services based on need, and disseminating this information—to ensure these efforts keep up with the best and current science on mental health and substance abuse; supporting state innovation via block grants; and promoting access to mental health services via grants for homeless populations, jail populations, integration of primary and mental health care, revisioning suicide prevention, and much more.

Throughout the Cures Act, there are several mentions of expanding the use of inpatient beds in a strategic fashion. One priority is to use technology to better understand the availability of inpatient resources, their utilization, and their fit in a broader continuum of care by region and across the country. Thus, this reimagination of mental health care is a key, and bold, effort since deinstitutionalization policies to address this persistent need of a vulnerable class of citizens. Notably, it expands Medicaid to cover a broader array of mental health services to stymie the use of jails and prisons as the new asylum for individuals with mental illness. Yet, these institutions will remain an important component of the "new" system of care it envisions.

1.3   Key Problems Today

The four following problem areas need to be introduced early in this text: stigma, trauma, co-occurring disorders, and cost of services. Together, they represent persistent barriers to successfully address mental health care in the United States. In fact, "stigma" is directly addressed 4 times in the Cures Act, "trauma" 27 times, "co-occurring" 37 times, and "cost" 98 times. Recall that cost is the glue that makes the effort to re-envision mental health care possible; thus, any innovation will only prove to be viable if it can prove cost savings. Always keep this in mind when considering the advances of science in future years.

1.3.1   Stigma

Davey (2013), writing for Psychology Today, has a great description of mental health stigma and both the outward discussion as well as internal: "Mental health stigma can be divided into two distinct types: *social stigma* is characterized by prejudicial attitudes and discriminating behaviour directed towards individuals with mental health problems as a result of the psychiatric label they have been given. In contrast, *perceived stigma* or *self-stigma* is the internalizing by the mental health sufferer of their perceptions of discrimination, and perceived stigma can significantly affect feelings of shame and lead to poorer treatment outcomes" (Davey, 2013; emphasis as in original; citing Link, Cullen, Struening, Shrout, & Dohrenwend, 1989; Perlick et al., 2001). The stigma associated with mental illness can be a barrier for many to seek treatment in the first place; in other words, people's resistance and reluctance to be labeled mentally ill—officially or unofficially—often makes them think twice about reaching out for help, even to those they trust. Also, friends and family members often struggle with overcoming stigma and stereotypes to remain supportive to those suffering from mental illness. Increasingly concerning, as with many illnesses, lack of treatment leads to worsening of symptoms and severity. Typically, better outcomes are tied to addressing an illness as early as it can be detected—mental health included. This is the basis of why the concept of stigma is so important, and it is vital to understand why it endures.

The typical stereotype of mental illness is a "crazy" person who commits acts of violence and could be a harm to themselves or others (Angermeyer, 1996; Nunnally, 1981; Pescosolido, Monahan, Link, Stueve, & Kikuzawa, 1999; Penn, Kommana, Mansfield, & Link, 1999). In reality, most individuals with mental illness are not violent. One widely cited study by Link, Phelan, Bresnahan, Stueve, and Pescosolido (1999) details the power of this misconception through an experiment with five vignettes placed on a massive social science survey in 1996 (the General Social Survey). The vignettes were written about people with mental illness in a nonclinical way to gauge people's reaction about (1) alcohol dependence; (2) major depression; (3) schizophrenia; (4) drug dependence; and (5) a "troubled person." Importantly, the "troubled person" vignette represented a person experiencing a rough time in their life, but did not meet any criteria for mental illness, giving the researchers a basis for comparison. For example:

> John is a [ETHNICITY] man with an [EDUCATIONAL LEVEL] education. Up until a year ago, life was pretty okay for John. But then, things started to change. He thought that people around him were making disapproving comments and talking behind his back. John was convinced that people were spying on him and that they could hear what he was thinking. John lost his drive to participate in his usual work and family activities and retreated to his home, eventually spending most of his day in his room. John was hearing voices even though no one else was around. These voices told him what to do and what to think. He has been living this way for six months.—the vignette for schizophrenia

The results from 1444 survey participants detail the depth of the issue of stigma and the stereotype of the dangerousness of mental illness. When directly asked, "In your opinion, how likely is it that [NAME] would do something violent toward other people—very likely; somewhat likely; somewhat unlikely; very unlikely," the average responses indicated that people viewed cocaine dependence as the most dangerous (87% of respondents either chose very or somewhat likely), followed by alcohol dependence (71%), and schizophrenia (61%). This reaction is in the face of volumes of empirical evidence consistently finding that only a minority of individuals with mental illness become violent. Perhaps even more telling, when Link and his colleagues asked whether the people surveyed would be willing to live next to this person, spend an evening with them, work closely with them, and react to them marrying a relative, most respondents sought to distance themselves from the person in the vignette. The results were in line with perceived dangerousness—the vast majority of people surveyed would distance themselves from cocaine dependence (90%), alcohol dependence (70%), and schizophrenia (63%). Even the individual depicted as having major depressive disorder would be isolated by many respondents (47%).

Importantly, the researchers also felt as though the respondents felt hesitant to use the term "mental illness" when asked about the people in the vignettes.

Specifically, when respondents were asked if they believed the person detailed in the vignette was experiencing a mental illness, most, but not all, responded affirmatively. This was especially the case with major depressive disorder (69% of respondents thought the person had a mental illness), alcohol dependence (49%), cocaine dependence (44%), and a troubled person (22%). Yet, when confronted with the specific condition of the people depicted in the vignettes, the vast majority of respondents were convinced that the individuals had alcohol dependence (98%), cocaine dependence (97%), major depression disorder (95%), and schizophrenia (85%). The differences in responses here show the weight of the words "mental illness."

Stigma, social distancing, and labels are incredibly powerful interrelated and complex concepts. Not only do these concepts shape the experience of mental illness, the science in this area details the interconnectedness of deviance (including drug use/abuse), crime and criminality, vulnerability and victimization, homelessness, and mental illness with stigma as a central component. Thus, it is important to fully explore stigma and its role in the lives of people with mental illness.

1.3.2   Trauma

Trauma is often related to a significant untoward and problematic event in a person's life (SAMHSA, 2017b, 2014). It is more common than one may expect and is not bound by age, gender, race, ethnicity, socioeconomic status, or other difference between people. While many people can persevere through traumatic events without experiencing lasting negative outcomes, a broadening array of research is revealing the importance of early treatment intervention. Individuals with a support system and those who have never or rarely experience trauma are typically more resilient, but not always. Unfortunately, this trauma can linger and become a larger problem, perhaps in the form of mental illness and/or substance abuse—especially when the trauma is persistent and/or occurs with increased frequency. Furthermore, it is important to note that the negative effects of trauma are magnified when they occur during childhood. Thus, children and teenagers are at most risk for developing lasting conditions such as substance abuse disorder (including smoking cigarettes and drinking alcohol) and mental health problems (including depression, anxiety, and post-traumatic stress disorder) or engage in risky behaviors such as self-injury and risk taking.

Trauma may be the result of harm, violence, and victimization from a variety of experiences. In fact, SAMHSA offers toolkits (2014) that offer an excellent summary across the broad domains of experiencing trauma and helpful resources that can help both laypersons and professionals link up with evidence-based treatments to address these sources of trauma. Broadly, these domains include sexual abuse or assault; physical abuse or assault; emotional abuse or psychological maltreatment; neglect (e.g., failure of a caretaker to provide care, food, shelter, and other basic necessities); serious accident, illness, or medical procedure; victim of or witness to

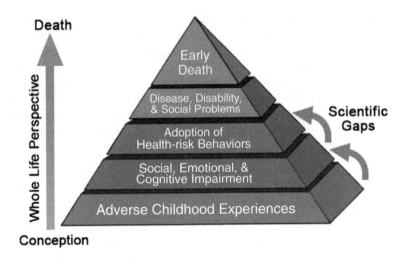

Fig. 1.8 Relationship among adverse childhood experiences and potential later life outcomes, courtesy of the Substance Abuse and Mental Health Services Administration

domestic violence; victim of or witness to community violence (e.g., gang violence, racial conflict, police-citizen confrontations, and riots); historical trauma (e.g., traumatic experiences tied to a group or culture, e.g., American slavery, Jim Crow, and post-Jim Crow); school violence and bullying; natural or man-made disasters; forced displacement; war, terrorism, or political violence; military trauma (e.g., for military members and their families as a result of deployment and/or military service); victim of or witness to personal or interpersonal violence; traumatic grief or separation; and system-induced trauma and retraumatization. While this list may not be exhaustive, it does offer a structure to begin to investigate the sources of trauma.

Further, a great deal of recent research has been focused on early life trauma, called adverse childhood experiences (ACEs). This research has clearly shown that these events pose a significant risk factor for the development of mental health disorders in later life (in particular, substance use disorders) and can have an impact on future prevention efforts (SAMHSA, 2017b). This research was kick-started by a collaborative effort between of the Centers for Disease Control and Prevention and Kaiser Permanente; in 1998, these entities published their research on ACEs in 17,337 participants studied across two waves in the *American Journal of Preventive Medicine* outlining. Their findings were remarkable: (1) ACEs are common (28% of participants reported some form of physical abuse and 21% reported some form of sexual abuse); (2) ACEs tend to occur in clusters or in multiples (i.e., 40% of participants reported a history of two or more ACEs and 12.5% experienced four or more); and (3) ACEs predict health problems with strong, positive statistical relationship (or, in other words, the more ACEs one experiences strongly predicts the risk of a variety of health problems in later life, including substance use and co-occurring disorders) (see Fig. 1.8; read the next section for a definition of co-occurring disorders).

The reason why trauma is considered a key problem here is that the effects of trauma can be tricky to diagnose and treat, and without addressing this root cause of mental health and/or drug abuse problems, symptoms, and negative outcomes can persist and can confound prevention efforts. For example, if an underage drinking prevention program with a proven track record of success is adopted in a high-risk community, it may not have the same level of success *or any success* if the programming does not address adverse experiences. Or, alternatively, if this program has the ability to recognize the signs of ACEs, it may link with other programming that can address coping skills, dysfunction in the home, the effects of divorce, and so on.

1.3.3   Co-Occurring Disorders

Co-occurring disorders, once known as dual diagnosis, exist when a person has both mental health and substance use disorders at the same time. According to the National Survey on Drug Use and Health in 2014, more than 7.9 million Americans had co-occurring disorders. With this large number, adding on issues related the criminal justice system can only further complicate recovery for individuals.

One of the major hurdles with co-occurring disorders is establishing high-quality and appropriate treatment. Treatment for this type of disorder lends itself to the "chicken or the egg" adage—does the mental health diagnosis occur before the substance use disorder or does substance misuse/abuse occur before other mental illness? The answer to this question can radically shape an appropriate treatment protocol in one direction or another very different direction. Even further, clinicians need to ask, do the mental health concerns fuel the struggles with substance use, or does the substance use struggle fuel the mental health concerns? From the clinician's perspective, the signs and symptoms of both mental health and substance use disorder can be difficult to separate, which leads to further difficulty in treating the disorders adequately. Clinicians may require longer periods of time to document and diagnose these issues, perhaps delaying the delivery of the best treatment to address these compounding symptoms. Yet, the system of care for mental health services in many locations may not allow for optimal care and treatment; many treatment programs may only treat one disorder while not addressing the other which often does not help in the overall wellness and health of the individual. For example, a person may suffer from bipolar disorder and cocaine use disorder. With bipolar disorder, the individual can experience both depressive episodes and manic episodes. Cocaine is a stimulant, so in this scenario, it could be difficult to differentiate between symptoms from the manic episode from bipolar disorder versus the "highs" of the cocaine use disorder. Additionally, the idea of "self-medicating" can be often brought up in the clinical discussion regarding co-occurring disorders. For example, a person suffering from depression may use alcohol to "self-medicate" and mask negative feelings when experiencing tough times. In this way, alcohol will also fuel the depression and symptoms. Therefore, in both of these examples, treatment professionals may have difficulties with treatment plans. Often, to fully realize the true nature of the mental illness side, the person must fully detox from the substance(s).

Additionally, and further complicating matters for mental health professionals, the level of severity of co-occurring disorder can vary wildly across and within individuals. For example, both of the following may fit the "co-occurring" definition: (1) a person experiencing mild anxiety who misuses alcohol to help with sleep by engaging in frequent binge drinking and (2) a person diagnosed with schizophrenia who may abuse opiates to avoid or shut out the hallucinations they may be experiencing. The intensity and frequency of the issues depicted here can vary in one's life depending on stressors, life circumstances, and so on. Since either the mental illness or the substance use disorder can develop first, it often can be difficult to determine which is fueling the other. Substances can pose a problem by also worsening or, at times, creating problems with a person's mood and throwing off one's brain chemistry leading to behavior issues. Therefore, most treatment options for co-occurring disorders involve an integrated approach.

According to information provided by the National Alliance on Mental Illness, "about a third of all people experiencing mental illnesses and about half of people living with severe mental illnesses also experience substance abuse" (NAMI, 2015). That is a significant number of people impacted by these illnesses, and these figures are important to keep in mind from a treatment perspective. In particular, helping the person and their loved ones understand how both mental illness and substance abuse interact and impact their daily life is important for transformative change. Further, "in the substance abuse community, about a third of all alcohol abusers and more than half of all drug abusers report experiencing a mental illness" (NAMI, 2015). It is also important to note that men are more likely to develop co-occurring disorders than women. Also, those of a lower socioeconomic status, people with more medical illnesses, and military veterans are more likely to be at risk of co-occurring disorders.

SAMHSA literature points out that "the consequences of undiagnosed, untreated, or undertreated co-occurring disorders can lead to a higher likelihood of experiencing homelessness, incarceration, medical illnesses, suicide, or even early death" (SAMHSA, 2016). In the criminal justice system, many people have co-occurring disorders, and using integrated treatment is essential to success. Further, appropriate screening to identify co-occurring disorders is important to ensure inmates are receiving the proper care within the system. Addressing both mental health and substance use both during and after incarceration can also reduce the likelihood of recidivism.

1.3.4 Dollars and ~~Cents~~ Sense

One of the biggest obstacles, and one major common theme throughout this book, is funding. Recall that the most recent landmark mental health law, the Cures Act, mentioned cost more than any other concept; thus, this is not only a theme for this book, it is the top driving force for American policy decision-making. At the more localized level, budgets for jails and state prisons are being cut substantially, primarily due to the overuse of incarceration as a solution for social problems (largely, drug problems). Incarceration is a very expensive solution to maintain at current levels; the addition of any financial strains, such as from the fiscal pressures of recession, has resulted in cutting services to bare minimums in many circumstances. Further, expenses related to the justice and mental health services are more vulnerable (if not *the most* vulnerable) to cuts as lawmakers tend to be more protective over services that directly affect their constituents—such as schools, roads, parks, and local community services. Divestment in justice and mental health services lead to not only increases in need but decreases in jobs and quality options. If funding for treatment is cut, then jobs and options for treatment providers are also diminished, making for a bleak outlook. Burnout and frustration in the workforce will also heighten; think—if our criminal justice and behavioral health systems were overwhelmed before budget cuts (as they have tended to be historically)—how are they professionals in the aftermath of divestment?

One struggle with lack of mental health treatment options is the waste of the little resources involved primarily due to the inefficiency of the system; many critiques of the system do not account for this. Professionals often know of "frequent flyers," or individuals who are well known for returning to facilities with recurrent symptomatology because their care is often incomplete. Their treatment is likened to a person with an open wound who is treated with a Band-Aid and an over-the-counter pain reliever instead of full ambulatory care (think stitches, antibiotics, and follow-up to ensure that an infection has not occurred). In other words, providing effective treatment for an individual suffering from mental illness costs a finite amount of resources, which depends on the type of treatment (inpatient, outpatient, etc.), medication, doctor visits, follow-ups, counseling services, and so on. Consider then, like any other illness, prolonging treatment by lack of options, resources, long wait times, or access to medication can often worsen the condition and time to achieve a healthy outcome—and cost volumes more in the long run. Further, the traumatizing experience of incarceration because one's symptoms cause legal problems can create additional negative mental health outcomes and may complicate treatment in the long run and cost even more money.

Incarcerating a person in need of treatment puts the financial burden onto the criminal justice system, thus creating a different problem. In this case, the criminal justice system now bears the burden of housing and treating a person with mental illness. Currently, the system is overcrowded and underfunded. Adding more people to the situation only furthers the burden while also complicating matters with their illness. Utah, like many other states, has seen an increase of deaths in jails, specifically to suicide. In one county alone, Weber County, there have been 31 deaths in the jail since 2000 and 14 of those were to suicide.

1.4   Rethinking Mental Health

Removing the stigma associated with mental illness and treating it as any other concern is one of the major needs of our society. However, more central to fundamental change are the interconnected linkages that need to be built throughout a comprehensive system of care. This system must be able to communicate effectively across its entire footprint, including those tangibly involved or providing services but are not formally connected with the system.

What if mental illness was treated the way that cancer or diabetes is treated? If it was even viewed in a similar light, the outcomes could drastically be different. For example, with cancer, primary care physicians commonly are knowledgeable about how to refer patients out to specialists—at times, high-profile specialists at the Moffitt Center or MD Anderson—and ensure that patients' follow-up to be seamlessly handed off to their specialists for treatment. This treatment can involve imaging, labs, consultants with specialists, and so on. Each of these appointments can also be made seamlessly, often with reminders that occur automatically. What if we put this practice into commonplace mental health care?

1.4.1 A Continuum of Care

The continuum of care is a difficult but essential element of the process to ensure the health of an individual. The continuum of care refers to all of the steps and actions involved in the overall care cycle for a person—including all the key players at and between each point of contact and between the "system" and patient. For example, an individual exhibiting symptoms of depression may make an appointment with their primary care doctor. During their visit, the primary care doctor may refer the person to a psychiatrist. Upon seeing a psychiatrist, the individual may be prescribed an antidepressant medication and/or referred to a therapist to begin talk therapy. In an ideal situation, the psychiatrist and therapist would discuss that patient/client's treatment on a regular basis to ensure the wellness of the person continues throughout the span of their care.

In the criminal justice realm, there are many more professionals involved, which can often lead to many more options for problems or issues "falling through the cracks." The care and obstacles depend on many variables: is this person incarcerated in a jail or prison? If prison, is it state or federal? Has this person been treated before for mental illness or is their onset within jail/prison? (Fig. 1.9)

The term continuum of care, also known as organized delivery systems, has certainly become a "buzz" word in the health-care delivery industry. As it progressed to include first responders, law enforcement, courts, and jails, the continuum of care is a complex concept that focuses on a simple outcome—that no patient or client falls through the cracks of a complex care system. In other words, as a patient enters the health-care system, this person will be properly triaged and evaluated and referred to the best source(s) to handle the next steps in his or her care, and if further care is needed, follow-ups occur, further referrals are given, treatment is delivered, and this continues until the issue bringing this person into the system is resolved. Additional aftercare is delivered to ensure that success continues. With first responders, correctional officers, officers of the court, and more professionals being pulled into a broader continuum of care for many individuals, this has set the American

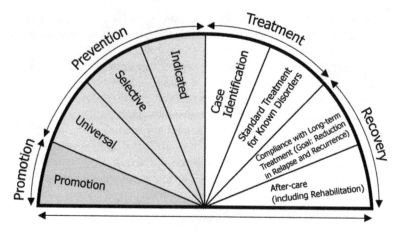

Fig. 1.9 The continuum of care protractor, courtesy of SAMHSA (2017a). Note that diagnosis occurs between prevention and treatment

mental health-care system on a new paradigm to reevaluate previous conceptualizations of continuums of care across the nation—this includes the criminal justice system as a starting point or referral point into health-care delivery systems.

1.5 Conclusion

With problems of awareness, in prevention, and with stigma, people will continue to suffer in their mental illness—particularly the vulnerable. Unfortunately, this can magnify the risk of contact by law enforcement and lead to the involvement in the criminal justice system. Further complicating the problem, mental health resources are scarce in most segments of the criminal justice system—whether it being federal or state prison, in local jails, or within community corrections. These institutions lack funding for programming and staff to fully attend to the needs of mental health inmates. Substance abuse often can further complicate mental health symptoms, creating an endless cycle of negative experiences for a vulnerable population.

This population was first brought into the public consciousness by Dorothea Dix. She brought compassion to a suffering class of people and sought to bring about the moral treatment of individuals with mental illness. While her efforts shifted people with mental illness from jails and prisons to state hospitals, most of these institutions ended up devolving into prisons themselves—with often "patient" treatment being worse than inmate life. This system continued until the abuses of the new system were brought to light by a new and powerful media. At the same time, psychiatric medicine (or psychopharmacology) experienced its most important breakthrough in the development of antipsychotic drugs. This enabled symptoms to be treated in what would be known as the least restrictive setting—often this means treatment in the community setting. From this moment through today, the ideal goal for the majority of special interests and advocacy groups alike was to enhance American communities to build the capacity to address mental health by setting up full systems of care. Thus, a trend sets in to divest from state mental hospitals with hopes of setting up a comprehensive network of community mental health treatment services. After many decades of development, many gaps continued to exist to effectively treat many of those in need. At first, the most vulnerable have ended up homeless and, at times, in jail; and then, after the significant criminal justice policy shifts in the 1980s, an exponential increase of individuals with mental illness has occurred in jails and prisons. This has caused a notable strain on the criminal justice system, further complicating the overall system of care.

One solution is to develop a comprehensive continuum of care that involved both the public behavioral health and criminal justice systems. Professionals working to seek this change use data and evaluation methods to examine points in the system can be the most successful in intervening in mental health episodes or crises. This can be an encounter with a law enforcement officer, upon intake into a jail, at the emergency room, at a community clinic, and even can begin with a call to 911, crisis hotlines, or resource lines. This solution does not try to eliminate the criminal justice system as earlier advocates have pioneered; it includes it as one segment of many intervention points. In a perfect world, it would be the point of the last resort. In many circumstances, justice intervention can be a very salient one, however. As researchers and professionals acknowledge this, it can lead to stronger partnerships and better outcomes for the vulnerable.

Finances and investment will continue to be an impendent toward progress, especially in dire fiscal times. Both behavioral health and criminal justice services take higher priorities for lawmakers when they consider budget cuts. It is important to note that this trend is no longer absolute. With the 21st Century Cures Act, legislators have signaled an impetus for change. It dedicates resources, gives direction, and provides a template for progress. This progress may be incomplete without comprehensive criminal justice reform; however, *progress will still occur without it*, albeit at a slower pace and in fewer places across the country.

References

Angermeyer, M. (1996). The effect of violent attacks by schizophrenic persons on the attitude of the public towards the mentally ill. *Social Science Medicine, 43*, 1721–1728.

Atkinson, J. M., & Garner, H. C. (2002). Least restrictive alternative—Advance statements and the new mental health legislation. *Psychological Bulletin, 26*, 246–247.

Buck, P., & Toro, P. (2004). Images of homelessness in the media. In D. Levinson (Ed.), *Encyclopedia of homelessness* (Vol. 1). Thousand Oaks, CA: SAGE.

Buck, P. O., Toro, P. A., & Ramos, M. A. (2004). Media and professional interest in homelessness over 30 years (1974–2003). *Analyses of Social Issues and Public Policy, 4*(1), 151–171.

Bureau of Justice Statistics. (1982). Prisoners 1925–81. Retrieved March 13, 2018, from https://www.bjs.gov/content/pub/pdf/p2581.pdf

Bureau of Justice Statistics. (2017a). *National prisoner statistics program.* Retrieved June 1, 2017, from http://www.bjs.gov

Bureau of Justice Statistics. (2017b). *Key statistic: Total correctional population.* Retrieved June 1, 2017, from https://www.bjs.gov/index.cfm?ty=kfdetail&iid=487

Carter, K. C., & Carter, B. R. (1994). *Childbed fever: A scientific biography of Ignaz Semmelweis.* Westwood, CT: Greenwood Press.

Davey, G. C. L. (2013). Mental health and stigma. *Psychology Today.* Retrieved June 1, 2017, from https://www.psychologytoday.com/blog/why-we-worry/201308/mental-health-stigma

Haller, J. S. (1981). *American medicine in transition, 1840–1910* (Vol. 185). Urbana, IL: University of Illinois Press.

Healy, D. (2009). *The creation of psychopharmacology.* Cambridge, MA: Harvard University Press.

James, D. J., & Glaze, L. E. (2006). *Mental health problems of prison and jail inmates.* Washington, DC: Bureau of Justice Statistics.

Kris, E. B., & Carmichael, D. M. (1957). Follow-up study on patients treated with thorazine. *The American Journal of Psychiatry, 114*(5), 449–452.

Lamb, H. R., & Weinberger, L. E. (2005). The shift of psychiatric inpatient care from hospitals to jails and prisons. *Journal-American Academy of Psychiatry and the Law, 33*(4), 529.

Link, B. G., Cullen, F. T., Struening, E., Shrout, P. E., & Dohrenwend, B. P. (1989). A modified labeling theory approach to mental disorders: An empirical assessment. *American Sociological Review, 54,* 400–423.

Link, B. G., Phelan, J. C., Bresnahan, M., Stueve, A., & Pescosolido, B. A. (1999). Public conceptions of mental illness: Labels, causes, dangerousness, and social distance. *American Journal of Public Health, 89*(9), 1328–1333.

Maisel, A. Q. (1946, May 6). Bedlam 1946: Most U.S. mental hospitals are a shame and a disgrace. *Time Magazine.*

Muckenhoupt, M. (2004). *Dorothea dix: Advocate for mental health care.* New York: Oxford University Press.

National Alliance on Mental Illness. (2015). Dual diagnosis. Retrived June 1, 2017, from Davey, G. C. L. (2013). Mental health and stigma. Psychology Today. Retrieved June 1, 2017, from https://www.psychologytoday.com/blog/why-we-worry/201308/mental-health-stigma

Nunnally, J. (1981). *Popular conceptions of mental health.* New York: Holt, Rinehart & Winston.

Packard, F. R. (1901). *History of medicine in the United States.* Philadelphia: Lippincott.

Penn, D. L., Kommana, S., Mansfield, M., & Link, B. G. (1999). Dispelling the stigma of schizophrenia: II. The impact of information on dangerousness. *Schizophrenia Bulletin, 25*(3), 437–446.

Perlick, D. A., Rosenheck, R. A., Clarkin, J. F., Sirey, J. A., Salahi, J., Struening, E. L., et al. (2001). Stigma as a barrier to recovery: Adverse effects of perceived stigma on social adaptation of persons diagnosed with bipolar affective disorder. *Psychiatric Services, 52*(12), 1627–1632.

Pescosolido, B. A., Monahan, J., Link, B. G., Stueve, A., & Kikuzawa, S. (1999). The public's view of the competence, dangerousness, and need for legal coercion among persons with mental health problems. *American Journal of Public Health, 89,* 1339–1345.

Rivera, G. (2017). *Geraldo Rivera.* Retrieved June 1, 2017, from http://geraldo.com/folio/willowbrook

Rothwell, J. (2015). *Drug offenders in American Prisons: The critical distinction between stock and flow.* Brookings Institute. Retrieved June 1, 2017, from https://www.brookings.edu/blog/social-mobility-memos/2015/11/25/drug-offenders-in-american-prisons-the-critical-distinction-between-stock-and-flow/

Substance Abuse and Mental Health Services Administration. (2007). *Funding and characteristics of State Mental Health Agencies, 2007.* Washington, DC.

Substance Abuse and Mental Health Services Administration. (2013). *Behavioral health, United States, 2012.* Washington, DC.

Substance Abuse and Mental Health Services Administration. (2014). *TIP 57: Trauma-informed care in behavioral health services.* Washington, DC.

References

Substance Abuse and Mental Health Services Administration. (2016). *Co-occurring disorders*. Retrieved June 1, 2017, from https://www.samhsa.gov/disorders/co-occurring

Substance Abuse and Mental Health Services Administration. (2017a). *Prevention of substance abuse and mental illness*. Retrieved October 21, 2017, from https://www.samhsa.gov/prevention

Substance Abuse and Mental Health Services Administration. (2017b). *Types of trauma and violence*. Retrieved June 1, 2017, from https://www.samhsa.gov/trauma-violence/types

Torrey, E. F. (1997). *Out of the shadows: Confronting America's mental illness crisis*. New York: Wiley.

Trent, J. W. Jr. (2017). Moral treatment. *Disability History Museum*. Retrieved June 1, 2017, from http://www.disabilitymuseum.org/dhm/edu/essay.html?id=19

World Health Organization. (1996). *Mental health care law: Ten basic principles*. Retrieved October 31, 2017, from http://www.who.int/mental_health/media/en/75.pdf

Chapter 2
Size and Scope of Justice-Involved Mental Illness

Research on mental health epidemiology shows that mental health disorders are common throughout the United States, affecting tens of millions of people each year, and that, overall, only about half of those affected receive treatment.—National Institute of Mental Health (2018).

Before starting a discussion on just how many justice-involved individuals have a diagnosable mental illness, what those diagnoses tend to be, their severity of symptoms, and their rates of relapse, it will be helpful to keep a few caveats in mind. First, diagnosing mental illness can prove difficult as it impinges on the full cooperation of the patient. This cooperation may be influenced by stigma; varying levels of acceptance of mental health care by gender, race, and culture; and, likely, the "us versus them" relationship of medical staff to inmate, probation and parole officer to client, drug court case manager to client, and so on. Second, there is evidence of moderate amounts of malingering in the justice-involved population; in other words, justice-involved individuals are known to feign illness, including mental illness, if doing so will provide a benefit, such as getting out of assigned work duties, obtaining higher-quality meals, to get out of their jail or prison cell, to be able to be in an air-conditioned facility, or just to feel the reward of gaining a privilege or advantage, no matter how trivial it is to an average person. Last, there is considerable variation in applying mental health screening tools in professional circles, and, further, there can be dynamic differences in how mental health professionals apply diagnoses over time, by place or region, or given other factors (that will be discussed later). To make the long story short, there is a substantial amount of gray area when trying to estimate the *prevalence* of mental illness among the justice-involved population. This chapter will discuss the most current prevalence estimates—or the overall rate of mental illness among each segment of the justice-involved population.

© Springer International Publishing AG, part of Springer Nature 2018
J. Hector, D. Khey, *Criminal Justice and Mental Health*,
https://doi.org/10.1007/978-3-319-76442-9_2

2.1 What We Know: It's Complicated

To begin, and most importantly, there has been no comprehensive record keeping of mental illness for justice-involved individuals. Further, the epidemiological tracking systems on mental health for all Americans are addressed by the Centers for Disease Control; yet, the organization only recently began its first deep assessment in 2011 by piecing together data from several of its monitoring programs (Center for Disease Control and Prevention, 2017a). Ideally, one centralized source would build the capacity to collect data on the extent of mental illness in the United States as well as within the subpopulation of justice-involved individuals; but instead, existing data on the topic comes from a series of special governmental reports, state reports, and sporadic independent research endeavors. This persistent problem was, in fact, acknowledged by the Twenty-First Century Cures Act. For example:

- Section 14015, entitled "Improving Department of Justice Data Collection on Mental Illness Involved in Crime," requires the US Attorney General to gather and report data on homicides (including homicides of police officers), serious injuries, assaults, serious injury or death by law enforcement officers "with respect to the involvement of mental illness in such incidences, if any."
- Section 14016, entitled "Reports on the Number of Mentally Ill Offenders in Prison," includes a mandate to the Comptroller General to estimate the cost of imprisoning individuals with "serious mental illness by the Federal Government or State or unit of local government."

While these efforts of expanding our tracking systems are ongoing and are beginning to be fleshed out, it is important to understand our most current tools. As a helpful resource, William Reeves (2013) of the Centers for Disease Control offers a comprehensive summary of the American mental health surveillance systems. Reeves begins by defining seven key public health functions of these systems, which underscores the importance of this section. First, the public health surveillance systems are put into place to inform interventions with the benefit of data to help shape decision-making. In other words, the systems are set up in a way that allows for trends to be monitored, providing an easy mechanism to discover, identify, and describe changes—or potential signs of problems—and act on them. Second, these systems provide a way to estimate the impact of health conditions, including mental illness. Third, surveillance provides an ability to experts to follow the progression of health conditions and how our responses and treatments shape outcomes. This "natural history" offers a learning tool to help professionals refine future responses and treatments. Fourth, they aid in providing a big picture description of how conditions are distributed in society and how often they occur. Fifth, and related to the second function above, these systems provide structure for hypothesis creation and seeds research ideas. Sixth, they further allow for the evaluation of prevention efforts and control measures. Last, they help professionals plan programs strategically.

As Reeves describes it, surveillance is accomplished through a diverse multilayered approach deployed in unison to give us "a complete mosaic" of the health issues being explored. Specifically, three broad types of surveillance systems exist that collected data on mental illness: population surveys, health-care surveys, and vital statistics. Each provides a slice of information that assist in the *triangulation* of data. According to George Rutherford and his colleagues, "public health triangulation is a process for reviewing, synthesizing, and interpreting secondary data from multiple sources that bear on the same question to make public health decisions" (Rutherford, McFarland, Spindler, White, Patel, Aberle-Grasse, Sabin, Smith, Tache, Calleja-Garcia, & Stoneburner, 2010). In fact, triangulation goes deeper than this; in other words, surveillance systems use different research methodologies and/or sampling strategies to access information in unique ways. The key triangulation is to look for convergence and divergence in the data for further exploration.

2.1.1 Population Surveys

Population surveys examine health issues of *all* citizens (or a subpopulation) through the use of representative samples of the American public at the national, regional, state, and local levels. This survey technique relies heavily on self-reported information to determine the occurrence of mental illness in the wider population. While there is not any one population survey that solely deals with mental health, the US Department of Health and Human Services embeds an array of mental health surveillance into a suite of ongoing programs. For example, the National Survey of Drug Use and Health (NSDUH—administered by SAMHSA) has been tracking mental health since 1994; this survey tool is an annual, nationally representative, self-report survey of Americans aged 12+ designed to capture a broad array of data on substance use and abuse as well as general and mental health. It has become a leading tool for surveillance and has led to an array of special governmental reports and independent research on overall mental health trends in the United States. As such, it can easily be considered the flagship mental health population survey tool at this time. Specifically, it was equipped with the ability to track two key mental illness measures in 2008, both at the state and national level: (1) severe mental illness and (2) any mental illness (SAMHSA, 2013). The drive for this upgrade to the NSDUH in 2008 was, in fact, made over 15 years earlier when Congress passed the Alcohol, Drug Abuse, and Mental Health Administration Reorganization Act, thus showing how slowly innovation can occur after policy shifts.

The NSDUH currently utilizes sets of questions, called scales, to determine whether a survey respondent has severe mental illness or any mental illness. Such scales include psychological distress and functional impairment, which largely makes up the clinical interview section of the survey—the Structured Clinical Interview (SCID-I/NP; includes mood, anxiety, eating, impulse control, substance use, and adjustment disorders as well as a screen for psychotic symptoms). In addition, the NSDUH includes questions on thoughts of suicide and depression within the last year, and these questions help shape the estimations of both severe mental illness and any mental illness in the population. Using the most up-to-date methods available, the survey estimated that 4% of American adults have a serious mental illness (17.9% have any mental illness) in 2015 (SAMHSA, 2017). Importantly, this prevalence is not impacted by diagnoses—that is, this information is gathered in a way that does not require a diagnosis if the scales deployed in the NSDUH have been vetted properly and are sufficiently reliable. Ongoing research is being done to ensure that these estimations are reflective of the American reality of mental illness. In fact, these most recent estimations were recently recalibrated in the 2011 edition of the NSDUH in a collaboration project between SAMHSA and the National Institute on Mental Health (NIMH). These recalibration efforts will continue to be ongoing as our understanding of mental illness evolves. For example, in October 2015, the American Psychiatric Association released its newest Structured Clinical Interview (First, Williams, Karg, & Spitzer, 2016). As such, it is important to remember that there will be a lag of ability to receive the latest intelligence of mental health prevalence on the American population using population surveys. It is also important to remember that the diagnostic criteria for many mental illnesses do not change substantially over the years. In other words, there will be relatively negligible amounts of error in the population data collected. It still is important to note the shortcomings of each data type, especially when trying to account for changes in mental health conditions over time (Fig. 2.1).

Additionally, it is also important to note that the NSDUH reaches respondents who have a physical address. While this can include some "noninstitutional group quarters" such as shelters, boarding houses, university dorms, migrant worker camps, and halfway and quarter houses, NSDUH *does not* reach many homeless or transient Americans who do not consistently seek shelter. Most importantly for the current discussion, NSDUH further excludes individuals in jails and prisons, nursing homes, state mental health hospitals, and individuals in long-term care facilities. In other words, it excludes a wide swath of the vulnerable populations we are interested in studying. These vulnerable populations must be accounted for in some other way; but, we also should consider the prevalence of mental illness will always be underestimated when reviewing the findings of the NSDUH results each year.

To expand and refine mental health surveillance further into states, and more importantly, down to the county level, the Centers for Disease Control and Prevention have relied on the Behavioral Risk Factor Surveillance System (BRFSS). This effort began in 1984 to annually interview a representative sample of Americans in all states to record and track information on health-related risk behaviors, chronic health conditions, and the use of local preventative services. It has since become one of the largest routine health surveys in the world with over 400,000 participants each year. In regard to mental health, the BRFSS has historically used some core questions to ascertain number of mentally unhealthy days and has since 2007 included optional modules (with states given the option to opt-in) for anxiety and depression as well as mental health and stigma. For the areas that

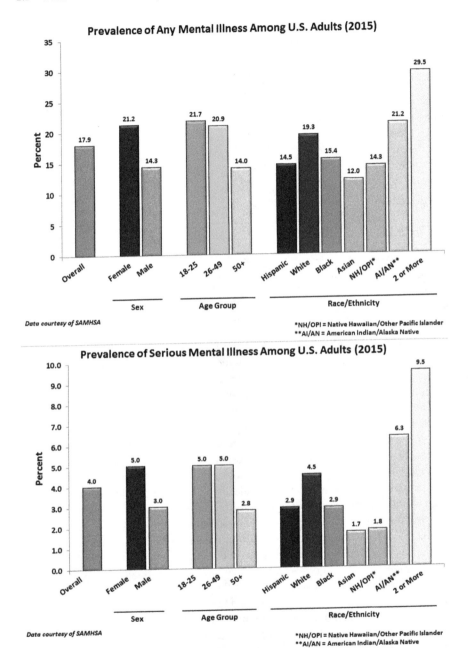

Fig. 2.1 Latest prevalence of mental health and serious mental health illnesses in American adults, reported in 2015 by SAMHSA

Table 2.1 Prevalence of mental health problems among prison and jail inmates (James & Glaze, 2006); note the levels of individuals with mental health problems

	Percent of inmates in —			
	State prison		Local jail	
Selected characteristics	With mental problem	Without	With mental problem	Without
Criminal record				
Current or past violent offense	61%	56%	44%	36%
3 or more prior incarcerations	25%	19%	26%	20%
Substance dependence or abuse	74%	56%	76%	53%
Drug use in month before arrest	63%	49%	62%	42%
Family background				
Homelessness in year before arrest	13%	6%	17%	9%
Past physical or sexual abuse	27%	10%	24%	8%
Parents abused a alcohol or drugs	39%	25%	37%	19%
Charged with violating facility rules[a]	56%	43%	19%	9%
Physical or verba: Assault	24%	14%	8%	2%
Injured in a fight since admission	20%	10%	9%	3%

[a]Includes items not shown

opt-in to examine mental health issues, the BRFSS can provide basic information about the prevalence of mental health issues at the local level. It can also assist mental health professionals in realizing the capacity of services in the local area or estimate the numbers of underserved individuals needing mental health care. This will become important for justice-involved populations as states and communities begin seeking alternatives to jails and prison and need the data to inform change. In 2007, the BRFSS mental health module was delivered in almost half of the United States: Alaska, Arkansas, California, Connecticut, District of Columbia, Georgia, Hawaii, Illinois, Indiana, Iowa, Kentucky, Louisiana, Minnesota, Mississippi, Missouri, Montana, Nevada, New Hampshire, New Mexico, Puerto Rico, Rhode Island, South Carolina, Vermont, Virginia, and Wyoming. In 2009, only eight states opted-in to receive follow-up data.

Reeves (2013) further points out that additional in-depth population surveys occur sporadically, typically at near 10-year intervals. Examples of these include the National Comorbidity Surveys and the National Epidemiologic Survey on Alcohol and Related Conditions. This also includes the special editions of surveys performed by the Bureau of Justice Statistics to expand this surveillance into the justice-involved population, the 1996/2002 Survey of Inmates in Local Jails, and the 1997/2004 Survey of Inmates in State and Federal Correctional Facilities. The most recent special editions of these surveys mimic the methodology of the NSDUH by utilizing a modified clinical interview (for the DSM-IV). The findings, not surprisingly, are very different from the general public. About 56% of state prisoners, 45% of federal prisoners, and 64% of local jail inmates indicated any mental health problem, with many symptoms being severe in nature (James & Glaze, 2006). The latest surveys also disentangled substance dependence (or abuse) from mental health problems. When doing so, the results show just how enmeshed these problems are (Table 2.1).

The special report (James & Glaze, 2006) entitled "Mental Health Problems of Prison and Jail Inmates" provides a summary of the findings from the special editions of the Survey of Inmates in Local Jails (2002) and Survey of Inmates in State and Federal Correctional Facilities (2004). The modified clinical interview in these surveys reliably estimated 23% of state prisoners and 30% of jail inmates had symptoms of major depression, and 15% of state prisoners and 24% of jail inmates had symptoms of a psychotic disorder. Notably, while a substantial portion of prisoners and inmates had a recent history of mental illness (24% of state prisoners, 21% of jail inmates, 14% of Federal prisoners), many more exhibited symptoms of mental illness (49% of state prisoners; 60% of jail inmates; 40% of Federal prisoners). More troubling, very few receive services to address these issues (33% of state prisoners who exhibited mental health problems, 17% of jail inmates who exhibited mental health problems, 24% of federal inmates who exhibited mental health problems). Much more detail will be provided in subsequent chapters on the nature of these findings:

- Roughly one in four of state prisoners and jail inmates with a mental health problem served three more prior incarceration periods relative to state prisoners and jail inmates without mental health issues.
- Female inmates exhibited higher rates of mental health problems relative to male inmates (73% of female State prisoners compared to 55% male; 75% of female jail inmates compared to 63% male).
- State prison inmates who exhibited a mental health problem were about twice as likely to experience homelessness relative to those without a mental health issue.

These issues are central to this text and will be explored into great depth. At this point, consider the value of this type of research and surveillance tool in understanding mental illness, particularly within vulnerable populations.

2.1.2   Health-Care Surveys

Health-care surveys are only recently gaining more significance in the surveillance of mental illness. The reason for this is that the data comes directly from health-care and insurance providers; historically, mental health professionals use the *Diagnostic and Statistical Manual of Mental Disorders*, or DSM, to diagnose a patient whereas hospitals, medical providers, and insurance companies use the *International Statistical Classification of Diseases and Related Health Problems* as managed by the World Health Organization or ICD. The latest edition of the DSM—the DSM-5—has only recently been aligned with the ICD, which is now in its 10th revision (ICD-10). While mental health is yet to be effectively tracked in this manner, it is only a matter of time before the professions adjust to report on more indicators than it has been able to reliably track in the past. To date, suicide is one of the few reliable indicators being tracked by this system of surveillance (Reeves, 2013).

Table 2.2 Primary diagnosis at office visits, classified by major disease category in 2013 (NAMCS; Center for Disease Control and Prevention, 2017b)

1. Supplementary classification (follow-up care, including routine care)	18.2%
2. Diseases of the musculoskeletal and connective tissue	10.1%
3. Diseases of the circulatory system	9.0%
4. Symptoms, signs, and ill-defined conditions	8.4%
5. Diseases of the nervous system and sense organs	8.1%
6. Diseases of the respiratory system	8.1%
7. Mental disorders	6.7%

One prime example of a health-care survey is the National Ambulatory Medical Care Survey, again led by the CDC. This survey, conducted annually since 1973, randomly selects physicians providing direct patient care to participate. It has since been expanded to cover community health centers in 2006. Specifically, the survey tool asks physicians to provide information on roughly 30 patient visits in a randomly selected 1-week time frame. Mental health-related questions have been asked in a few different ways since the 2001. Other examples of health-care surveys include the National Hospital Discharge Survey and the National Nursing Home Survey (Table 2.2).

To date, there has not been any survey to medical providers in jails or prisons that replicates these surveillance techniques. Even if most of these providers wanted to engage in a surveillance program, the lack of resources proves to be a significant roadblock in doing so. For example, medical records may not be kept electronically, or if they were, the systems in which the information is kept may be out of date and incompatible with modern surveillance systems. It is for these reasons that reports of this nature are limited to states with well-resourced criminal justice systems.

2.1.3   Vital Statistics

Vital statistics generally include births, deaths (and fetal deaths), marriages, and divorces. For the current discussion, deaths are the important component of public health surveillance. Suicide is the leading mental health indicator that can easily be tracked by current surveillance methods. As of 2016, suicide is the second to accidents as the leading cause of death for Americans aged 15–19 and the tenth leading cause of death in all Americans (Center for Disease Control and Prevention, 2017c). Another notable indicator that can be included among vital statistics is substance use disorder. For example, medical examiners or coroners can determine that substance abuse contributed to a decedent's cause of death, such as in a case of a long-term cocaine abuser who died from a heart condition. It could very well be determined that this user's heart was damaged by chronic cocaine use, which is very possible with the stimulant family of drugs. Yet, it is important to note here that death investigation systems are quite varying across the United States. It is true that the vast majority of deaths (99% according to the CDC) are recorded, not every jurisdiction has equal access to a comprehensive death investigation system. As such, many deaths many not be classified correctly or completely. In the same example of a long-term cocaine abuser, it may be that his death is simply recorded as cause of death, myocardial infarction (immediate cause), and manner of death, natural without any mention to cocaine dependence as a mechanism of death. Thus, the heart attack would not be noted as a direct consequence of the long-term cocaine use on a death certificate and in vital records.

Suicide has been the leading cause of death for jail inmates for quite some time (deaths in custody was first tracked by the Bureau of Justice Statistics in 2000, so certainly since then, Noonan, 2015). About one-third of jail inmate deaths are attributed to suicide (or 46 suicides per 100,000 inmates), with deaths from heart disease close behind. Compare this to 5.5% of prison inmate deaths attributed to suicide (or 15 suicides per 100,000 prisoners), and the vulnerable population becomes clear—much more about this will be discussed in later chapters.

2.1.4 Putting It All Together: A Summary of Mental Health in America Today

The National Alliance of Mental Illness, a leading advocacy organization for mental health, keeps an array of easy-to-follow briefs on the most up-to-date compilation of mental health statistics available to aid in spreading its message. For example, in their most recent *Mental Health Facts in America* infographic, the following facts are the most salient:

- 43.8 million American adults experience mental illness in any recent year; that is one in five adults in the United States.
- A subset of these Americans—ten million, or close to 1 in every 25 adults—lives with a serious mental illness.
- Half of all chronic mental illness begins to occur by age 14, with the average delay between the onset of symptoms and initial intervention being 8–10 years.
- Depression is the leading cause of disability worldwide.
- Serious mental illness is estimated to cost the United States $193.2 billion in earning losses each year.
- 90% of those who commit suicide have an underlying mental illness; suicide is the tenth leading cause of death in the United States.
- The majority of adult American living with mental illness—60%—did not receive mental health services in the previous year; half of youths (aged 8–15) with mental illness did not receive services in the previous year.
- Black and Hispanic Americans are half as likely to seek and use mental health services compared to their white American counterparts; Asian-Americans utilize mental health services even less, about 1/3 the rate of their white American counterparts.

In their most recent *Mental Health Facts: Multicultural* infographic, these points are also crucial to summarize here:

• American Indian or Alaskan Native adults have the highest prevalence of mental illness at 28.3%, almost three in every ten adults, followed by white adults (19.3%), black adults (18.6%), Hispanic adults (16.3%), and Asian adults (13.9%).
• Individuals who identify as LGBTQ are more than twice as likely to have a mental health condition relative to those who identify as straight/heterosexual; LGBTQ youth are two to three times more likely to commit suicide than straight youth.

This information largely draws from the National Institute of Mental Health resources and is updated frequently to promulgate the latest intelligence on mental health in the most user-friendly way.

2.2 What We Don't Know

With only five targeted population surveys on justice-involved individuals, the two most recent being much more comprehensive than the previous ones, we still may not know the "true" size and scope of justice-involved mental illness. Also disconcerting, the latest available data dates to 2004—over a decade ago—and much has changed since then. In particular, a steady stream of Federal investment in evidence-based practices and programming has shown the potential to ameliorate the issues being discussed here; on the other hand, a perfect storm was also brewing for massive cutbacks in criminal justice and mental health within the same time frame: (1) the level of mass incarceration crested at a peak of 506 inmates and prisoners per 100,000 citizens in 2007–2008. (2) This coincides perfectly with a substantial economic recession, the so-called Great Recession, beginning December 2007. Consider these findings from a recent SAMHSA, (2016) review of behavioral health spending and use: the broad trend in mental health spending from 1986 to 2014 indicated a deeper divestment in inpatient and residential treatment coinciding with an increase in the use of and expenditures in outpatient treatment; during the same time frame, Medicare, Medicaid, and private insurance use increased, while out-of-pocket expenditures decreased; conversely, decreases in Medicaid (26 to 25%) and local spending (16 to 14%) occurred from 2008 to 2014. If one were to dig deeper into these expenditures, they would find a mix bag of successes and failures—with the successes masking the failures when observing this summary data.

For example, the National Alliance on Mental Illness (2015) published its results of an annual survey on state legislation on, and investment in, mental health. In this study, NAMI cites a loss of $4.35 billion in state cuts to mental health-care systems since the recession. From the initial results of this survey published in 2013, many states have begun to reinvest in these systems upon recovery, yet some states have been unable to reform, while others have been in decline. Perhaps more troubling, the results in 2015 show slowed growth and progress relative to previous years for states that were able to make headway. Alaska, North Carolina, and Wyoming are cited by NAMI to be in states of steady decline, with signs of problems occurring in Kentucky, Arkansas, Iowa, Kansas, Ohio, and the District of Columbia. While not mentioned directly in the narrative of the study's findings, Louisiana also has been struggling to reform; in fact, its state constitution will only allow for cuts to higher education and health care during non-budget legislative sessions (e.g., every other year). While other states may not be so restrictive, mental health and criminal justice are often higher on the chopping block for cuts than other essential services.

Thus, information about the level of need that exists for mental illness and substance use disorder treatment, or both, is ill defined. What is clear is that the number of individuals in jails and prisons who requires treatment far exceeds the number who receives it—the latest justice-involved population surveys verified this. Specifically, "over 1 in 3 State prisoners and 1 in 6 jail inmates who had a mental health problem received treatment since admission" (James & Glaze, 2006). In other words, *66% of prisoners and 83% of jail inmates do not get the mental health treatment that they need according to the most up-to-date and comprehensive investigation into the justice-involved mental health population.* Remember, these bleak figures were obtained before mental health systems were further stressed by the recession.

Not knowing much more beyond this is a barrier to progress. Recall that Reeves (2013) describes seven key functions of public health surveillance systems: (1) to inform interventions with the benefit of data, providing an easy mechanism to discover, identify, and describe changes—including signs of problems—and act on them, (2) to estimate the impact of health conditions, (3) to provide a natural history of health conditions and how our responses and treatments shape outcomes, (4) to provide a big picture description of how conditions are distributed in society and how often they occur, (5) to structure hypothesis creation and seeds research ideas, (6) to enable thorough evaluation of prevention efforts and control measures, and, perhaps most importantly, (7) to help professionals engage in strategic planning. Without further investment into mental health surveillance, these functions become much more difficult to achieve. One truth in all of this is that, historically, the United States has prioritized mental illness behind other matters.

2.3   What We Know We Don't Know: Hidden Mental Illness

It is entirely possible—in fact, it is very probable—that not all illnesses are addressed, while an individual is incarcerated. Further, these illnesses may not be addressed in time to help the patient, fully addressed in the best way possible, or diagnosed in a way to offer the best treatment. On that last point, proper diagnosis may require several visits and observations by a mental health professional, all of which may benefit greatly by comprehensive medical records for the current provider to understand prior assessments, treatments, and so on. Often, for many reasons, a person's medical history may be disjointed and/or lack current information.

Consider visiting a doctor as an adult and being asked for a complete medical history from childhood. Even for a person with little to no medical history, it may be difficult to recount all that is needed for a current report. Now, imagine this scenario again from someone who has felt stigmatized many times for a mental health concern and criminal history. The mental illness alone may have prompted denial or a reluctance to report symptoms. Add in a criminal history, all the more reason for a person to fear stigma. Further, the chain of information is broken after incarceration and return to society. Often, this continues to repeat again and again resulting in stagnation for the individual in the process of recovery and health.

Broadly speaking, inmates may not disclose their illness for fear of discrimination, negative treatment, or just plain lack of knowledge. Often, individuals feel shame surrounding their mental health. Mental health concerns are often seen as a sign of weakness—a label that is perhaps one of the most problematic for inmates— which only further perpetuates the stigma. Masking the signs and symptoms of depression or anxiety, or any other psychological disorder, can be a major setback for a person as these issues will go untreated, potentially leading to significant problems, decompensation, and higher risks of bad outcomes (e.g., suicide, drug overdose, violent confrontations, and so on). Seeking help as soon as symptoms arise is important to the health of the person affected, yet this has not historically been the case for jail inmates or prisoners, thanks largely to the effects of stigma. Additionally, knowing one's own triggers is essential for future prevention and proactive efforts to remain healthy.

Taking that ideal a step further, mental illness in a male prison, there is less likelihood of disclosure of mental illness and seeking of treatment. According to the World Health Organization (2017), there are differences in both prevalence of mental health and substance abuse as well as reporting by gender. This gap is supported by a stream of literature; for example, Doherty and Kartalova-O'Doherty (2010) published their analysis of the HRB National Psychological Wellbeing and Distress Survey in 2010. The data in this telephone survey revealed significant gender differences between males and females that influence seeing general practitioners for mental health concerns. In particular, an array of sociodemographic and psychological factors (such as feelings of limited physical activity and social activity, educational level, employment status, marital status, self-reported physical health, self-reported quality of life, and whether these men live in a rural or urban setting) influenced male visits to general practitioners, while females were only influenced by social factors (e.g., feeling like mental health limits social activities) and access to health care (e.g., price), thus leading to broader differences among the genders in seeking mental health help from practitioners. The main point here is that we generally know less about individuals who do not seek help or are not willing to seek help and that the rate of untreated mental illness is likely higher in some groups relative to others, gender being a prime example.

Another issue surrounding the idea of prisons or jails as it relates to mental health is time. The intake process is limited, and only a small amount is spent addressing the immediate needs of the incoming inmate as well as acclimating them to the policies and procedures of the prison. Also, keep in mind the mindset of the individual being brought into the facility. Obviously, none of this is ideal for the typical psychosocial interview. In a hospital setting, a trained mental health professional would complete a psychosocial interview upon intake with a patient. This interview would include questions regarding background and history on both physical and mental health in order to gain a baseline for the individual. This allows the treatment staff to have somewhat of a comparison for behavior. Additionally, this information is kept in the patient's medical record for future use if needed. If the same patient returns for treatment, the staff would then be able to review past notes and information to best treat the person. Jails and prisons, however, do not have similar processes in place (oftentimes), leading to an utter lack of knowledge about the people within these facilities. Thus, mental health diagnoses often remain undiagnosed, yielding to a lack of ability to adequately describe the issues within justice-involved populations. Other than the few major surveys of jail and prison inmates, which offer limited glimpses into the "true" picture of mental health within these facilities, there is a major disadvantage in the lack of ability to track issues over time, track the emergence of new problems, understand the impact of policies on mental health, and so on.

2.3.1 Marginalized Groups and Cultural Differences

Marginalized groups struggle within the criminal justice system as they do in regular society. Persons of different races, religions, sexual orientation, etc. often experience difficulties in seeking help, maintaining treatment regimes, or even being considered for treatment services (e.g., in the case of justice-involved transgender individuals). These groups often experience higher rates of victimization, isolation, stigmatization, and so on and often are less likely to report mental health concerns and seek treatment. Without knowing the full picture and extent of these issues with relevant data, it is difficult to intervene in the lives of these vulnerable individuals. This certainly can add to their trouble receiving help. Without factual information to support the need, most facilities cannot justify providing further programming—particularly when trying to justify costs. And unfortunately, with little to no information and data being collected on these vulnerable subpopulations (let alone, on individuals with mental illness, generally), it is difficult to assess the extent of the problem(s) in the first place. Part of the lack of information lies in the lack of understanding of different marginalized groups or cultures even outside of the criminal justice system. Even further, without research and information, it is also difficult to determine any further disparities that may exist; most research suggests this to be the case.

For example, recent stories of violence against transgender persons have emerged as a widely publicized issue in late 2016 and early 2017. With recent national attention on issues of this population, advocates are helping to aid in equality for transgender persons in criminal justice settings as well by tapping into this surge of attention. The National Center for Transgender Equality (NCTE)—a leader in this movement—"continues to press for stronger protections and accountability and create new tools for advocacy focused on transgender and gender non-conforming people's interactions with the criminal justice system with local, state and federal law enforcement officials and public at-large" (2017). Within the literature found on their website, the NCTE makes reference to the daily humiliation, increased risk of physical and sexual abuse, and fear of harm if individuals use legal solutions to report these problems. In particular, the Prison Rape Elimination Act (PREA) was designed specifically to include dedicated provisions to help protect incarcerated transgender individuals against sexual assault. However, prisoners (and staff) often lack respect for the PREA process, with many left thinking that it could be considered "a joke" or just a window dressing on the realities of prison life (Khey, unpublished research).

Mental health professionals are trained on cultural competencies to work with different cultural groups, particularly with an understanding of the issues described above to encourage sensitivity to the deficiencies primarily caused by the social realities of vulnerable populations. The dilemma, as mentioned many times within in this book, often rests with a lack of professional staffing to accommodate all inmates within a jail or prison. This means, that despite adequate training for mental health professionals, there being one person for an entire jail or prison means that there may not be the means to assess all inmates to ensure proper care and adherence to cultural etiquette. At that point, administrators tend to focus their efforts on meeting and maintaining what is currently understood as the constitutionally acceptable level of mental health services. Much more on this concept will be explored in subsequent chapters; however, it is important to understand that typical levels of mental health services throughout American corrections tend to only allow for crisis care and exigent problems as they may present themselves. Vulnerabilities can often be magnified in criminal justice settings, including those inherent in cultural differences.

To be sure, there are many various cultural barriers that may exist within society that also are relevant within the criminal justice system. For example, language barriers can be difficult to overcome in everyday life, let alone the difficulties that language barriers can present when entering a jail upon arrest. A language barrier can particularly exacerbate the issue of obtaining proper and accurate information (of special note: health information). Also, it is further important to recognize that certain cultures are far less likely to adhere to American cultural norms. Some people of Asian descent tend not to make eye contact, which to some may be perceived negatively or disrespectful—or more notably in this instance—may be a sign of deception for some trained law enforcement and corrections personnel. In addition, in some Asian cultures, as well as in others such as Orthodox Hasidim, it is wholly inappropriate to have any interaction between females and males who are not married. With this in mind, consider the harsh environment of a jail or prison; if a male inmate were to be approached by a female corrections officer and who subsequently avoids eye contact and does not respond, there could be potential trouble (e.g., insubordination). The inmate would be doing this as a sign of respect to his culture, but for the officer and other staff, this would be viewed as disrespect and could lead to possible infractions inside the jail/prison. Furthermore, different races, religions, and other cultural subgroups may have other barriers and specific behaviors. Consider differences among Islamic inmates, women of color, American Indians, and so forth.

On a final note, it is often important to consider one's perceived social status when discussing mental health outcomes. In other words, it may not be enough only to consider membership in a vulnerable subpopulation or class (e.g., transgender male prisoner) in isolation. Importantly, mental health problems may be attenuated by one's own perception of being marginalized. In research published by Friestad (2010), male Norwegian prisoners were surveyed to understand how perceived social status in prison affected potential inequalities in health (and mental health). As expected, prisoners who perceived that they were marginalized exhibited increased odds of experiencing mental health problems. More work needs to be done in this area to better understand the impacts of vulnerable individuals, particularly at the point when these individuals are set to reenter society.

2.4 Conclusion

Many professionals suspect that most mental illnesses are underreported. In fact, this chapter remains brief as the American epidemiological understanding of mental illness continues to take a back seat to other, less- or non-stigmatized problems. This is truly the result of the lack of investment in mental health research relative to other American priorities. There appears to be a shift in this trend, however. The twenty-first Century Cures Act was recently enacted into law; it sharply responds to this problem through policy, by earmarking funds, and by shifting governmental agencies in a way that will enable progress in this area. While it is not exactly clear when these changes will start producing results, changes have already started to occur to ensure transformation in America's struggle with mental health.

One key issue that is not always discussed or even thought of in regard to the lack of mental health treatment options is the waste of the resources earmarked for this purpose. This waste can take many forms. Consider then, like any other illnesses, the effect of prolonging/delaying treatment in that this can often result in an increase the cost/investment necessary to achieve a healthy outcome. Further, the traumatic experiences of incarceration, one of America's primary responses to mental health diagnosis, often serves to only push vulnerable people toward further or compounding negative outcomes. Therefore, if treating the person in the community early in the disease process could be given a certain dollar amount, it most certainly would be monumentally less than the amount necessary when the cost of incarceration is factored in for those individuals that fall in the cracks of this safety net. Incarcerating a person in need of treatment has placed a large financial burden onto the criminal justice system, thus creating a different problem. To date, this problem has been largely ignored; yet, progress is slowly occurring in the form of broad partnerships and fresh ideas to address this problem.

References

21st Century Cures Act. Public Law 144-255. 2016.

Center for Disease Control and Prevention. (2017a). *CDC report: Mental health surveillance among U.S. adults*. Retrieved June 1, 2017, from https://www.cdc.gov/mentalhealthsurveillance/

Center for Disease Control and Prevention. (2017b). *Ambulatory health care data*. Retrieved June 1, 2017, from https://www.cdc.gov/nchs/ahcd/index.htm

Center for Disease Control and Prevention. (2017c). *National suicide statistics*. Retrieved June 1, 2017, from https://www.cdc.gov/violenceprevention/suicide/statistics/

Doherty, D. T., Kartalova-O'Doherty, Y., (2010). Gender and self-reported mental health problems: Predictors of help seeking from a general practitioner. *British Journal of Health Psychology 15*(1):213–228.

First, M. B., Williams, J. B., Karg, R. S., & Spitzer, R. L. (2016). *SCID-5-CV: structured clinical interview for DSM-5 disorders, clinician version*. American Psychiatric Association.

Friestad, C., (2010) Socio-economic status and health in a marginalized group: the role of subjective social status among prison inmates. *The European Journal of Public Health 20*(6):653–658.

James, D. J., & Glaze, L. E. (2006). *Mental health problems of prison and jail inmates*. Washington, DC: Bureau of Justice Statistics. Retrieved June 1, 2017, from https://www.bjs.gov/content/pub/pdf/mhppji.pdf

National Alliance on Mental Illness. (2015). *State mental health legislation 2015: Trends, themes, and effective practices*. Retrieved June 1, 2017, from https://www.nami.org/About-NAMI/Publications-Reports/Public-Policy-Reports/State-Mental-Health-Legislation-2015/NAMI-StateMentalHealthLegislation2015.pdf

National Center for Transgender Equality. (2017). *Issues: Police, jails, and prisons*. Retrieved June 1, 2017, from http://www.transequality.org/issues/police-jails-prisons

National Institute on Mental Health. (2018). *Statistics*. Retrieved March 12, 2018, from https://www.nimh.nih.gov/health/statistics/index.shtml

Noonan, M. (2015). *Mortality in local jails and state prisons, 2000–2013 - Statistical tables*. Washington DC: Bureau of Justice Statistics. Retrieved June 1, 2017, from https://www.bjs.gov/content/pub/pdf/mljsp0013st.pdf

Reeves, W. (2013). Mental health surveillance. In M. D. Gellman & J. R. Turner (Eds.), *Encyclopedia of Behavioral medicine*. New York: Springer.

Rutherford G. W., McFarland, W., Spindler, H., White, K., Patel, S. V., Aberle-Grasse J., Sabin, K., Smith, N., Taché, S., Calleja-Garcia, J. M., Stoneburner, S. L., (2010). Public health triangulation: approach and application to synthesizing data to understand national and local HIV epidemics. *BMC Public Health 10* (1).

Substance Abuse and Mental Health Services Administration. (2013). *Revised estimates of mental health from the National Survey on Drug Use and Health*. Retrieved June 1, 2017, from https://www.samhsa.gov/data/sites/default/files/NSDUH148/NSDUH148/sr148-mental-illness-estimates.htm

Substance Abuse and Mental Health Services Administration. (2016). *Behavioral health spending & use accounts: 1986–2014*. Retrieved June 1, 2017, from https://store.samhsa.gov/shin/content/SMA16-4975/SMA16-4975.pdf

Substance Abuse and Mental Health Services Administration. (2017). *Reports and detailed tables from the 2015 National Survey on Drug Use and Health*. Retrieved June 1, 2017, from https://www.samhsa.gov/samhsa-data-outcomes-quality/major-data-collections/reports-detailed-tables-2015-NSDUH

World Health Organization. (2017). *Gender and women's mental health*. Retrieved June 1, 2017, from http://www.who.int/mental_health/prevention/genderwomen/en/

Chapter 3
The Front Line: EMS, Law Enforcement, and Probation and Parole

Mental health continues to be a topic people would rather ignore, especially management.—Survey Respondent, National Association of Emergency Medical Technicians (2017)

First responders—which typically include emergency medical services (EMS), "line" (or patrol) law enforcement officers, and firemen—are workers who are dispatched to crime scenes, accidents, and emergencies. Aside from bystanders and witnesses, they are often the first to encounter people in crisis and even more likely to be the first to engage with these individuals. These professionals routinely encounter the turmoil, panic, and pain in its rawest form and thus are often dealing with difficult and serious situations—perhaps even daily. In regard to confronting mental illness, the primary concern lies in the lack of relevant training for the vast majority of these professions. For example, EMS personnel commonly have *some* level of training to enhance their ability to work with individuals experiencing mental health crises and/or who have a mental illness (diagnosed or undiagnosed); on the other hand, law enforcement officers commonly have *little to no required training* in mental health-related topics. This training deficiency is beginning to be addressed as some departments are moving to require officers, or a subset of law enforcement agencies' patrol units, to be trained to serve on Crisis Intervention Teams (CIT), but this is not yet universal. Therefore, it is imperative to carefully consider the unintended consequences of having citizens routinely encountering professionals who are not properly trained to work with individuals experiencing mental health crises when emergency services are dispatched. While many urban and suburban areas have created a mobile crisis unit that provides immediate services in the event of a mental health crisis, these units are often underfunded or work in isolation. Ideally, these mobile crisis units work together with local law enforcement when emergency services are called. This chapter discusses the current picture of first responders' work with individuals with mental illness and citizens

© Springer International Publishing AG, part of Springer Nature 2018
J. Hector, D. Khey, *Criminal Justice and Mental Health*,
https://doi.org/10.1007/978-3-319-76442-9_3

experiencing mental health crises. It further identifies probation and parole officers as part of the first responder definition as these professionals confront the very same issues as do their colleagues in patrol law enforcement and EMS.

3.1   Know the Role

Dealing with people who are ill day in and day out can be difficult for almost anyone. Much like any other illness (in particular, chronic illness), those with mental illness also may seek treatment repeatedly with varying levels of success (and failure and/or setbacks). Also, many illnesses can progressively worsen over time particularly with lack of treatment, including undertreatment. Seeing the same person over and over as a first responder or treatment provider—often colloquially called frequent flyers—can take its toll. Imagine, if you perceive that whatever you do on your job, that very little of it seems to be helping or that you feel like you are simply "doing the motions" without anything to show for it.

"Helping professionals" often get into the business directly due to a passion or desire to want to help people. For example, on a top police news and blogging site—PoliceOne.com—a recent post entitled "7 reasons I'm still a police officer" explained that the unnamed author cherished "protecting those who cannot protect themselves," and "getting help to someone who needs it" as his or her main reasons for continuing to serve while the recent political climate seems to have given rise to a downturn in confidence in American law enforcement officers (PoliceOne, 2016). With a broken continuum of care and a consistent lack of systematic resources, protecting vulnerable citizens and proving help to those who need it can be a very difficult and often frustrating task. If you factor in the bureaucracy of local, state, and federal government, one can begin to envision a series of roadblocks that can often demotivate American first responders, leading to further unintentional consequences. For example, these barriers commonly lead to burnout, and this burnout leads to mental health concerns for these helping professionals and first responders.

Unfortunately, these concerns have become self-evident in the amount of suicides within these professions. In a recent study by the Centers of Disease Control and Prevention, "protective service" professionals including law enforcement and firefighters were found to have the sixth-highest suicide rate and will over double the national average suicide rate of that year (30.5 per 100,000 versus 12.6 per 100,000 average for American Adults, both in 2012; McIntosh, Spies, Stone, Lokey, Trudeau, & Bartholow, 2016). Even more stark, female protective service professionals experienced the highest suicide rate relative to other adult females in any other occupation (14.1 per 100,000).

It is far from clear what level of impact deinstitutionalization has had on the mental health of these professionals themselves; however, it is clear that deinstitutionalization has starkly increased the interaction of helper professions with individuals with mental illness and/or individuals at high risk to experience mental health crises. On its website, the National Alliance on Mental Illness strongly suggests that "law enforcement agencies have increasingly become the de facto first responders to people experiencing mental health crisis" while citing indirect evidence to support this claim. From the evidence presented in the last chapter, this bold claim appears to have a lot of truth to it in the absence of direct study; either way, it is certain that these interactions are common, frequent, and have an impact on both responders and respondees in ways we are yet to completely understand.

Probation and parole officers also struggle with these very issues yet have been largely forgotten in the growing research in this area. Further, probation and parole officers often have to contend with increased caseloads and decreased resources due to the nature of recent justice reforms and policies set in place to decrease prison overcrowding/populations. As revealed in the previous chapter, the vast majority of individuals in need of services are not receiving them in jail or prison settings. At this point, the vast majority of treatment resources continue to remain in the communities probationers and parolees return to; however, connecting these individuals with services often remains challenging. Research is direly needed in this area as probation and parole officers often have caseloads that include individuals with varying degrees of mental illness and co-occurring disorders who may require routine care.

For supervisees with serious mental illness, community corrections agencies have often adapted a special agent role or "unit" to address "extreme" cases and thus focuses training resources on agents with the most challenging caseload (Lurigio, 2001). Yet, the job also demands that *all* agents confront individuals when they are having mental health crises. Relative to patrol police officers, it appears that many in community corrections have broader experiences with individuals with mental illness and/or at risk of experiencing mental health crises. A litany of research questions arise from these interactions and are yet to be explored.

For example, probation and parole officers aid in the success of individuals in lieu of incarceration or post-incarceration. The transition of leaving jail, prison, or court-ordered treatment can be the most difficult period for person; in fact, a wide array of literature focuses on this transitional period as a particular moment of high risk of problems (most likely, relapse, recidivism, rearrest, and/or re-incarceration; Begun, Early, & Hodge, 2016; Jacob & Poletick, 2008; Stewart & George-Paschal, 2017). Consider that the mission of community corrections agencies often highlights and prioritizes the assurance of accountability among their supervisees to promote successful outside of jail and prison facilities and to ensure public safety. One must rhetorically consider, then, the level of accountability to be placed on individuals with mental illness and co-occurring disorders. Perhaps the following question should be carefully considered: how should probation and parole officers respond to supervisees who are in violation with their conditions of supervision or release directly due to mental illness and/or substance abuse?

The front lines of first responders are people who truly get to be pillars of support in times of crisis. They often help those in need when the worst has happened, quickly becoming the worst moments in people's lives and memories. The level of empathy and concern for others is truly a remarkable feat that often gets overlooked when assessing the problems of tending to individuals with mental illnesses.

3.1.1   EMS and Trained Firefighters

Emergency Medical Services (EMS) refers to the medically trained professionals (and their agencies) who are dispatched to incidents of medical emergencies to provide acute out-of-hospital care, triage, and transportation services to medical facilities for further assessment and treatment (District of Columbia Department of Health, 2017). They include (1) paramedics—highest level of training and licensure of their class, paramedics are skilled in ambulatory medicine delivery, heart monitoring, intubation, establishing an airway when it is occluded, and other advanced life support procedures (e.g., defibrillation); (2) emergency medical technicians (EMT) of varying levels of training and expertise including EMT-Intermediate (one step lower in training relative to paramedics—to be phased out in upcoming years), Advanced-EMT (limited range of ambulatory medicine delivery, yet fully trained in advanced airway procedures and set to replace the EMT-I level of certification), and EMT-Basic (limited range of emergency care procedures, yet include the most important such as defibrillation, procedures in case of potential spinal injury, and oxygen therapy); and (3) ambulance personnel (who are, at times, cross-trained in a certification listed above). As mentioned earlier, EMS personnel work closely with law enforcement and fire departments when responding to various types of emergencies. In fact, in most major metropolitan areas, when EMS is run as a public venture, it often falls under fire services in organizational charts. Further, EMS has been increasingly privatized as noted in a recent *The New York Times* expose entitled "When you dial 911 and Wall Street answers" (Ivory, Protess, & Bennett, 2016), leading to new challenges yet to be adequately researched and assessed.

As with most medical-related occupations, EMS personnel do receive some training as it relates to mental health, albeit minimal at this time. Most critically, it should be noted that EMS personnel and firefighters have consistently and historically retained a medical orientation to care coming from a *non-law enforcement* perspective. In other words, as first responders to incidents featuring mental illness and/or mental health crises, law enforcement professionals have been criticized for their paramilitary orientation and approach which often is contraindicated for these types of incidents. So, while the level of training may not be substantially different in the certification and licensure process (and re-certification process) for law enforcement and EMS personnel, the orientation should theoretically produce significantly different results on the street.

In Florida, training often consists of lectures relating to excited delirium (e.g., symptoms of bizarre and aggressive behavior, psychomotor excitement (high rate of breathing and feelings of "on edge"), paranoia, panic, and potential violence), combative patients, and the use of restraint and drugs such as ketamine. In all actuality, these topics are covered within broader lectures on interfacing with patents, often lasting a few hours (at best; Strate, 2017). In New Orleans, similar coverage was confirmed with a local training manager and community liaison (Belcher, 2017). As such, the majority of the EMS and firefighter workforce remain critically undertrained in mental health across the nation. Further, there is a dearth of literature on the impact of privatization of these services on the quality of care given to individuals with mental health concerns. This is a critical issue as privatization has become more prevalent since the economic downturn and recession in the United States in 2008. Anecdotally, it appears that there is a great potential for more problematic interactions between private sector EMS personnel and firefighters; *The New York Times* expose detailed worsening response times, failing and faulty equipment, and poor service that have led to the death of at least two patients (Ivory, Protess, & Bennett, 2016).

3.1.2 Law Enforcement

The vast majority of "line" law enforcement personnel across the country attend standardized training, called Peace Officer Standards and Training (POST). The POST standards are created and maintained by state-level commissions and vary across state. As such, the level of mental health training police cadets receive varies. For example, in California, cadets attending POST-certified police academies across the state will receive at least one module that addresses the following: (1) an introduction to the laws put into place that protect people with mental illness and disabilities, (2) training in recognizing the behaviors that can be a red flag or serve as indicators of mental illness or disability, (3) training in de-escalation skills, (4) training in responses that are appropriate to differing situations that include indirect referrals for the individual and direct referrals to community partners, and (5) educate cadets in mental health and disability stigma to ensure reduction in stigma (California Commission on Peace Officer Standards and Training, 2017). This content was developed in partnership with the National Alliance on Mental Illness, local mental health professionals, and POST subject matter experts to ensure best results; and while the hours of training dedicated to this module may vary, mostly this Regular Basic Course receives a minimum of 664 h of training (yet most academy average over 850 h of overall training, signifying that most academies go above and beyond the minimum to ensure adequate training of new cadets).

In 2017, California leads the United States in the development of this type of embedded training in POST academies. This is directly due to state legislation that was signed into law in October of 2015. California Senate Bill 11 created a statutory mandate directing the Commission on Peace Standards and Training to include "adequate instruction in the handling of persons with developmental disabilities or mental illness, or both…[and] to establish and keep updated a continuing education classroom training course relating to law enforcement interaction with developmentally disabled and mentally ill persons" (2015). As time passes, it will be interesting to see if other states follow suit, take an alternative approach to ensuring better training practices, or remain stagnant. At this time, most law enforcement training mirrors the status quo for EMS personal explained above. This status quo tends to focus on "containment and transportation" (Strate, 2017). Such training can include tactics of restraint, which again, can be contraindicated in some situations. To, at minimum, make mention of how to approach encounters with individuals with mental illness and/or citizens experiencing a mental health crisis, law enforcement training may include de-escalation skills in the form of "Verbal Judo" or something quite similar. Verbal Judo is training program developed by George Thompson (whose doctorate was in English and was further trained in rhetoric) that focuses on the power of persuasion and verbal communication to redirect behavior. It remains empirically unclear whether these tactics show statistical improvement in outcomes when encountering individuals with mental illness and/or citizens who are experiencing a mental health crisis. Yet, Verbal Judo remains incredibly popular as a training option for developing crisis intervention skills in the United States and abroad.

The most concentrated and promising investment in affecting change among law enforcement, EMS, and trained firefighters has been in building Crisis Intervention Team (CIT) programs and its related training. This in-service training has become robust, evidence-based, and is thought to be the leading solution to the current state of affairs of underserving vulnerable mental health populations and individuals with disabilities. CIT is explained further below.

3.1.3   Probation and Parole

Probation and parole officers face a different challenge working with individuals post-conviction and post-incarceration. The agent's role involves supervising individuals who have been arrested of a crime and are sentenced to a probationary period or individuals who are being released from incarceration. Typically, supervision involves case management, frequent and (often) random drug tests, and regular visits and/or check-ins. Policies can differ across states as well as with the federal approach; however, the basics and routines are essentially very similar (United State Courts, 2017).

In urban areas with adequate resources, special units within community corrections have been created to address the mental health caseload that these agencies may have. For example, in New York City, the New York City Probation offers a forensic mental health unit to "help their clients adjust to probation supervision while also addressing…mental health needs…, [including] working individually with clients and tracking their progress, sometimes through periods of hospitalizations and homelessness" (2017). This is a relatively new unit, with mandates to begin forming in 2008 after a formal review gaps in services performed by New York City. It is difficult to determine the effectiveness of this type of program; yet, it does appear that it and others like it deploy evidence-based practices and services designed to show improvements in outcomes for this target population. Much more research on the effectiveness of these programs are slated to emerge in upcoming years.

One recent study, by Wolff and her colleagues, shows that there is great promise in deploying specialized mental health caseloads (Wolff, Epperson, Shi, Huening, Schumann, & Sullivan, 2014). This study used a mixed-methods approach to first ensure that trained special agents in New Jersey were staying true to their training and evidence-based approaches while also following up to observe any potential differences in outcomes among probationers with mental illness who are supervised on a specialized caseload versus those who are not. Their findings show that the special caseloads were deployed with rigor and probationers who received these special services had statistically improved criminal justice and mental health outcomes (e.g., fewer violations of probation resulting in arrest and jail days, improved mental health symptoms, better quality of life, etc.) relative to those who were not placed on a special caseload (although they did qualify). This study is robust, yet the researchers urge future researchers to examine special caseloads with a random control treatment design to be able to understand whether other potential confounding factors are interfering with these results.

Probation and parole officers will be as important as first responders in managing mental health in American communities in the upcoming years. In fact, there will likely be more burden directly placed on their shoulders to be on the front lines of this response.

3.2 Common Interactions

The vast majority of interactions between first responders and individuals with mental illness and/or experiencing a mental health crises are often perceived as negative. Textbooks, advocacy groups, and research often use a lens of the perspective of individuals with mental illness, which is compelling and offers great insight into the plight of this target population. This text does make light of this perspective, often heavily, to ensure adequate assurance of busting myths that plague this topic, to improve understanding in the area, and to help make sense of the broken nature of our mental health care systems. Yet, exploring these interactions from this perspective alone will only be able to depict a smaller part of the broader problem. To gain better understanding into and compassion for the issues explored in this text, it will be important to understand both sides of the interaction.

3.2.1 Frequent Flyers: An Example of Typical and Common Interactions (and Frustrations)

In Austin, Texas, Travis County Emergency Medical Services grew curious about a number of repeated calls to 911, often from the same patients time and time again (Plohetski, 2008), a common occurrence experienced by EMS professionals across the country (Belcher, 2017; Strate, 2017). One such example described a man calling emergency dispatchers three times in 1 day, resulting in three separate trips to local hospitals. Further research into this same case uncovered that over the course of 2 years, paramedics were called to this man's home 290 times (an average nearing three times a week). As a result of such cases, Travis County began to track these data in order to better serve the community and identify a better solution for such patients with extraordinary need. In particular, this study found:

- Ten patients made up more than 1 percent of the system's 130,000 contacts with patients in two years. Their most common complaints were stomach or chest pain, injuries or respiratory problems. Paramedics also responded to calls when the patients exhibited behavioral problems.
- Nearly all of the patients went to a hospital emergency room each time, sometimes crowding into already overflowing facilities.
- The patient who was seen 290 times in the two-year period was evaluated by paramedics twice on 36 days and nine times in a separate seven-day period.

This new tracking system and database has allowed for Travis County EMS to take a better look at their processes and where their time and resources were being spent (and wasted). For example, and at that time (in 2008), Travis County was spending $300 on labor, gasoline, and medical equipment costs for the average call and was putting in more than an hour of time commitment. The cumulative drain repeated and unsuccessful calls for service have on the system had become a critical issue with regard to the *quality* of services for the entire service area. Adding to the emerging crisis, cutbacks were occurring contemporaneously to Austin's mental health centers and hospitals, resulting in increased activity in emergency rooms (and, by default, emergency medical services) in addition to the lack of resources and reduced quality care available in the area at the time.

Common problems arise in situations where these inefficiencies in the system promulgate. In other words, frequent flyers in the system can cause a ripple effect. For example, patients may end up in emergency room beds for too long, possibly even days or weeks without medical history or medication information. The emergency room, particularly at hospitals serving the vulnerable and underserved populations, can also have less capacity to provide thorough treatment or assistance for patients experiencing mental illness. In Travis County's case, local stakeholders were compelled to search for alternatives after this critical introspection into its mental health-care system's inefficiencies in order to overcome these obstacles and have even attempted to resolve things directly with patients in need. They have since explored better triage plans and policies for mental health patients by EMS, adding a nurse to emergency services dispatch to assess patients over the phone, who appear to have mental health concerns, and developing a community health paramedic position. In one instance, Travis County EMS actually met with a patient and her caregiver directly to discuss ways to help and avoid frequent calls/hospital trips. The effort was successful temporarily until the patient was arrested and, upon her release, the cycle of frequent calls began again. Yet, the willingness to explore out-of-the-box options is now on the table for many jurisdictions dealing with the very same issues.

"Frequent flyers" are common jargon among first responders (Belcher, 2017). Interventions with particular focus on the emergency room have been created and tested and show promise (Michelen, Martinez, Lee, & Wheeler, 2006). For example, a relatively recent study of in New York City showed that an emergency department diversion program featuring health priority specialists and community health workers successfully reduced the return rate to the hospital. It appears that many areas are exploring broader community partnerships to engage on fixing this problem rather than having an approach spearheaded from a sole source (such as EMS like in Travis County or by a hospital, such as in this case in Manhattan).

3.3 Common Problems

The Treatment Advocacy Center is a nonprofit working to safeguard for the "effective treatment of severe mental illness" by removing barriers to services and care; this nonprofit also clearly documents the common problems facing American mental health services today (Treatment Advocacy Center, 2017a, 2017b, 2017c). Relevant to this discussion, the center recently released a study discussing the interactions between law enforcement and individuals with mental illness. The study laid out some alarming statistics initially to drive its focus; for example, "people with untreated mental illness are 16 times more likely to be killed during a police encounter than other civilians approached or stopped by law enforcement" (Fuller, Lamb, Biasotti, & Snook, 2015). This particular study, entitled "Overlooked in the undercounted: The role of mental illness in fatal law enforcement encounters," explores additional data angles and alternative sources for estimates when data is unavailable to continue its point. Using publicly available data, Fuller, Lamb, Biasotti, and Snook uncover that while only a few individuals shy of 1 in 50 Americans are said to have untreated and severe mental illness, this segment of the population seems to be involved in *at least* a quarter of fatal shootings by law enforcement. In fact, their estimates put this statistic closer to half of these shootings involve this particular segment. When looking deeper, these researchers estimate that roughly one in ten citizen-police encounters also involve this segment. While it may be tempting to also assert that these statistics are being sourced by an advocacy group who may be well served by articulating these problems in the most negative light to get a reaction or to seed change, the report clearly recognizes its close partnership with the National Sheriffs' Association in evaluating these issues facing law enforcement.

Recall our discussion above about frequent flyers as well. Imagine having 10% of your workload (roughly) dedicated to citizens who have untreated severe mental illness, many of whom you (and/or your fellow coworkers) routinely encounter. Also imagine feeling powerless to do anything about it as your training offers you few options, certainly fewer options *that work*. The viewpoint of the center is to develop a strategy to scale down confrontations between individuals with mental illness and law enforcement in order to diminish the number of fatal police shootings; it has worked closely with law enforcement over the years to begin promulgating solutions. Coauthor and Executive Director John Snook makes his point clear—"By dismantling the mental illness treatment system, we have turned from a

Table 3.1 Summary of undercounted: The role of mental illness in fatal law enforcement encounters (Treatment Advocacy Center, 2017c)

Overview: This study reviews law enforcement homicide reporting, examines the role of mental illness in the use of deadly force by American law enforcement, and recommends practical changes in policy to aid in reducing fatal police shootings
Findings
• The risk of being killed while being approached or stopped by law enforcement in the community is 16 times higher for individuals with untreated serious mental illness than for other civilians
• By the most conservative estimates, at least one in four fatal law enforcement encounters involves an individual with serious mental illness. When data have been rigorously collected and analyzed, findings indicate as many as half of all law enforcement homicides ends the life of an individual with severe psychiatric disease
• The arrest-related death program operated by the Bureau of Justice Statistics within the US Department of Justice is the only federal database that attempts to systematically collect and publish mental health information about law enforcement homicides. The program was suspended in 2015 because the data available to the agency was not credible enough to report
Recommendations to policymakers
• Restore the mental illness treatment system sufficiently that individuals with serious mental illness are not left untreated to the point that their behavior results in law enforcement action
• Accurately count and report the number of fatal police encounters in a reliable federal database
• Accurately count and report all incidents involving use of all deadly force by law enforcement, not only those incidents that result in death
• Systematically identify the role of mental illness in fatal law enforcement encounters
Since the study
• The twenty-first century cures act, passed by congress and signed by President Obama in December 2016, included a mandate for the US attorney general to collect and report data on the role of serious mental illness in fatal law enforcement encounters
• The Bureau of Justice Statistics overhauled its system for collecting law enforcement homicide data and, in December 2016, resumed reporting arrest-related death statistics. Using the new methodology approximately doubled the number of arrest-related deaths that were verified and reported by the Department of Justice. The role of mental illness in them has not yet been reported

mental health crisis from a medical issue to a police issue. This is patently unfair, illogical, and is proving harmful to both the individual in desperate need of care and the officer who is forced to respond." To address these concerns, the report recommends (1) a reinvestment and "restoration" of mental health-care services, particularly for individuals with severe mental illness; (2) to establish a centralized (at the federal level) tracking and reporting system of police use of deadly force, even if these incidents do not result in death; and (3) to assure that any data collection has the capacity to identify the role when law enforcement utilizes use of deadly force. See Table 3.1 for a summary of the report.

While death is the most extreme result of problematic encounters between law enforcement and an individual with mental illness, this remains a very rare event and relatively uncommon. It could be said that these events are becoming increasingly common; however, it is the goal of this section to emphasize routine results from these often problematic encounters. This is explored further below.

3.3.1 Police-Citizen with Mental Illness Encounters

Unfortunately, with the prevalence of mental health and dwindling treatment options, come the prevalence of conflicts, as made clear with the Treatment Advocacy Center report. These issues have since clearly spilled over into the public consciousness as partially evidenced by recent incidents in the news involving law enforcement and those suffering from mental illness—particularly when these encounters turned deadly. For example, there was the incident in July 2016 with social worker of an autistic man being shot by police in Miami that reverberated in news cycles around the country, with shares on social media with links to Internet sources rehashing the incident (Rabin, 2016). Perhaps the level of attention this story received sparked some conversations about the real issue: fear and misunderstanding as it relates to mental illness. Was this a case of fear and misunderstanding? With all of the officer-involved shootings and social unrest as of late, has the fear of violence led to more aggressive response by police? Would understanding autism have helped to ensure everyone's safety in this situation?

In this Miami incident, police were dispatched to a scene with the information that a man was on a city street threatening to commit suicide with a gun. This turns out to be not the case. After the chaos settled, police learned that a 23-year-old man with autism was holding a toy truck. When the officers reached the scene, they rightly identified the man who created the disturbance that prompted the call to 911; yet, this man was not responding to their orders. A caretaker from a nearby mental health facility attempted to intervene and explain the nonthreatening situation. Somehow the situation escalated to the point that the officers on the scene fired upon the autistic man and his caretaker and both were injured. Bystander's cell phone video was delivered quickly to the local media, which depicted the caretaker laying prone, hands clearly in the air, next to the man creating the disturbance who was sitting Indian style with an object in his hand. The caretaker's attempts to intervene were obviously unsuccessful. This bystander-shot video is one of the many recently shared on the Internet that have been a potent tool of critique of law enforcement tactics. These videos can also be a useful training tool and conversation starter on common problems that have been long simmering beneath the surface of public scrutiny.

Law enforcement officers hold difficult jobs for many reasons, as it is the nature of the position and the need for quick, split-second thinking that can have considerable consequences. Further, complicating police use of force decisions described above is an instance colloquially called "death by cop" or "suicide by police." In this scenario, an individual provokes and intends to be shot and killed by a police officer. This is not only disturbing for the individual involved but also by law enforcement. For example, in the suburban and rural areas just north of New Orleans—an hour's drive away from the city—two citizens recently confronted law enforcement with the intent of having officers end their lives by forced execution (within 2 days of each other; Rodrigue, 2017). In one case, officers attempted to engage in a traffic stop for a simple violation; the man in the car began to speed away and led officers on a high-speed chase. This resulted in a crash, with the man leaving the car with a machete and subsequently yelling at officers to "shoot me, just shoot me." In the second case, a woman in a rural area armed with a gun was engaging in similar behaviors when police were called to her house. In both cases, police were successful in de-escalating the situation and able to connect these "suspects" with mental health services in lieu of arrest. These starkly different outcomes from Miami story versus the one out of the New Orleans area are striking. The case where no deadly weapon was found to be in play turned out to be potentially fatal for two citizens, while the cases where deadly weapons were clearly identified resulted in no one being harmed. Actually, the latter resulted in real help for the two individuals that needed it.

Maybe further investing in SWAT (or Special Weapons and Tactics team) training can help in these situations. According to the National Tactical Officers Association (NTOA, 2008), "A Special Weapons and Tactics (SWAT) team is a designated law enforcement team, whose members are recruited, selected, trained, equipped and assigned to resolve critical incidents involving a threat to public safety which would otherwise exceed the capabilities of traditional law enforcement first responders and/or investigative units." These teams are often used on missions including "hostage rescues, barricades, snipers, high-risk warrant service and high-risk apprehensions, dignitary protection, terrorism responses, special assignments, and other incidents which exceed the capability and/or capacity of an agency's first responders and/or investigative units." Here, both law enforcement and emergency personnel train and work together to complete the missions of the specialized team. Also, as one would assume with the term "high risk," these missions can involve some potentially life-threatening or violent scenarios. For instance, take high-risk warrant service and apprehensions. Often these involve a person who is wanted for murder or a violent crime. The SWAT team would be engaged and briefed on the mission to serve the warrant and apprehend the wanted individual prior to going out in the field. Then, the team would travel to the location and attempt and ideally successfully apprehend the individual. Obviously, much of this process involves potentially risky engagement. It is possible that the wanted individual is armed and willing to "put up a fight" if needed. Additionally, there may be a group of individuals armed with weapons at the location of interest. Also, if the individual does resist arrest in any way, the SWAT team may use force, including deadly force. All of these potential scenarios put the law enforcement, medical personnel, wanted individual(s), and even bystanders/witnesses at risk of injury or death.

Yet, the often-aggressive tactics and appearance of SWAT are almost certainly contraindicated in most cases discussed here. A simple Internet search of SWAT and mental health uncovers some signs of trouble regarding the use of SWAT for individuals with mental illness. For example, an expose of the Chicago Police Department's use of SWAT for mental health-related events revealed at least 38 clear cases that met these criteria, some with tragic outcomes (Lazare & Southorn, 2017). In fact, it appears that Chicago Police Department's use of SWAT in these situations is increasing. A Boston Globe reported recently featured a heartbreaking interview with a father in Hingham, Massachusetts, who lost his son in a mental health-related SWAT raid. On July 8, 2017, Austin Reeves locked himself in his bedroom with his dog and a gun and told his family he needed some time alone. Leading up to this situation, Austin, age 26, was speaking with his ex-girlfriend on the phone. He was reeling from their recent breakup and he was clearly distraught—to the point she hung up with Austin and quickly called the police to check on his welfare. As a result, the police had called the Reeves' house phone and got a hold of Russell Reeves, Austin's father. Learning about what was going on, Russell checked the guns in his house and found that they were all locked, as always. Austin arrived at the family house shortly thereafter and was met by his father explaining the situation and asking if he was okay. Austin grew upset when he learned the police had called the house, which he fled to his bedroom to be alone as a result. Russell, feeling out of options, called the police back asking for help. This escalated over a period of 10 h from the moment two uniformed police arrived to a full SWAT response and standoff with the police. How did a routine call about a family in distress turn into SWAT response? His father pleaded with police just to leave the family alone at that point, yet the police did not stand down. Eventually, the SWAT team infiltrated his bedroom and shot Austin, resulting in his death. To further intensify the pain of the Reeves family, the Hingham Police Department left a message on the family answering machine sometime after the standoff that was intended for the neighbors also impacted by this event: "Hello, this is a message from the Hingham Police Department. The Hingham Police Department would like to thank you for your cooperation this morning and notify you that the incident on Edgar Walker Court has been resolved. Thank you" (Russell, 2017).

Can some of the SWAT training can be applicable to or hinder decision-making when officers are serving on their regular duties? Many SWAT training materials cover crisis response, but it is unclear exactly how much (if at all) mental health is referenced in SWAT training receive across the country. Much more research is direly needed in this area to address these emerging and potentially more common interactions, particularly as these trends are perceived to be on an upward trend.

3.3.1.1 Baltimore, Maryland: A Model Story for Systemic Failure on the Front Line

The Baltimore Police Department (BPD) has been in the news a number of times, unfortunately most have been for extremely negative circumstances and events relating to mental illness (Young, 2016). According to the US Department of Justice's (DOJ) Civil Rights Division report on the BPD:

- BPD's use of force against individuals with mental health disabilities or experiencing crisis violates the Americans with Disabilities Act.
- BPD's officers routinely use unreasonable force against individuals with mental health disabilities or those experiencing a crisis in violation of the Fourth Amendment. Additionally, by routinely using unreasonable force against individuals with mental health disabilities, BPD officers repeatedly fail to make reasonable modifications to void discrimination in violation of Title II of the American Disabilities Act of 1990.

- Since 2004, BPD has provided some specialized training to its new officers on how to interact with individuals with disabilities and those in crisis. But this training has not been provided to all officers (United States Department of Justice, 2016).

In many investigated situations, officers have assaulted vulnerable citizens, many of which have not committed a crime. Some of these assaults escalated into the use of unnecessary nonlethal force (e.g., deploying a Taser device) and lethal force resulting in at least one death. According to a recent Baltimore Sun article, "ACLU-Maryland reports that of the 109 people who died in police interactions from 2004-2014, 38 percent (41 people) were likely individuals with mental health and/or substance abuse issues" (Young, 2016). Again, these conflicting statistics under-score the need of monitoring such practices as indicated in the Treatment Advocacy Center report highlighted earlier in this chapter.

The BPD is only one department with clear and substantiated evidence of "engag[ing] in systemic disability-based discrimination" despite the many investi-gated across the nation done by DOJ. This is extremely disheartening for many reasons since these issues include both concerns with regard to individuals with disabilities as well as race concerns. The article discusses further that the police being the first responders to mental health calls is part of the overarching problem in not only Baltimore but the criminal justice system as a whole. Community responses have begun to offer suggestions to overcome the struggles of those with mental ill-ness in the area. Those responses begin with the idea of addressing this issue as a "health-care matter" rather than a criminal justice/law enforcement issue. As stated over and over in this book and research surrounding this topic, the outlook by both the community and the DOJ is to gear toward more community care to those with mental illness. The goal here is not only to reduce individuals re-entering the crimi-nal justice system but also to avoid entry to begin with in the first place. Baltimore is in dire need of a crisis response team to help with the increasing problem of caring for those with mental illness. This would not only take the burden from the police department but also ensure those who need would receive proper care.

3.3.1.2 Not All Is Lost: Positive Law Enforcement Interactions

A little training can, in fact, go a long way. Consider an expose featured on Vox, entitled, "How America's criminal justice system became the country's mental health system," which details the story of Kevin Earley of Fairfax County, Virginia. At the time the article was published in 2016, Kevin was 37, and the interviews of himself and of his father shed light on the struggles he has had with his own mental health and how this has subsequently intersected with law enforcement. Both Kevin and his father, Pete, share multiple experiences with police in Kevin's time of crisis with his mental illness. In one instance, Kevin explains his experience with a police officer during an encounter that resulted in his arrest and further paranoid, while in his last serious encounter is much more positive:

> One encounter began shortly after a psychotic episode that briefly landed him in an emer-gency room in 2002. Within 48 hours, Kevin wrapped tinfoil around his head, claiming that

the CIA was reading his thoughts. He slipped out of the house and broke into a stranger's home to take a bubble bath, and eventually several officers and a police dog arrested him and took him into custody.

[Yet, in] Kevin's last serious encounter with police in 2006, he was staying at a safe house, where people with mental health problems could relax for a night. There, he took off his clothes — thinking it made him invisible — and walked outside. A police officer, with training for mental health crises, approached Kevin. Kevin was scared, remembering the last time police approached him (and tased him). But this officer talked softly, reasoned with him, and, finally, convinced him to get into the car – no violence necessary. The cop didn't take Kevin to jail – he took him to a hospital. There, Kevin got a case manager. She fended off criminal charges, got Kevin into a "housing first" program for aid, and helped him sign up into a jobs program where he learned to become a peer-to-peer support specialist. (Lopez, 2016)

This last encounter with police in Fairfax County significantly changed Kevin's life situation. For the past 10 years, he has not had any negative police contact and has been under proper medication and care for his illness. Just a change in the approach taken by first responders can have lifelong positive outcomes. Kevin's story is a success story. He and his father believe that his final encounter resulted in transformative change as he was treated as a mental health patient and not a criminal. He was approached in a different manner by professionals who understood his illness and were focused on providing help in his time of need. While the systemic changes needed for agencies such as the Baltimore Police Department will take time, the good news is that there are plenty of documented stories of success to keep the faith that, in time, things can improve with dedicated positive momentum.

3.3.2   Interfacing with the Homeless or Near-Homeless Population

One interrelated issue worth mention here is the lack of trust vulnerable populations have with police and emergency medical services, largely due to years of misunderstanding, miscues, and problematic encounters. This trust may be further eroding giving the unresolved issues described above, exacerbating the crisis on the street. In 2004, Zakrison, Hamel, and Hwang published a study focusing on the trust homeless people in Toronto who have with local police and paramedics and potential health-related outcomes. Perhaps their findings are not so surprising; among their sample of 160 homeless Canadians staying at a local shelter when surveyed, there was a wide margin of difference in willingness to call the police in times of emergency relative to emergency medical services (69% of the sample compared to 92%, in the same order as listed). This was surely related to the differences in the level of trust these homeless individuals had in these professionals (a median of 3 out of 5 for police versus a 5 out of 5 for emergency medical services personnel, with 1 representing the lowest trust and 5 representing the highest trust). Additional responses from this sample are quite compelling: about one in ten self-reported an assault by a police officer in the last year, while none reported such an action by emergency medical services personnel.

What if there is no assurance on who would arrive on a scene of an emergency if emergency dispatch was called? What if, since 2004, these levels of trust have further eroded, especially in the United States that does not feature universal health-care coverage as its neighbor to the north? Answers to such questions still allude us, as is common theme for this text.

3.4   Evidence-Based Solutions

Great strides have been made in the development of evidenced-based services and programs to address the ongoing mental health crisis in the United States. For law enforcement, the Bureau of Justice Assistance (2017) and its partners have produced the Police-Mental Health Collaboration Toolkit that can educate key stakeholders and community partners on the most progressive and research-informed practices available today. The dedicated website for the toolkit features an easy-to-follow, step-by-step guide to the ten essential elements of police and mental health collaborations that have been proven to be successful in the jurisdictions that have implemented it: (1) collaborative planning and implementation; (2) program design, (3) specialized training; (4) call-taker and dispatcher protocol assessment and revision; (5) stabilization, observation, and disposition; (6) transportation and custodial transfer; (7) information exchange and confidentiality; (8) treatment, supports, and services; (9) organizational support; and (10) program evaluation and sustainability.

Currently, the website includes the learning experiences and successes of the Houston, Los Angeles, Madison (Wisconsin), Portland, Salt Lake City, and University of Florida Police Departments in customizing programming to meet their needs as well as their communities' needs. The common features of each are explored below.

3.4.1   *Crisis Intervention Teams:* **The** *Preferred Solution*

Crisis Intervention Team (CIT) programs "[are] community partnership[s] of law enforcement, mental health and addiction professionals, individuals who live with mental illness and/or addiction disorders, their families and other advocates" (Crisis Intervention Team International, 2017). First developed in Memphis, and sometimes known as the "Memphis Model," CIT programming offers police-based training from an inventive first-responder model. The *team* aspect of CIT primarily involves law enforcement and local mental health providers and other related service providers. The overarching goal of the partnership is to aid in working with a person in crisis and route these individuals to medical treatment in lieu of criminal justice processing that has become so common, creating a seamless flow for individuals with mental health concerns to receive services in the community. This often starts with dispatch flagging calls for service, relaying relevant information over to officers who receive dedicated CIT training and linking up with professionals in the community who are plugged into the CIT partnership to address potential clients' needs. Each CIT is customized to the local community and, as such, is nimble to adapt to changes in the community. The model prioritizes and promotes the best welfare for people in crisis as well as concretely connecting them with the best option for success and recovery. Additionally, CIT provides for a safer interaction for law enforcement in the event of a crisis situation.

The National Alliance on Mental Illness and their local affiliates have been key in promulgating CIT training across the country. These trainings have become standardized and feature 40 h of training on the following topics:

- **Learning from mental health professionals and experienced officers in your community**. One of the reasons CIT is successful is that it connects officers with a team of clinicians and fellow officers who can advise, problem solve, and support them when a challenging situation occurs.
- **Personal interaction with people who have experienced and recovered from mental health crisis and with family members who have cared for loved ones with mental illness**. NAMI members present at the training, providing officers a first-hand opportunity to hear stories of recovery, ask questions and learn what helps (and harms) when a person is in a crisis.
- **Verbal de-escalation skills**. CIT teaches a new set of skills for ensuring officer safety – the words, approach, and body language that convince a person to get help or defuse a potentially violent encounter.
- **Scenario-based training on responding to crises**. With the help of volunteers or actors, officers practice their skills in common crisis situations and get immediate feedback from instructors and classmates. (National Alliance on Mental Illness, 2017)

The standardized curriculum was developed through a partnership of the National Alliance on Mental Illness, the University of Memphis Crisis Intervention Team Center, CIT International, and the International Association of Chiefs of Police. Since implementation, research has shown the difference coordinated training can make: in Memphis, dispatch calls for "mental disturbances" fell substantially, by 80%; CIT-trained officers surveyed by researchers reveal that they feel they spend less time on such calls and feel more effective on meeting the needs of people with mental illness in their community; and CIT makes a clear difference in connecting citizens to the services that they need (e.g., counseling, medication, and other forms of treatment) relative to individuals being processed by the criminal justice system (Deane, Steadman,Borum, Veysey & Morrissey, 1998; Compton, Demir Neubert, Broussard, McGriff, Morgan, & Oliva, 2011; Dupont, Cochran, & Bush, 1999; National Alliance on Mental Illness, 2017; Massaro, 2004; Tully & Smith, 2015).

With such enthusiasm and empirical support, many cities are moving toward positive and proactive measure to help educate local law enforcement and better help the citizens they serve. One way this is happening is to have officers trained in mental health practices. For example, New Orleans Police Department (NOPD) now trains officers regularly in CIT with the hopes to continue with more and more both new and veteran officers trained. This is a new concept and will hopefully prove to be effective for the city of New Orleans when dealing with individuals in crisis. On the downside, the state of Louisiana continues to have budget cuts that directly affect the amount of treatment, specifically inpatient hospitals, in order to treat those with mental illness properly.

Having law enforcement trained in handling individuals with mental illness and those in crisis is essential because they are often the first to arrive on the scene when emergency services are called. Also, keeping in mind that not all information provided by the caller is accurate when a phone call is made for emergency assistance. For example, a bystander may call 911 if a person is wandering through a public setting yelling at strangers. The bystander may have little to no information about the person or the situation but observes an individual in an irate situation. A police officer is then dispatched to the scene with no information regarding the mental status of the irate person. It is important that the officer approach the scene with caution for many reasons.

3.4.2 Mental Health First Aid

Originating in Australia, the Mental Health First Aid curriculum was developed in 2001 by a nurse with a background in health education, named Betty Kitchener, and a professor of mental health literacy, named Tony Jorm. It has become known to be a rigorous yet "light" course that is delivered in 8 h. Mental Health First Aid has been likened to the mental health equivalent of CPR for non-clinicians when attending to a heart attack, with the goal of being able to appropriately and effectively intervene until "the real help arrives"—the trained professionals (Mental Health First Aid USA, 2017). The curriculum features ways to understand stigma, basic mental health knowledge, and related topics; however, the main focus of the course is to be competent in a five-step action plan in cases of a panic attack, suicidality, or an overdose situation. As such, it gives a practical and evidence-based approach to tending to these situations when they occur. Further, Mental Health First Aid appears on SAMHSA's National Registry of Evidence-Based Programs and Practices as a promising strategy in improving knowledge, attitudes, and beliefs about mental illness as well as non-specific mental health disorders and symptoms (SAMHSA, 2017).

For first responders, Mental Health First Aid appends their knowledge, skillset, and tools to effectively attend to mental health crises. Anecdotally, this evidence-based practice is proving effective in these professions. For example, in a recent article from the Department of Homeland Security First Responder division (formerly under the website firstresponder.gov), a fire and rescue captain expressed his observations of the Mental Health First Aid Curriculum:

> Law enforcement is beginning to recognize that some of the situations they have found themselves in recently have been misjudgments of people with mental health issues…and if they had been able to recognize certain symptoms, they may not have taken the, you know, forcible action that they took….[If first responders] don't have a baseline training for these guys,… they can only draw on their own experience. And if they don't have any experience [dealing with mental illness], then they're going to come up with their own idea of whether it's right or wrong. We'd rather make a decision than not make a decision. (Department of Homeland Security, 2015)

The article expresses other first responder leadership's impression of the training in a positive light while explicitly suggesting others consider joint investment in both CIT and Mental Health First Aid. Notably, Mental Health First Aid is much cheaper and quicker to deploy while also allowing for easily local sustainability through the form of "train-the-trainer" curriculum. That is, Mental Health First Aid offers standardized courses for individuals interested in becoming certified instructors. Thus, if a local jurisdiction wishes to make Mental Health First Aid available to a wide array of consumers, including first responders, they may simply invest in an initial round of training while also selecting a subset of trainees to receive instructor certification. These local instructors would then continue training until the local goal is met. This is the approach a regional National Alliance on Mental Health affiliate of Louisiana took in late 2015, continuing on through the current day. As of this writing, this NAMI office has trained several 100 trainees, including local judges, law enforcement, probation and parole, emergency medical services personnel, jail correctional officers and staff, and so on. While the impact of this initiative is unknown, the perception of the trainees has been positive (Richard, 2017).

3.4.3 Alternative Destination Pilot Project: North Carolina

North Carolina developed a novel approach to for emergency medical services working with patients with mental illness—called the Alternative Destination program. Rather than transporting the patients to the emergency room and waiting for a psychiatric evaluation, EMS enabled their personnel to transport them directly to a psychiatric facility. This was piloted initially in 2009 and has been expanded upon in recent years. The wait times in North Carolina emergency rooms were looming, medical professionals were overwhelmed, and resources were strapped. The Alternative Destination pilot project in Wake County, North Carolina, set out to alleviate these problems in a smarter way.

The Alternative Destination protocol was strictly defined to focus resources on those who need it the most yet who are not in exigent need of *emergency* medical services: (1) primarily, patients must not be experiencing a mental health crisis to a point that may require sedation or show an acute change in mental health status, (2) a patient's pulse is no more than 120 (e.g., signifying potential agitation or excited delirium), (3) a patient cannot present with other acute medical symptomatologies, (4) an extremely liberal blood alcohol content level must be met (up to 0.40, or anything less than five times the legal limit; note: if this condition is met with a high BAC while the other conditions presented here are met, this is an indicator of high alcohol tolerance), (5) each patient must be able to perform the activities of daily living (ADLs, or self-feeding, bathing, personal hygiene, dressing, using the bathroom and toilet hygiene, and walking and/or mobility), and (6) a patient must have a blood glucose level of less than 300 mg/dL. If all of these qualifiers are met, EMS can redirect the patient to other medical facilities qualified to handle these patients with available space. To implement this protocol and its strict guidelines, "advanced practice paramedics" were trained using a 240 h course, including topics such as available mental health resources within their own community as well as patient evaluation and assessment. By 2015, 20 trained advanced practice paramedics were active in Wake County, with over 30 others trained and ready to activate. Initial internal evaluations have been compelling: Miller (2015) reports that the pilot project has reduced emergency department transports by 20% from 2013 through 2015 by directing 764 patients to other facilities out of 3831 total mental health and/or substance abuse evaluations by advanced practice paramedics.

Over the length of a year, it was estimated that the program saved $500,000 in Medicaid costs. Unfortunately, as often in the case with innovative programming, the pilot has led to some stumbling blocks. For instance, despite the decrease in costs to Medicaid, the local EMS budget was strained due to reduced reimbursements as premiums are placed on transports to the emergency departments. This becomes a difficult paradox in that transportation directly to the psychiatric facility for treatment is best for the patient in need yet does not allow for reimbursement most of the related activities (including the increased work of the newly trained advanced practice paramedics), although, in the grand scheme of things, this pilot program is better for the emergency medical care system as well—and the system as a whole has been committed to seeing the program work.

The Alternative Destination pilot program appears to be a beneficial option for individuals who experience mental illness symptoms regularly but are not actively in the midst of a crisis. Those that may need a medication adjustment have not been harmed in any way and have or were always not in a panic attack or related moment. On a positive note, programs like the Alternative Destination pilot program are beginning to catch the attention of governments and other areas across the nation. The North Carolina State Government has recognized the program which has helped to spread information. Similarly, over 260 programs throughout the United States have begun to implement similar protocols.

3.4.4   Community Paramedic Program: Grady EMS (Atlanta)

Meanwhile, in Atlanta, the Grady County EMS (GEMS) Vice President of Operations, Michael Colman, began a search for a better option for the mental health calls in the area. Colman was able to identify that about 6%, or 6410, of the 911 calls to GEMS were determined to be psychiatric or suicide related. He reviewed the call volume data and was able to further determine that those that called EMS at least five a month were often made from individuals that had a mental illness. "A financial analysis using a sample of 156 patients from this group determined that it cost Grady EMS over $100 more than they received in reimbursement for each of these transports. In addition, the emergency department spent over $400 more on each patient than they received in reimbursement" (Stanaway, 2016). Consider here this amount is *in addition to* what is already being reimbursed by Medicaid, insurance, etc.

In response to this information, Grady EMS implemented a community paramedic project. According to the California Emergency Medical Services Authority, which offers fine details about this model:

- Community paramedicine (CP) is an innovative and evolving model of community-based health care designed to provide more effective and efficient services at a lower cost. Community paramedicine allows paramedics to function outside their traditional emergency response and transport roles to help facilitate more appropriate use of emergency care resources while enhancing access to primary care for medically underserved populations.
- Community paramedics are licensed paramedics who have received specialized training in addition to general paramedicine training and work within a designated community paramedicine program under local medical control as part of a community-based team of health and social services providers. Paramedics are uniquely positioned for expanded roles as they are geographically dispersed in nearly all communities, inner city, and rural, always available, work in home- and community-based settings, are trusted and accepted by the public, are trained to make health status assessments, recognize and manage life-threatening conditions outside of the hospital, and operate under medical control as part of an organized system approach to care (California Emergency Medical Services Authority, 2017).

Grady EMS looked to find a solution to help patients experiencing a mental health crisis other than the typical means. Those in crisis "were routinely subjected to unplanned physical restraint, chemical restraint, police restraint and even arrest" (Stanaway, 2016). This is to say that a person experiencing a mental health crisis were often not able to be de-escalated without the use of physical force and/or medication. These are also extra costs as well as safety concerns for all involved.

This pilot program was developed in 2012 and put into operations in early 2013. Grady EMS created a crisis response team which includes a paramedic, a Grady Health System licensed counselor, a Behavioral Health Link clinical social worker, and even, at times, a third-year psychiatry resident. This crisis team responded with the regular EMS staff during the pilot phase of the project. Additionally, the crisis team could be dispatched at the request of those on scene but did not respond alone and was only available on weekdays. Their part in the on-scene process was to provide an assessment and a medical evaluation for the patient in need.

Later, after completion of the pilot phase, the program began implementing the full program. In the full program, the crisis intervention team was then able to respond as an independent unit without regular EMS accompaniment. Further, rather than just the original 40 h per week availability, the program was expanded to 80 h to allow for additional services to be provided. GEMS personnel used the Georgia Crisis Action Line (GCAL) in the field when the team was not available:

GCAL is the 24/7 hotline for accessing mental health services in Georgia. The Georgia Department of Behavioral Health and Developmental Disabilities (DBHDD) provides treatment and support services to people with mental illnesses and addictive diseases, and support to people with mental retardation and related developmental disabilities. (Georgia National Alliance on Mental Illness, 2017)

Community Paramedicine Pilot Sites Testing 7 Concepts

Fig. 3.1 Latest community paramedicine projects offered by the Emergency Medical Services Authority of California, a leader in community paramedicine innovation

Calling GCAL involves a mental health professional who has the ability to evaluate a patient via phone contact. This evaluation can take place in a matter of minutes and results in a number of options with the best interest of the patient upheld. If necessary, the mental health professional could have the paramedics on scene transport the patient directory to a psychiatric facility. Further aiding in the success of the program, Grady EMS created a process that allows 911 dispatchers to transfer some calls directly to the GCAL, if certain criteria are met. GCAL can also call Grady EMS back if an ambulance is in fact needed to respond (Fig. 3.1).

Coordinated programs like this one have allowed patients who would otherwise have been arrested or possibly restrained in a most disruptive situation to receive care in a better manner while also saving money and resources. This can be shown by the data, "In 2013, Grady EMS dispatch transferred 175 calls directly to Behavioral Health Line saving Grady EMS about $13,000. The Grady EMS

Upstream Crisis Intervention Group responded to 20 percent of EMD category 25 calls totaling 1,250 responses. The team obtained 275 refusals/no transports. Many of those patients were provided with safety plans and outpatient appointments, which prevented unnecessary emergency department visits totaling about 1,925 bed hours" (Stanaway, 2016). Michael Colman described the financial aspect of the changes within the program and has estimated it to be over $140,000 and adding in the referrals that did not require transports savings of $248,000 for 2013. Additionally, "In 2014 the psych unit responded to 1778 calls, potentially saving EMS over $100,000. In 2015, Grady EMS received 7668 calls that were psychiatric in nature. Of those, the psych unit handled over 20%, again saving EMS over $100,000" (Stanaway, 2016).

Another added benefit of the program is also the job satisfaction increase for Grady EMS. As discussed in another chapter, burnout and compassion fatigue are common occurrences of jobs as first responders often responding to crisis on a regular basis. According to the program director Tina Wright, staff reported a "higher-than-normal" job satisfaction as the program kicked into high gear. Wright discussed that many staff members feel as though they are really making a positive change in their community which has led to a personal sense of satisfaction.

3.4.5 A Survey of Other Approaches Across the Country

There are many more instances of successful and budding programs being sown across the United States. Indeed, there does appear to be progress in the disarray of the current state of the mental health system of care. For example, the state of California is engaging in 13 community paramedicine projects, adopting this model to localized needs (California Emergency Medical Services Authority, 2017). Madison, Wisconsin, is one of the six law enforcement-mental health learning sites and serves as a model for other sister jurisdictions (City of Madison, 2015). Statewide efforts have been made in Colorado, Connecticut, Florida, Georgia, Illinois, Maine, Ohio, and Utah to provide specialized training in police responses in cases of mental illness and mental health crises (Bureau of Justice Assistance, 2017). In Alabama, the Birmingham Police Department has a number of programs within their Community Services Division that help to improve the overall relations between the public and law enforcement. These improvements are sought to be done through a variety of community services initiatives. One program specifically works to improve the process of police call outs dealing with individuals with mental illness. The program involved specially trained officers called Community Services Officers (CSOs) that "provide crisis intervention social services through direct service, referral and consultation. Their objective is to stabilize a crisis, attempt to prevent further crises, and enhance their client's well-being. They network and maintain professional relationships with relative community resources and strive to provide exemplary crisis intervention services" (Birmingham Police Department, 2017).

Much more innovation is occurring in recent years, many of which are smaller pilots that have promise for broader adoption. One thing is for certain, much of the innovation is occurring on the local level, as guided by national resources and broader research trends. While this section does not offer a comprehensive review of the innovations occurring across the country, it is important to note that there has been an explosion of activity of collaborative projects in recent years. This is likely to continue for some years to come. Perhaps in the near future, there will be a clearinghouse of projects similar to other resource databases that have grown popular in recent years.

3.5   Conclusion

A persistent issue presented in this chapter is the lack of awareness and training of mental illness among those who currently need it the most, American first responders. This often leads to problematic, and sometimes deadly, police-citizen encounters. While the American public often only learns of the most troublesome of these encounters through the media, bystander accounts and video, and so on, there has been a great deal of innovation to ameliorate the volatility of these encounters through training, partnerships, policy changes, and strategic alterations of systemic responses to potential mental health calls for service. With so much focus placed on law enforcement, it is important to take a step back and take full stock of the collaborative nature among medicine, paramedicine, and law enforcement and understand each role for each of their potential to intervene in mental health crisis events.

These collaborative relationships are critical in one of the most comprehensive and promising models to address the consistent problems regarding mental illness today—the persistent contact of individuals with mental illness has with the police and the criminal justice system often without addressing any of the underlying mental health concerns. This model, the Crisis Intervention Team, is increasingly a part of the solution for many communities looking to address the persistent issues discussed in this book. Further, this model tends not to be deployed in absence of other evidence-based solutions to address the underlying problems. Programs such as Mental Health First Aid and community paramedicine projects are gaining popularity to add additional layers of awareness and system processes to intercept potential criminal justice concerns with community-based services that typically cost taxpayers much less while offering better outcomes.

Finally, it is important to clearly define the role of probation and parole officers (e.g., community corrections) in regard to serving individuals with mental health concerns. These professionals are often overlooked, just when their role appears to be increasing given the pressures to move away from overutilization of American prisons and to alleviate overcrowding in these facilities. At the time of this writing, community corrections have received far less attention in regard to serving Americans with mental illnesses relative to their first responder counterparts. One exception is the utility of specialized caseloads or units, which seem to offer promising advantages over mixed caseloads for probationers and parolees with mental illness.

References

Begun, A.L., Early, T.J., Hodge, A., (2016) Mental health and substance abuse service engagement by men and women during community reentry following incarceration. *Administration and Policy in Mental Health and Mental Health Services Research 43*(2):207–218.

Belcher, E. (2017). Personal communication.

Birmingham Police Department. (2017). *Community services*. Retrieved on June 1, 2017, from https://police.birminghamal.gov/bureaus/support-operations/community-services

Bureau of Justice Assistance. (2017). *Police-mental health toolkit*. Retrieved June 1, 2017, from https://pmhctoolkit.bja.gov

California Commission on Peace Officer Standards and Training. (2017). *Mental health training in the regular basic course*. Retrieved December 21, 2017, from https://www.post.ca.gov/mental-health-training-in-the-regular-basic-course.aspx

California Emergency Medical Services Authority. (2017). *Introduction to community paramedicine*. Retrieved December 21, 2017, from https://emsa.ca.gov/community_paramedicine

City of Madison. (2015). *Mental health liaison/officer programs*. Retrieved June 1, 2017, from https://www.cityofmadison.com/police/community/mentalhealth

Compton, M.T., Demir Neubert, B.N., Broussard, B., McGriff, J.A., Morgan, R., Oliva, J.R. (2011). Use of force preferences and perceived effectiveness of actions among crisis intervention team (CIT) police officers and non-CIT officers in an escalating psychiatric crisis involving a subject with schizophrenia. *Schizophrenia Bulletin 37*(4):737–745.

Crisis Intervention Team International. (2017). *Learn about CIT programs*. Retrieved June 1, 2017, from http://www.citinternational.org/Learn-About-CIT

Deane, M., Steadman, H., Borum, R., Veysey, B., & Morrissey, J. (1998). Policemental health system interactions: Program types and needed research. *Psychiatric Services, 50*(1), 99–101.

Department of Homeland Security. (2015). *Responder news: Responding to people with mental illness*. Retrieved June 1, 2017, from https://www.dhs.gov/science-and-technology/news/2015/11/23/responder-news-responding-people-mental-illness

District of Columbia Department of Health. (2017). *What is EMS?* Retrieved June 1, 2017, from https://doh.dc.gov/service/what-ems

Dupont, R., Cochran, S., & Bush, A. (1999). *Reducing criminalization among individuals with mental illness*. In US Department of Justice and Department of Health and Human Services, Substance Abuse and Mental Health Services Administration (SAMHSA) Conference on Forensics and Mental Illness, Washington, DC.

Fuller, D.A., Lamb, H.R., Biasotti, M., & Snook, J. (2015). *Overlooked in the undercounted: The role of mental illness in fatal law enforcement encounters*. Retrieved June 1, 2017, from http://www.treatmentadvocacycenter.org/storage/documents/overlooked-in-the-undercounted.pdf

Georgia National Alliance on Mental Illness. (2017). *Georgia crisis and access line*. Retrieved July 1, 2017, from https://namiga.org/georgia-crisis-and-access-line

Ivory, D., Protess, B, & Bennett, K. (2016). *When you dial 911 and Wall Street answers*. Retrieved June 1, 2017, from https://www.nytimes.com/2016/06/26/business/dealbook/when-you-dial-911-and-wall-street-answers.html

Jacob, L., & Poletick, E.B. (2008). Systematic review: Predictors of successful transition to community-based care for adults with chronic care needs. *Care Management Journals, 9*(4), 154–165.

Lazare, S. & Southorn, D. (2017). *How do Chicago Police treat mental health? With SWAT raids*. The Intercept_. Retrieved December 21, 2017, from https://theintercept.com/2017/08/06/chicago-police-mental-health-swat-raids-militarized

Lopez, G. (2016). *How America's criminal justice system became the country's mental health system*. Vox. Retrieved June 1, 2017, from https://www.vox.com/2016/3/1/11134908/criminal-justice-mental-health

Lurigio, A.J., (2016) Effective Services for Parolees with Mental Illnesses. *Crime & Delinquency 47*(3):446–461.

Massaro, J. (2004). *Working with people with mental illness involved in the criminal justice system: What service providers need to know* (2nd ed.). Delmar, NY: Technical Assistance and Policy Analysis Center for Jail Diversion.

McIntosh, W.L., Spies, E., Stone, D.M., Lokey, C.N,, Trudeau, A.T., Bartholow, B. (2016). *Suicide rates by occupational group - 17 states, 2012*. Centers of Disease Control and Prevention. Retrieved June 1, 2017, from https://www.cdc.gov/mmwr/volumes/65/wr/mm6525a1.htm

Mental Health First Aid USA. (2017). *Mental health first aid*. Retrieved June 1, 2017, from https://www.mentalhealthfirstaid.org

Michelen, W., Martinez, J., Lee, A., Wheeler, D.P. (2006). Reducing Frequent Flyer Emergency Department Visits. *Journal of Health Care for the Poor and Underserved, 17*(1):59–69.

Miller, D.L. (2015). *Pilot project trains EMS to Bypass the ED with mental health patients*. Emergency Physicians Monthly. Retrieved June 1, 2017, from http://epmonthly.com/article/pilot-project-trains-ems-to-bypass-the-ed-with-mental-health-patients

National Alliance on Mental Illness. (2017). *What is CIT?* Retrieved June 1, 2017, from https://www.nami.org/Law-Enforcement-and-Mental-Health/What-Is-CIT

National Association of Emergency Medical Technicians. (2017). *2016 national survey*. Retrieved July 1, 2017, from http://www.naemt.org/docs/default-source/community-paramedicine/ems-data/naemt_ems_data_report_6_17_2016-5-1.pdf?status=Temp&sfvrsn=0.06606199361250287

National Tactical Officers Association. (2008). *SWAT standards for law enforcement agencies*. Retrieved June 1, 2017, from https://ntoa.org/massemail/swatstandards.pdf

Plohetski, T. (2008). Mental health patients strain Texas EMS resources. *Journal of Emergency Medical Services*. Retrieved June 1, 2017, from http://www.jems.com/articles/2008/01/mental-health-patients-strain.html

PoliceOne. (2016). *7 reasons I'm still a police officer*. Retrieved June 1, 2017, from https://www.policeone.com/community-policing/articles/217192006-7-reasons-Im-still-a-police-officer

Rabin, C. (2016). Cop shoots caretaker of autistic man playing in the street with toy truck. *Miami Herald*. Retrieved June 1, 2017, from http://www.miamiherald.com/news/local/crime/article90905442.html

Richard, N. (2017). Personal communication.

Rodrigue, A. (2017). Two attempted suicides-by-cop in two days highlight law enforcement struggle with mental illness. *WWLTV*. Retrieved June 1, 2017, from http://www.wwltv.com/mb/news/local/northshore/two-attempted-suicides-by-cop-in-two-days-highlights-law-enforcement-struggle-with-mental-illness/440607429?utm_campaign=trueAnthem%3A+Trending+Content&utm_content=591d2b7e04d3015559d40170&utm_medium=trueAnthem&utm_source=facebook

Russell, J. (2017). *His parents said he just needed to sleep*. A SWAT team came instead. Boston Globe. Retrieved June 1, 2017, from https://www.bostonglobe.com/metro/2017/07/15/his-parents-said-just-needed-sleep-swat-team-came-instead/1sTWdBw2MNqqFGCOUfLnHL/story.html

Stanaway, N. (2016). *Community paramedic program cuts mental health patient call volume*. EMS1. Retrieved June 1, 2017, from https://www.ems1.com/community-paramedicine/articles/93357048-Community-paramedic-program-cuts-mental-health-patient-call-volume

Stewart, C.C., George-Paschal, L. (2017). Barriers to reentry into society: Listening to parolees' perceptions. *American Journal of Occupational Therapy, 71* (4_Supplement_1):7111505066p1

Strate, J. (2017). Personal communication.

Substance Abuse and Mental Health Services Administration. (2017). *National registry of evidence-based programs and practices*. Retrieved December 21, 2017, from https://www.samhsa.gov/nrepp

Tully, T., Smith, M. (2015). Officer perceptions of crisis intervention team training effectiveness. *The Police Journal: Theory, Practice and Principles, 88*(1):51–64.

Treatment Advocacy Center. (2017a). *TAC reports*. Retrieved June 1, 2017, from http://www.treatmentadvocacycenter.org/evidence-and-research/studies

Treatment Advocacy Center. (2017b). *People with untreated mental illness 16 times more likely to be killed by law enforcement*. Retrieved June 1, 2017, from http://www.treatmentadvocacycenter.org/home-page/71-featured-articles/2976-people-with-untreated-mental-illness-16-times-more-likely-to-be-killed-by-law-enforcement-.

Treatment Advocacy Center. (2017c). *Overlooked in the undercounted: The role of mental illness in fatal law enforcement encounters*. Retrieved October 1, 2017, from http://www.treatmentadvocacycenter.org/evidence-and-research/evidence-and-research/3845

United States Department of Justice. (2016). *Investigation of the Baltimore Police Department*. Retrieved June 1, 2017, from https://www.justice.gov/crt/file/883296/download

United States Courts. (2017). *Probation and pretrial officers and officer assistants*. Retrieved June 1, 2017, from http://www.uscourts.gov/services-forms/probation-and-pretrial-services/probation-and-pretrial-officers-and-officer

Wolff, N., Epperson, M., Shi, J., Huening, J., Schumann, B.E., Sullivan, I.R. (2014). Mental health specialized probation caseloads: Are they effective?. *International Journal of Law and Psychiatry, 37*(5):464–472.

Young, L. (2016). Police should rarely be the first responders for those in mental health crisis. *The Baltimore Sun*. Retrieved June 1, 2017, from http://www.baltimoresun.com/news/opinion/oped/bs-ed-response-team-20161201-story.html

Zakrison, T. L. (2004). Homeless people's trust and interactions with police and paramedics. *Journal of Urban Health: Bulletin of the New York Academy of Medicine, 81*(4):596–605.

Chapter 4
Treatment: Intersection with Criminal Justice

> Well, the part I really don't understand – if you're looking for self-help [books], why would you read a book written by somebody else? That's not self-help, that's help! There's no such thing as self-help. If you did it yourself, you did not help! You did it yourself.—George Carlin

When hearing the terms "mental health" or "mental illness," the stereotype is to think of "crazy." This stereotypical image is of a person suffering from radical delusions and/or hallucinations, which is also often associated with violence. This common distortion of the realities of mental illness is certainly one leading reason why data collection is important. That is, the best way to combat stereotypes and educate the public on the true face of mental health or mental illness is to gather and deploy factual information. These facts detailing the actual number of people diagnosed with a mental illness help with educating the public of problems in their community. Additionally, friends and families can better understand the needs of their loved ones. Communities can create ways to address the needs of those with a diagnosis or help to prevent symptoms before onset occurs.

This chapter addresses a variety of interventions possible and services available in communities to address mental illness, its symptoms, and the collateral consequences of mental health issues (e.g., family stress and strains, homelessness, unemployment/underemployment, etc.). Oftentimes, local social service agencies keep a resource guidebook on hand to assist employees working with clients in connecting people with the resources they may need or serve as a self-help tool for individuals to seek the services which they may feel that they need. The resources and services listed in this chapter serve as a generic blueprint of the core of the majority of these resource guides that every student of crime and mental health should have in their mental rolodex—the essentials of mental health care in American communities (see Fig. 4.1).

© Springer International Publishing AG, part of Springer Nature 2018
J. Hector, D. Khey, *Criminal Justice and Mental Health*,
https://doi.org/10.1007/978-3-319-76442-9_4

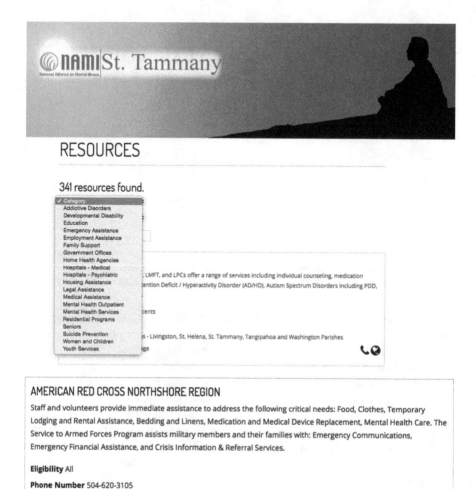

Fig. 4.1 A screenshot of the online version of NAMI St Tammany's (Louisiana) resource guidebook (2017)

4.1   Where Do People Fall Through the Cracks?

Treatment is essential in any health-related area for the overall wellness of an individual and for the communities they reside. The justice-involved population is certainly no exception and is particularly in need of treatment in several ways as it relates to mental health and, at times, also substance use. The unmet need for treatment is great for persons without a criminal background let alone for individuals with more complex mental health histories; this issue lends itself to the crux part of the problem—how can treatment change so *all Americans* can remain healthy? How does a person get help, especially when stigma presents such a roadblock to seeking help in the first place? How does a community overcome the lack of funding and the difficulties often present when citizens try accessing services?

Luckily, the conversations regarding change and improvement are happening across the country. As a society, the United States is beginning to acknowledge the need for criminal justice reform; further, many communities have taken decisive strides to address the largest gaps in complex criminal justice systems in which people tend to fall through the cracks without the help they need to succeed in everyday life. With that, the idea of working toward more proactive measures to help other concerns with each individual has and will hopefully continue to be part of the discussion. Yet it is important to review the critical lapses in mental health-care systems that persist as policymakers and stakeholders move to address these gaps.

As with most politically relevant topics, especially those critical of government-run or government-related systems, "cracks," fault lines, weak points, and gaps seem inevitable. Specifically, government-run systems and programs often stereotype the beleaguered nature of complex bureaucracies. This is certainly not to say that all bureaucracies are problematic. Yet, even well-run bureaucracies can have secondary problems, such as being difficult to navigate by average citizens unfamiliar with bureaucratic processes. A popular and fitting example is to pick on state Department of Motor Vehicles. One recent case known to the authors speaks volumes:

ATTENTION FLORIDA DRIVERS LICENSE HOLDERS WHO DO NOT HAVE CARS: I just went to local DMV to transfer FL license to [Pennsylvania]. Could not do it--after three hours of rigmarole-- because my FL license could not be verified by PA. I call FL DMV, they tell me license is "suspended." I ask why. They tell me "for lack of car insurance." I tell them "but I haven't had a car since 2012, and that's why I got rid of car insurance." And I get silence on the phone.

Then I ask how/when was I notified of this suspension, and I get silence on the phone. They tell me they can fix it on phone since "it has been longer than three years," but that it takes 24-48 hours to update system. I ask them if they can send confirmation to PA DMV, they say yes, we'll fax it. 45 minutes later, no fax.

This is on top of ridiculous PA ...ID requirements which include the following documents to be presented in order to transfer license:

Passport, or raised seal birth certificate--note photo ID from Florida NOT acceptable for ID at PA DMV

TWO of following: tax records, current gun permit, mortgage, lease, w2, utility bill in my name

ALL addresses must match.

AND social security card

So, gotta hit DMV again in "24-28 hours" I guess. (Khey, unpublished research—unnamed informant)

Imagine trying to navigate these issues if you did not feel physically well. Similar comparisons could be made to trying to navigate these issues when not feeling mentally well.

In addition, bureaucracies are certainly not easy to change; adjustments to federal, state, and local law/policy require time, systems need to lay out how to address these changes to stay in compliance with the law/policy, and these plans require action that may take a while to perfect. While the intent of this text is not delve into complexities of public administration, it may be helpful to highlight some of the issues in civic processes to answer questions like "why doesn't someone just change it?" Of course the answer is that this is easier said than done, but it helps to remind ourselves why. State legislatures, for example, operate in sessions in which new bills or amendments to bills can be introduced. One problem lies in the amount of time it takes for legislation to be reviewed and the number of hands it must pass through to get approved. This process could take weeks or months and still fail in the end. Further, it could take years to even develop into a bill worthy of bringing to the legislature in the first place, let alone the issues of political gridlock and partisanship, the influence of special interests, and so on.

Governmental processes aside, one persistent "crack" in mental health-care systems lies more in the control of the communities they reside; specifically, and simply, access to care—and further, quality care—has been a core issue since the early development of mental health care. Accessibility issues can be borne from seemingly simple barriers, such as the lack of transportation options to seek treatment or a consumer's ability to pay. Alternatively, appropriate treatment options for mental health and substance use disorder patients, much less those that are justice involved, may not be readily available in some area yielding long waits or even available at all. While outlining these issues, the former director of the National Institute of Mental Health (NIMH), Thomas Insel, released a report in 2010 discussing the changes needed in the treatment of serious mental illness. The report notes:

> There are several facts about mental illness in the United states that always seem to surprise those who are not directly involved:
>
> - Each year, there are nearly twice as many suicides (33,000) as homicides (18,000)
> - The life expectancy for people with major mental illness is 56 years (the average life expectancy in the U.S. is 77.7 years)
> - Mental disorders and substance abuse are the leading cause of disability in the United States and Canada
>
> To this list we can now add another statistic—according to the Treatment Advocacy Center, and based on an analysis of data provided by the Substance Abuse & Mental Health Services Administration, **people with mental illness are three times more likely to be in the criminal justice system than hospitals**. In some states, such as Nevada and Arizona, the ratio is closer to 10 times more people with mental illness in jails and prisons (Insel, 2010).

As mentioned earlier in this text, there has been a drastic decrease (about 90%) in the number of state hospital beds over the past 50 years. Yet, the number of Americans with mental illness continues to increase as the population expands. Policy changes have significantly impacted the number of individuals with mental illness being sent to jails and prisons. As discussed earlier, people with mental illness are more likely to also have a substance abuse problem. Keeping this in mind, mandatory sentencing requirements for drug crimes mean that these individuals are now being incarcerated without any (or at minimum with little) consideration to the underlying mental health concerns in fueling drug-related offending. "Most of all, however, [the] statistic [above] reveals a failure to provide alternatives in the mental health care system for people requiring hospitalization" (Insel, 2010).

Individuals with mental health concerns begin to fall through the cracks in the systems of care in American communities. Recall that the National Alliance on Mental Illness commonly cites an important National Institute of Mental Health statistic—typically, it takes an average of 8–10 years after the onset of mental health symptomatology to *begin to* formally address these mental health concerns (NAMI, 2017a). This does not take into consideration any gender or cultural differences that may even further delay the time it takes to seek help. Rhetorically, it appears as though the popular perception of mental illness in the form of a crazy, delusional, and violent individual aggravates this delay in seeking help; or alternatively, the lack of mental health awareness blunts our ability to detect mental health concerns until mental health symptomatology reaches some critical mass. This critical mass could present itself when an individual winds up homeless, in an emergency room, or as a jail inmate; yet, it does seem that, many times, these costly issues to remedy tend to be a starting point in addressing underlying mental health concerns. The following section takes a deeper look into mental health safety net and its continued inherent problems.

4.2 Common Problems

One leading and pervasive problem is access to services within a local area, particularly among the most vulnerable individuals in our communities. Ex-offenders reentering society post-incarceration certainly fall among this broader class of vulnerable individuals. Simple gaps in access can be merely transportation (*reliable* transportation) to get to treatment services, participate in group and support meetings, travel to the pharmacy or doctor's office to obtain medication (even if they were affordable or free), and so on. Depending on the location in which a person resides, rural versus urban area in particular, there may be insufficient to nonexistent public transportation services available. As such, the lack of transportation can be a primary barrier to treatment, services, and employment – something that most of us would take for granted. Fortunately, some treatment facilities and new programs (including grant-funded programs and program streams) are adding in the funding to supply clients with transportation options, such as taxi reimbursement, gas cards, transit "tokens" or pre-loaded cards, etc. (Fraze, Lewis, Rodriguez, & Fisher, 2016). For example, a recent workshop of the National Academies of Sciences, Engineering, and Medicine recently evaluated the available data and metrics on the value of connecting patients to transportation services. Of particular value, the experts present at the workshop opined on the return on investment of these services:

> There is stiff competition for limited transportation resources, Ed Christopher said, and Congress requires justification for the spending of public money to ensure that the money spent achieves a positive return…. He observed that return on investment is viewed differently by different stakeholders. For transportation access to care, he said, the questions

Table 4.1 Summary of the main points of speakers of the workshop on the value of connecting patients with treatment services, National Academies of Science, Engineering, and Medicine

• Inclusive planning is a key element of success. It is important to directly engage the people who will be served by community transportation in the planning process and to understand what their specific needs are
• Education can improve transportation. Transportation providers might not understand what accommodations the patient needs; health-care providers often do not know the transportation options available and therefore cannot advocate for patients; and patients are often unaware of or do not understand how to use the transportation that is available in the community
• Different stakeholders view return on investment differently, depending on their individual goals
• Cross-sector collaboration will be aided by developing a shared vocabulary and shared metrics.
• There is an immediate need to make the business case that investing in transportation to care is of economic value, and there is also a need for longer-term research that demonstrates improvement in quality of life and the impacts of prevention

revolve around whether the efforts are making people healthier. Lefler noted that return on investment is difficult to ascertain in health care because it depends on illness, age, income level, and other factors of the many individuals involved. The ultimate question is whether quality of life is being improved…. Cronin highlighted the need for new and innovative cross-discipline research and stressed the need to "speak the language" of those you are trying to convince. He described some of his early work on return-on-investment calculations for medically related transportation services. One approach is to calculate cost avoidance (as a result of, for example, reduced ED visits, hospitalizations, or missed days of work). He said that much of the work at that time was based on assumptions about relationships between transportation and care (e.g., how many trips to care might correlate with avoidance of a 1-day in-hospital stay). He agreed that medical trips are about quality of life improvement, but he added that those controlling the funding (i.e., the tax dollars) want to show that they are generating a financial return (NASEM, 2016).

Often, transportation can be one of the costliest parts on a treatment budget, and this can have an impact on the treatment quality given the high cost of gasoline, insurance (including liability), motor pool maintenance, and so on; some care providers may be a great distance from clients, particularly in suburban and urban areas. Or there may be only one provider in a large area because the funding and options are based on population rather than size of the area. In these cases, creativity is needed to ensure proper treatment. For example, some programs offer treatment providers to go to the clients (e.g., make house calls) rather than the other way around. This is part of the benefit of "assertive community treatment," described more in depth in an upcoming section within this chapter (Table 4.1).

With ongoing budget cuts and political barriers, mental health and substance abuse services have become increasingly scarce in many communities across the United States. Less public facilities, less providers (and less quality providers), and less beds/space available continue to be the primary concerns among mental health-care leaders. Statistics show that behavioral health needs are increasing but the availability of treatment is decreasing. This leads to the major focus of this text: the obstacles described here lay the foundation of the key problem that has existed for years. Now more than ever, more individuals are using jails and prisons as a means to get clean. Families and friends are also encouraging this idea due to the fact that there are no other options. Ironically, for those suffering from a mental illness, "getting clean" can increase the possibility of mental health concerns surfacing—leading to a particularly vulnerable moment in people's lives.

4.2.1 Medical Coverage

A very obvious obstacle to seeking treatment is the lack of insurance, particularly access to Medicaid, to cover the cost of care. "Medicaid is the single-most important financing source of mental health services in the [United States], covering nearly 27% of all mental health care in [the country] and nearly half of the public mental health spending, according to SAMHSA" (NAMI, 2017b). Further, if a person is unable to acquire gainful and *meaningful* employment due to a criminal background, they are often unable to secure private health insurance of any kind. Without health insurance, the options for treatment are very limited, require the most severe symptoms before consideration, often have considerable waitlists, or are completely unavailable. Fortunately, some states have been moving forward with plans to help people leaving prison; this change typically comes in the form of adopting Medicaid expansion under the Affordable Care Act.

Louisiana offers a recent example. In 2016, after a long period of resisting Medicaid expansion, a bipartisan effort was spearheaded to join over 30 states which have expansion in place. This policy shift allows for ex-prisoners to be eligible for Medicaid upon release, with the potential of having benefits the moment these individuals leave prison facilities. While not currently in place, the goal is to initiate and complete the process to receive Medicaid (as well as other relevant benefits) in the months leading up to release. To do so, the Louisiana Department of Health (LDH) is collaborating with the Department of Public Safety and Corrections (DOC) to develop the ability to maintain a "suspended" status on Medicaid benefits that can be activated on a particular date (e.g., a release date). To date, it is routine to simply cancel benefits, forcing individuals to handle reapplication on their own upon reentry; as an interim process, sporadic reentry programs across the state employ case managers who assist with the application process. Allowing inmates to gain access to health benefits will hopefully allow improvements in health and decrease in returns to prison. "LDH and DOC implemented phase one of the prerelease enrollment initiative in January for offenders in the seven DOC state facilities. As of February 27, 2017, 230 offenders have been linked to a health plan, and it is expected that approximately 2,800 offenders will qualify for coverage annually, with about 30 percent of these former offenders being eligible for case management" (Louisiana Department of Health, 2017).

With the Affordable Care Act, and Medicaid for that matter, in peril due to loud calls for reform in the current political discourse, it is very difficult to anticipate how these trends will continue into the intermediate or distant future in regard to individuals with a criminal record (particularly, felons). While it is easy to cast political opponents of Medicaid expansion as adversaries of mental health, bipartisan political forces seem to be sending mixed messages. For example, the Twenty-First Century Cures Act continues to receive bipartisan support. Any movement to defund Medicaid may be supplanted with the support embedded in the Twenty-First Century Cures Act to some extent. Since the fates of the Affordable Care Act and Medicaid are still being debated and the policy changes of the Twenty-First Century Cures Act are being put into place, positive gains in mental health infrastructure appear to be secure in the near future, with the distant future having a murkier outlook.

4.2.2 Medical Records

Electronic health records (EHR) or electronic medical records are digital copies of an individual's clinical history. Hospitals are working to adopt these electronic records for many reasons. First, the ease of use is highly beneficial in most medical settings. A doctor can use a laptop or iPad throughout the hospital to have a patient's current medical information in seconds. Additionally, the information can be much more accurate and real-time since staff has the ability to input information immediately. EHRs allow for less use of resources since there is less need for storage, copies, and physical transfers of information. On a bigger scale, EHRs can offer access to information among many facilities, across many areas. If a person moves out of state, their electronic file can be easily obtained by the new treating physician to maintain care without any "cracks." Perhaps the most important reason of any listed here, EHRs have become required for any organization to seek federally funded research dollars.

The use of EHRs can be vital in working with individuals with mental illness. Maintaining accurate history regarding physical issues, medications, or even family contacts can be difficult with some who suffer from a mental health diagnosis. Additionally, individuals who have a mental health diagnosis and begin medication management often stop taking their medication once they "feel better." Having issues such as these well documented can empower each provider, stakeholder, and/or partner to engage in informed decision-making with their patient/client. In other words, EHRs can be vital in maintaining a continuum of care for an individual, especially those with mental illness and in the criminal justice system (particularly, those who are passing from one system to the other and vice versa). Often with mental illness, and not unlike other illnesses, treatment may not be immediate. Individuals can use resources like medication management and other therapies to help treat their diagnosis. Using electronic medical records, other doctors and treatment professionals can understand the medical history of the individual being treated. Understanding a person's medical history can help treatment professionals identify best practices and hopefully prevent future setbacks. Ideally, jails and prisons will also move toward the use of electronic medical records to also ensure the best care for individuals involved in the criminal justice system with a mental health diagnosis. With this process, the hopes would be to eliminate further "cracks" in treatment.

SAMHSA discusses the use of health records for patients and their families. Often, over the course of care, an individual will coordinate with multiple different providers including doctors, mental health professionals and other service providers. The use of EHRs will allow for less information to be lost, resulting in better overall wellness. SAMHSA explains using health information technology, "Health IT also offers you these benefits:

- Secure access to your personal health information
- Easy care coordination between providers
- Access to remote care from your home
- Self-management tools for you and your caregivers (SAMHSA, 2017)

While the concept of EHRs is far from new, the issue is that health-care systems have been slow to adopt this tool or have yet to fully integrate this tool into all facets of each system (Palabindala, Pamarthy, & Jonnalagadda, 2016). Yet, much progress has been made in the wake of the Health Information Technology for Economic and Clinical Health Act (enacted 2009; United States Department of Health and Hospitals, 2017). Data on EHR adoption can be found at the Office of the National Coordinator for Health Information Technology (https://dashboard.healthit.gov), which details that the vast majority of American physicians using some form of EHR and over 90% of critical access hospitals of various sizes throughout the country (2017). Thus, at this point, the issue is not whether or not the tool is in use but *how* it is used. As providers gain more experience using EHRs, the benefits of using these systems—improved clinical decision-making, better communication among providers and between providers and patients, and reducing medication errors—can be fully realized. In addition, and of critical value for mental health professionals, the quality of case notes placed in EHRs can vary from provider to provider. While having access to medical histories can provide a rich resource to current providers, an abundance of poor case notes within an EHR may present a lost opportunity to make use of previous treatment encounters. For example, a recent review of a local agency providing mental health services in Louisiana showed considerable variation in the quality of case notes entered into a popular EHR. One provider working at the agency tended to use very brief and often repetitive narratives to describe his/her interactions with clients. As such, the case notes did not offer any individualized narratives for each client. This finding was shared with the agency's quality assurance manager as it is highly unlikely that all clients are presenting the same circumstances, experiences, and symptoms nearly in the same way (Khey, unpublished research—Findings from an audit of a local Louisiana mental health provider).

At this time, it is unclear just how much of the narrative type of information placed in EHRs can be considered valuable and usable. What is clear is that medication histories have been reliable, and EHRs have a proven track record of reducing medication errors relative to medication errors of patients in systems not using EHRs. This medication history can also offer mental health professionals clues as to prior treatment decisions and, in conjunction with even moderate-quality case notes, can continue to be invaluable for making contemporary decisions. As these systems continue to flourish, their capacity to aid patients will certainly continue to grow.

4.2.3   Double and Multiple Stigma

As discussed earlier, stigma can be a difficult obstacle to overcome. Within the criminal justice system, the label of "criminal" can be harsh, misunderstood, and almost impossible to wipe clean. In the mental health realm, stigma can be just as harsh and limit or prevent an individual from seeking treatment. Now, imagine the stigma of incarceration *and* mental illness together. Having both labels and negativity piled on can be the catalyst to harmful and tragic outcomes. For example, the statistics for suicide in both populations are high in isolation, but the compounded stigma of both being a "criminal" and "crazy" often places these individuals at greater risk of self-harm and/or suicide.

Double stigma is defined as the presence of two stigmatized qualities present in one person. This can be a criminal history and mental health concerns. Some researchers have attributed a double stigma to be present among transgendered individuals who have mental health concerns, others have argued a double stigma among Muslim Americans who have mental health concerns, and so on. Beyond double stigma, multiple stigma is simply the presence of additional stigmatized qualities in one person. Each stigmatized status arguably confounds and magnifies each other, leading to poorer and poorer outcomes, and lessens the likelihood of healthy, "normal" lives.

While this simplistic terminology does not appear in many mainstream sources, its underlying assertions are clear. This will be addressed more fully in a subsequent chapter, but it is important to note here that stigma and labels can often be likened to a snowball effect—in other words, stigma and labels and build off of each other to knife off potential opportunities the legitimate and pro-social world, pushing those with stigma away from society and leaving them vulnerable to victimization, self-medication, homelessness, and much more.

4.2.4   Barriers of Public Housing

Often, individuals with mental illness and/or a criminal background have difficulty finding housing. This can be as a result of either or both "classifications"—the mentally ill or the criminal. Family and loved ones may not have the resources necessary to care for a person with higher needs or may not want to help, particularly with the cumbersome and/or expensive process of securing housing. Additionally, with stigma for both mental health and crime, shame and guilt can be factors influencing the involvement of loved ones. Housing difficulties are often the result of criminal history:

Public Housing Occupancy Guidebook provided by the United States Department of Housing and Urban Development

Ineligibility Because of Criminal Activity (24 CFR § 960.204) PHAs are required to prohibit admission of families with members:

Who were evicted from federally assisted housing for drug-related criminal activity for 3 years following the date of eviction (unless the family can demonstrate that the person who engaged in the drug-related activity has been rehabilitated or is no longer a member of the household); or

Who are currently engaging in illegal use of a drug; or

Who have shown a pattern of use of illegal drugs that may interfere with the health, safety, or right to peaceful enjoyment of the premises by other residents; or

Who are subject to a lifetime registration requirement under a State sex offender registration program; or

Whose abuse of alcohol or pattern of abuse of alcohol would interfere with the health, safety or right to peaceful enjoyment of the premises by other residents; or

Who have ever been convicted of drug-related criminal activity for manufacture of methamphetamine on the premises of federally assisted housing.

The Guidebook goes on to discuss in more detail on what would eliminate a person from eligibility:

Involvement in Criminal Activity on the Part of Any Applicant Family Member that Would Adversely Affect the Health, Safety or Right to Peaceful Enjoyment of the Premises by Other Tenants (24 CFR § 960.203(c)(3) and 960.204) PHAs are required to check an applicant's history of criminal activity for a history of crimes that would be lease violations if they were committed by a public housing resident. Before the screening steps are examined, consider that certain actions and behaviors require a rejection of an applicant: [emphasis added] · Persons evicted from federally assisted housing for drug-related criminal activities may not be admitted for three years from the date of eviction. In cases where the statute prohibits admission for a certain period of time, PHAs may now set a longer period of time for the prohibition (24 CFR § 960.203 (c) (3) (ii)). - Where the regulations specify a prohibition period for certain behavior, PHAs can consider the mandatory period and any extension of the discretionary period. - The discretionary time period for prohibition of admission can vary based on the type of activity. For example, a PHA may have a policy that an eviction where the applicant was manufacturing or dealing drugs results in a 5-year prohibition. In the case of life-time sex offender registrants, a PHA may establish long periods or a lifetime ban. · Persons engaging in the illegal use of a drug.... (U.S. Housing and Urban Development, 2017)

Solutions to housing restrictions are described below in the following section.

4.3   Common Resources

Outside of incarcerated settings and in the "free world," there are a number of treatment options for and resources available to individuals suffering from mental health concerns. Traditional treatment options often include individual or group therapy and even family therapy. Individual therapy features regular one-on-one sessions with a licensed mental health professional and, on its own, offers a light and effective treatment for common mental health symptomatology. Also known as counseling or psychotherapy, individual therapy sessions often occur weekly in the therapist's office. Therapists can be licensed professional counselors, licensed clinical social workers, and psychologists, and ideally, these mental health professionals would work in conjunction with a psychiatrist who could potentially prescribe medication to the patient, if/as needed. Each session generally lasts around 1 hour, with the length depending on the needs of the client. Sessions can discuss an array of topics including social skills, coping skills, and relationships, to name a few.

On the other hand, assertive community treatment (ACT) is considered one of the most intensive treatment options available for severe mental illness that demands an "all-hands" approach. ACT is a team-based model designed to treat individuals on a 24-h-a-day, 7-day-a-week basis while the patient remains in the community. Described in detail below, an ACT team features professionals across several disciplines and perspectives that can aid treatment provision. Thus, there are many different types of treatment that vary depending on the severity of illness, time available, and, as always, funding. Further, treatment options include a variety of settings, each with advantages to consider when customizing a patient's individualized treatment plan.

Additionally, group therapy can be beneficial for some individuals. Group therapy consists of a therapist and a group of clients. The ideal number for a successful group should be less than 12 clients, but this can vary in different settings. Also, groups can be topic based as well and range from grief to substance abuse to parenting and beyond. Often, group therapy is most readily available to a majority of mental health "consumers" due to its relative low cost and effectiveness. More frequently, support groups are also leveraged for the same reasons. In many circumstances, support groups lack the lead of a trained clinician; however, and more often, support groups feature peer support specialists that can aid individuals with mental illness and/or substance use disorder cope with their disease, learn more about their triggers, and heal through shared experiences.

Each of these modalities is described below, along with other resources available in the community to help individuals with mental illness heal, learn to live with their illness, live comfortably, and live life to the fullest extent possible.

4.3.1   Transitional Housing and Recovery Residences: Halfway Houses, Sober Houses, and Three-Quarter Houses

For some leaving prison or a secure medical facility, a "halfway house" or other form or transitional housing is a great option (oftentimes, the only tangible option) that allows an individual to learn how to reenter society. This type of housing helps to slowly re-acclimate to everyday life, learn life skills and coping skills, and begin the process of recovery on solid footing alongside others who can benefit from the group therapy dynamic. An individual begins to regain their independence while also maintaining structure and support to ensure ease in the most difficult transition time.

The vernacular for transitional housing varies across the country. Broadly speaking, transitional houses—or recovery residences—refer to an array of housing options that offer different levels of rule strictness, obligations to attend treatment, and structure. For example, halfway houses have stricter rules, often have requirements of attending AA/NA or other 12-step (or similar) meetings, and engage in drug testing to ensure abstinence in comparison to three-quarter houses. In addition, halfway houses may place restrictions on residents in their ability to leave the house freely as they wish. In reality, a variety of transitional housing resources exist throughout the country with varying levels of rules, restrictions, and resources; the goal would be to find a resource that would match the facility to the needs of the client with the overarching goal, in most cases, to gradually step down the restrictions on this client until he or she can live independently and healthy and engage in broad pro-social behaviors.

4.3.2 Detox

Some substance use disorders must be treated immediately with medically monitored detoxification or "detox." In this process, the patient will be forced into withdrawal from their drug(s) of choice in the safest way possible, which many times requires medication to moderate the discomfort of withdrawal symptoms, to stabilize vital signs, and to protect a patient from harm and death directly due to withdrawal or indirectly due to the psychological effects of withdrawal. Medical detox is most important for the cessation of chronic alcohol, barbiturates, and opioids; in particular, the withdrawal syndromes produced by chronic alcohol and/or barbiturates consistently produce life-threatening effects.

To be specific, SAMHSA defines detoxification as "a set of interventions aimed at managing acute intoxication and withdrawal. It denotes a clearing of toxins from the body of the patient who is acutely intoxicated and/or dependent on substances of abuse" (SAMHSA, 2006). Typically, the detoxification process takes place within an inpatient setting to allow for the proper monitoring of the person by trained medical staff around the clock. "During inpatient detoxification, a person is monitored 24/7 by a trained medical staff for up to 7 days. Inpatient detoxification is generally more effective than outpatient for initial sobriety. This is because inpatient treatment provides a consistent environment and removes the person battling addiction from exposure to people and places associated with using" (NAMI, 2017c). Importantly, detoxification alone is not sufficient in the treatment and rehabilitation of substance use disorders (Table 4.2).

It is further helpful for individuals unfamiliar with the inner workings of detoxification services to note its principles for care as promulgated by SAMHSA. These nine principles are often mantra-like in the industry, a phenomenon that occurs often in the treatment business:

1. Detox is not a cure for substance abuse or substance use disorder. Instead, it is likely to be a first step into drug recovery (and a recovery orientation) and can be the first entry point into an array of treatment events in one's life.
2. Substance use disorder can be treated and patients can have hope to progress into recovery.

Table 4.2 Guiding principles and assumptions of detoxification and substance abuse treatment (SAMHSA, 2006)

1. Detoxification alone is not sufficient treatment for substance dependence but it is one part of a continuum of care for substance-related disorders

2. The detoxification process consists of the following three components:
  • Evaluation
  • Stabilization
  • Fostering patient readiness for and entry into treatment
  A detoxification process that does not incorporate all three critical components is considered incomplete and inadequate by the consensus panel

3. Detoxification can take place in a wide variety of settings and at a number of levels of intensity within these settings. Placement should be appropriate to the patient's needs
4. Persons seeking detoxification should have access to the components of the detoxification process described above, no matter what the setting or the level of treatment intensity
5. All persons requiring treatment for substance use disorders should receive treatment of the same quality and appropriate thoroughness and should be put into contact with a treatment program for substance use disorders after detoxification
6. Ultimately, insurance coverage for the full range of detoxification and follow-up treatment services is cost-effective. If reimbursement systems do not provide payment for the complete detoxification process, patients may be released prematurely, leading to medically or socially unattended withdrawal
7. Patients seeking detoxification services have diverse cultural and ethnic backgrounds as well as unique health needs and life situations. Organizations that provide detoxification services need to ensure that they have standard practices in place to address cultural diversity
8. A successful detoxification process can be measured, in part, by whether an individual who is substance dependent enters, remains in, and is compliant with the treatment protocol of a substance abuse treatment/rehabilitation program after detoxification

3. Substance use disorder is a chronic brain disease that often features relapse. This disease should not be mistaken for moral weakness.
4. Patients are to be treated with respect and in a dignified manner.
5. Further, patients are to be treated supportively and without judgment.
6. Individualized treatment plans should be made in partnership with the patient and, as warranted, with his or her support network (e.g., family, friends, partners, and/or employers).
7. All treatment personal should promote rehabilitation and maintenance activities at all times, as appropriate, and should be prepared to link the patient with subsequent services immediately after discharge from detox.
8. Active participation and involvement of a patient's support system should be encouraged when appropriate while ensuring patient's privacy, confidentiality, and HIPAA rights.
9. Treatment professionals must consider differences in background, culture, preferences, sexual orientation, disability, vulnerabilities, and strengths of each patient when providing care (SAMHSA, 2006). Emphasis must be placed on the fact that detox often serves as an entry event that begins the path to recovery (also known as a treatment "career") but also may be necessary several times across one's substance use "career."

Fig. 4.2 Continuum of mental health services, courtesy of the Minnesota Department of Human Services (2017)

4.3.3   Inpatient Treatment Services

Inpatient treatment can be beneficial and possibly necessary for a person experiencing serious mental illness and/or severe substance abuse. The inpatient setting allows for 24/7 care in both medical and mental health. Individuals often receive a multitude of complementary treatments, supports, and care while in an inpatient treatment center. An individual receives social support, medication management, medical care, individual therapy, group therapy, at times recreational therapy, and possibly art therapy. All facets work together with the overall goal of recovery from mental illness and substance use. This comprehensive treatment approach can also work to aid in overcoming past trauma or other underlying causes of the mental illness or substance use yet is the costliest of options (outside of incarceration; NAMI, 2017c).

The popular culture references to 28-day programs, particularly for substance use disorder treatment, often colors our perception of inpatient treatment services. In reality, inpatient treatment is very diverse and includes several types of facilities, including hospitals. Further, duration of inpatient services is often dictated by ability to pay and insurance coverage, while also considering a patient's underlying mental illness. As has been discussed throughout this text, the capacity to offer inpatient treatment services has been sharply decreased relative to past decades. Thus, these services are reserved for severe illness and for mental health crises that require these services (Fig. 4.2).

4.3.4   Intensive Outpatient (IOP) Treatment

Intensive outpatient treatment or IOP is akin to "partial hospitalization" in that a person receives treatment on a regular basis in a medical setting but returns home each night (NAMI, 2017e). In an IOP program, an individual has multiple treatment sessions each week. This type of treatment is often used in a transition after inpatient and leads to a step-down to outpatient treatment. It can also be coordinated with a sober or halfway house for a fuller range of treatment support. Some programs differentiate between IOP and partial hospitalization in that the former is the less intensive version of the latter, but essentially, both require attendance during the day for several days a week and will release patients into the community in the afternoon or late afternoon.

4.3.5   12 Steps: AA/NA

Alcoholics Anonymous and Narcotics Anonymous (AA/NA) are group *support* meetings, not therapy, that take place with a community-like approach to support recovery from alcohol and drugs. These meetings are run and attended by individuals that suffer from addiction. Meetings can be open to the public or closed, specific groups. Additionally, some meetings can be segregated to just women only. The purpose of AA/NA meetings is to hold members accountable for their processing of the 12-steps of the program. As the title implies, group members remain anonymous in that what is discussed in the meeting is not discussed outside in public.

Twelve-step programs like Alcoholics Anonymous have become ubiquitous in all treatment systems in the United States and are widely adopted worldwide, in general. Overall, this support group orientation is effective in promoting recovery: individuals who attend 12-step programs are twice as likely to remain abstinent relative to those who do not, and more frequent attendance of 12-step meetings is statistically correlated with higher rates of abstinence (Kaskutas, 2009). Further, and perhaps most critically, these programs are incredibly cheap to run (ostensibly free). These support groups should always be part of a broader individualized treatment plan; however, individuals using AA/NA as their sole source of support and "treatment" have been successful in improving their progress in recovery (Fig. 4.3).

4.3.6   Assertive Community Treatment (ACT) Teams

Assertive community treatment (ACT) is a multidisciplinary team-based approach that provides around the clock care to patients in situ (i.e., where the patients are in the community and not at any particular facility; NAMI, 2017d). Rather than a work through referral process, ACT provides treatment directly to clients by offering a team of professionals to handle any would-be referral among the team and not "refer out." In other words, any service a patient may need can be handled among team members immediately, cutting out any "middlemen" of treatment provision. ACT operates as a 24/7 treatment team just like inpatient services; however, ACT services are provided at the location of the client rather than in a hospital/inpatient setting. The team members are trained on multiple areas of topics including nursing, substance abuse, social work, psychiatry, and vocational counseling.

1. We admitted we were powerless over alcohol —that our lives had become unmanageable.

2. Came to believe that a Power greater than ourselves could restore us to sanity.

3. Made a decision to turn our will and our lives over to the care of God as we understood Him.

4. Made a searching and fearless moral inventory of ourselves.

5. Admitted to God, to ourselves, and to another human being the exact nature of our wrongs.

6. Were entirely ready to have God remove all these defects of character.

7. Humbly asked Him to remove our shortcomings.

8. Made a list of all persons we had harmed, and became willing to make amends to them all.

9. Made direct amends to such people wherever possible, except when to do so would injure them or others.

10. Continued to take personal inventory and when we were wrong promptly admitted it.

11. Sought through prayer and meditation to improve our conscious contact with God as we understood Him, praying only for knowledge of His will for us and the power to carry that out.

12. Ha ving had a spiritual awakening as the result of these steps, we tried to carry this message to alcoholics, and to practice these principles in all our affairs.

Fig. 4.3 The 12 steps of Alcoholics Anonymous (Alcoholics Anonymous, 1981)

According to NAMI, assertive community treatment began in 1972 as the brainchild of Arnold Marx, Leonard Stein, and Mary Ann Test at Mendota State Hospital in Wisconsin. ACT was initially meant to serve as a support system for patients reentering the community from state hospitals during the early stages of the deinstitutionalization movement. In particular, these mental health professionals noted that many gains in mental health quickly tended to devolve after patients return back into their communities. As ACT services are reaching its half-centennial of existence, its proven success has earned it the distinction of being an evidence-based service by SAMHSA.

The key features of ACT are:

1. "*Treatment*: psychopharmacologic treatment, including new atypical antipsychotic and antidepressant medications, individual supportive therapy, mobile crisis intervention, hospitalization, substance abuse treatment, including group therapy (for clients with a [co-occurring disorder] of substance abuse and mental illness)"
2. "*Rehabilitation*: behaviorally oriented skill teaching (supportive and cognitive-behavioral therapy), including structuring time and handling activities of daily living, supported employment, both paid and volunteer work support for resuming education"
3. "*Support services*: support, education, and skill teaching to family members, collaboration with families and assistance to clients with children, direct support to help clients obtain legal and advocacy services, financial support, supported housing, money-management services, and transportation" (NAMI Minnesota, 2017)

4.3.7 The Value of Compulsory Treatment

Specialty courts are discussed in a different chapter within this book, but there are other ways that treatment can be required for those involved in the criminal justice system. In fact, *compulsory treatment* often leads to the most successful treatment experiences among patients, particularly when evaluating the likelihood of treatment completion. Importantly, successful completion of treatment is correlated with lasting success in recovery and healthy lives.

With court-mandated treatment, the added "benefit" of legal ramification with treatment noncompliance helps to keep patients on the path to successfully complete treatment regimes, often giving them the best chances of future success. Further, treatment can be an option in lieu of incarceration or prosecution, which also aids in giving people reason to stay clean, compliant, and out of trouble. According to the NIDA, "most studies suggest that outcomes for those who are legally pressured to enter treatment are as good or better than outcomes for those who entered treatment without legal pressure. Individuals under legal pressure also tend to have higher attendance rates and remain in treatment for longer periods, which can also have a positive impact on treatment outcomes" (2017).

4.4 Treatment Settings

Treatment can be provided in a number of settings and locations. The settings depend on the goals and recovery process of the individual seeking treatment. The benefit of multiple options is that there can be multisystemic approach. In other words, what works for one person may not work for another, so trying different settings to find the "right fit" may be best.

Private practice for a therapist is similar to a doctor's office. Often a therapist has their own office or is with a group in a building. This setting lends to a more open environment that is designed and decorated by the therapists themselves rather than a more hospital-type vibe. Typically, if in a group, each therapist has their own office in which to meet with clients. Insurance can be used in private practice settings to help offset the cost of sessions. Individual, family, and group sessions can take place in private practice offices. The following sections offer a review of other treatment settings available to patients in the community setting.

4.4.1 Community Mental Health Centers

Community mental health centers (CMHC) provide mental health services to the public. Generally, those visiting a community mental health center receive Social Security disability and/or Medicaid benefits (Centers for Medicare and Medicaid

Services, 2017). Local governments of the parish or county operate these centers, which offer a variety of services to the public. Those services can include outpatient treatment, group therapy and/or support groups, medication management, and case management, and some offer specific substance abuse addiction services. CMHCs can be very helpful in that they can offer referrals to other treatment providers and useful programs in the community. Most people who seek help at a CMHC experience a severe impact of symptoms on their activities of daily living. This can range between a variety of needs which result in a variety of referrals from day programs to longer-term inpatient supportive housing.

4.4.2   Emergency Rooms and Hospitalization

As with certain medical situations, there are times when an emergency arises and immediate treatment is needed for mental health as well. Additionally, in times of suicidal ideations or homicidal ideations, seeking emergency help is in the best interest for safety of the individual and/or others. A person can be brought to the emergency room for immediate attention for a mental health concern. As NAMI describes, "Situations that might require a trip to the emergency room include: a suicide attempt, assault or threatening actions against another person, hearing voices, paranoia, confusion, et cetera, or drugs or alcohol escalating to a person's mental health issue" (2017e). Often, going to an emergency room, whether voluntarily or involuntarily (loved one, ambulance, law enforcement, etc.), can be the first step in beginning the process of treatment. Luckily, many emergency rooms in major metropolitan areas have psychiatric areas specifically used to treatment-emergent situations with a mentally ill person. Also, the staff is trained to handle a psychiatric crisis and make the best decision for continued care.

4.4.3   Group Homes

At times, a group home may be a necessary type of supportive housing for a person who needs more attention and care. For individuals who are in need of medication management, but not in mental health crisis, a group home can be an option (NAMI, 2017f). As SAMHSA describes, "research literature documents that persons with serious mental illnesses, and substance use disorders die younger than the general population—mainly due to preventable risk factors (e.g., smoking) and treatable conditions (e.g., cardiovascular disease and cancer)" (SAMHSA, 2012, p. 7). Part of the measures taken to work to overcome these risk factors includes improving access to primary care. In some cases, that care can be provided "in-house" while a person is living in a group home or supportive housing, in collaboration with medical partners in the community. Individuals who are chronically ill can have access to both medical and mental health treatment within the setting of the group home or be transported by the group home to attend appointments for these services in the community. Additionally, individuals can live with other peers and work toward social improvements. Group homes often offer the opportunity to learn skills and activities all with the extra care.

4.5   Federal/National Resources

The federal system for criminal justice and health-care changes with each change in administration. These changes can be both good and bad. First, the instability on the system and all involved every 4–8 years can be a struggle. Additionally, each administration can vary wildly in regard to views and ways to handle the needs of the country, including by setting priorities and funding schemes to match these priorities (particularly among major federal grant-funding agencies). Fortunately or unfortunately, each state in the United States operates differently on some systems. There are federal standards to adhere to for hospitals and levels of treatment, but with other matters, policies can be changed or adjusted by state government. Further, the issue of treating mental health as a separate issue allows for more "flexibility" with treatment and funding at the state level. State governments make decisions about the allocation of money to each different entity, like public-run hospitals. If a state is in need of making financial adjustments, they can choose to defund those programs and even hospital. The following sections feature nationwide or federal resources that offer support to the issues documented in this book.

4.5.1   SAMHSA

The Substance Abuse and Mental Health Services Administration (SAMHSA) is a federal government agency that oversees many programs related to both mental health and substance abuse. Under the umbrella of SAMHSA include many different programs, campaigns, and initiatives including advisory councils to lead behavioral health policymaking; strategic initiatives "to help provide treatment and services for people with mental and substance use disorders [and support their family]"; social media campaigns; literature for professionals, individuals, and families; and current data on substance use and abuse as well as mental illness. Additionally, SAMHSA offers opportunity for funding via grants for state governments, local governments, and other related agencies (e.g., NAMI). These grants can offer opportunities for agencies, localities, and states to develop and expand existing programs or innovate to create new programs (Table 4.3).

Table 4.3 SAMHSA-funded programs (2017)

Grant program	Program description
State Pilot Grant Program for Treatment for Pregnant and Postpartum Women	"supports family-based services for pregnant and postpartum women with a primary diagnosis of a substance use disorder, including opioid disorders; 2) help state substance abuse agencies address the continuum of care, including services provided to women in nonresidential-based settings; and 3) promote a coordinated, effective and efficient state system managed by state substance abuse agencies by encouraging new approaches and models of service delivery"
Cooperative Agreements for Expansion and Sustainability of the Comprehensive Community Mental Health Services for Children with Serious Emotional Disturbances	"This cooperative agreement will support the provision of mental health and related recovery support services to children and youth with SED and those with early signs and symptoms of serious mental illness (SMI), including first episode psychosis (FEP), and their families…The SOC Expansion and Sustainability Cooperative Agreements will build upon progress made in developing comprehensive SOC across the country by focusing on sustainable financing, cross-agency collaboration, the creation of policy and infrastructure, and the development and implementation of evidence-based and evidence-informed services and supports"
State Targeted Response to the Opioid Crisis Grants	"The program aims to address the opioid crisis by increasing access to treatment, reducing unmet treatment need, and reducing opioid overdose related deaths through the provision of prevention, treatment and recovery activities for opioid use disorder (OUD) (including prescription opioids as well as illicit drugs such as heroin)"
Cooperative Agreement for the Provider's Clinical Support System—Medication Assisted Treatment Supplement	"Program purpose is to expand on the Drug Addiction Treatment Act (DATA) of 2000 and continue SAMHSA's currently funded PCSS-MAT initiative…This supplement will provide additional support to the current PCSS-MAT grantee by enhancing/expanding medication assisted treatment (MAT) training and educational resources to health professionals on evidence-based practices for preventing, identifying, and treating opioid use disorders"
Promoting Integration of Primary and Behavioral Health Care	"The purpose of this cooperative agreement is to: (1) promote full integration and collaboration in clinical practice between primary and behavioral healthcare; (2) support the improvement of integrated care models for primary care and behavioral health care to improve the overall wellness and physical health status of adults with a serious mental illness (SMI) or children with a serious emotional disturbance (SED); and (3) promote and offer integrated care services related to screening, diagnosis, prevention, and treatment of mental and substance use disorders, and co-occurring physical health conditions and chronic diseases"
Grants for the Benefit of Homeless Individuals	"The purpose of this program is to support the development and/or expansion of local implementation of a community infrastructure that integrates behavioral health treatment and services for substance use disorders (SUD) and co-occurring mental and substance use disorders (COD), permanent housing, and other critical services for individuals (including youth) and families experiencing homelessness"

(continued)

Table 4.3 (continued)

Grant program	Program description
Cooperative Agreement for the Historically Black Colleges and Universities Center for Excellence in Behavioral Health	"The purpose of this program is to continue to enhance the effort to network the 105 HBCUs throughout the United States to promote behavioral health, expand campus service capacity, and facilitate workforce development. The HBCU-CFE seeks to address behavioral health disparities among racial and ethnic minorities by encouraging the implementation of strategies to decrease the differences in access, service use, and outcomes among the racial and ethnic minority populations served and trained by the program. The goals of the HBCU-CFE are to promote student behavioral health to positively impact student retention; expand campus service capacity, including the provision of culturally and linguistically appropriate behavioral health resources; facilitate best practices dissemination and behavioral health workforce development; and increase awareness of the early signs of emotional distress and resources for early intervention"
Comprehensive Addiction and Recovery Act: Building Communities of Recovery	"The purpose of this program is to mobilize resources within and outside of the recovery community to increase the prevalence and quality of long-term recovery support from substance abuse and addiction. These grants are intended to support the development, enhancement, expansion, and delivery of recovery support services (RSS) as well as promotion of and education about recovery"
Grants to Expand Substance Abuse Treatment Capacity in Family Treatment Drug Courts	"The purpose of this program is to expand and/or enhance substance use disorder (SUD) treatment services in existing family treatment drug courts, which use the family treatment drug court model in order to provide alcohol and drug treatment (including recovery support services, screening, assessment, case management, and program coordination) to parents with a SUD and/or co-occurring SUD and mental disorders who have had a dependency petition filed against them or are at risk of such filing. Services must address the needs of the family as a whole and include direct service provision to children (18 and under) of individuals served by this project"
The Substance Abuse and HIV Prevention Navigator Program for Racial/Ethnic Minorities Ages 13-24 Cooperative Agreement	"The purpose of this program is to provide services to those at highest risk for HIV and substance use disorders, especially racial/ethnic males ages 13-24 at risk for HIV/AIDS including males who have sex with other males (MSM). The program will place a particular emphasis on those individuals who are not in stable housing in communities with high incidence and prevalence rates of substance misuse and HIV infection. It will provide opportunities to enhance outreach to the population of focus and assist them in receiving HIV medical care"

(continued)

Table 4.3   (continued)

Grant program	Program description
Resiliency in Communities After Stress and Trauma	"The purpose of this program is to assist high-risk youth and families and promote resilience and equity in communities that have recently faced civil unrest through implementation of evidence-based, violence prevention, and community youth engagement programs, as well as linkages to trauma-informed behavioral health services. The goal of the ReCAST Program is for local community entities to work together in ways that lead to improved behavioral health, empowered community residents, reductions in trauma, and sustained community change"
Cooperative Agreements to Implement the National Strategy for Suicide Prevention	"The purpose of this program is to support states in implementing the 2012 National Strategy for Suicide Prevention (NSSP) goals and objectives focused on preventing suicide and suicide attempts among adults age 25 and older in order to reduce the overall suicide rate and number of suicides in the U.S. nationally"
Grants for the Benefit of Homeless Individuals	"The purpose of this program is to support the development and/or expansion of local implementation of a community infrastructure that integrates behavioral health treatment and services for substance use disorders (SUD) and co-occurring mental and substance use disorders (COD), permanent housing, and other critical services for individuals (including youth) and families experiencing homelessness"
Cooperative Agreement for the Historically Black Colleges and Universities Center for Excellence in Behavioral Health	"The purpose of this program is to continue to enhance the effort to network the 105 HBCUs throughout the United States to promote behavioral health, expand campus service capacity, and facilitate workforce development. The HBCU-CFE seeks to address behavioral health disparities among racial and ethnic minorities by encouraging the implementation of strategies to decrease the differences in access, service use, and outcomes among the racial and ethnic minority populations served and trained by the program. The goals of the HBCU-CFE are to promote student behavioral health to positively impact student retention; expand campus service capacity, including the provision of culturally and linguistically appropriate behavioral health resources; facilitate best practices dissemination and behavioral health workforce development; and increase awareness of the early signs of emotional distress and resources for early intervention"
Comprehensive Addiction and Recovery Act: Building Communities of Recovery	"The purpose of this program is to mobilize resources within and outside of the recovery community to increase the prevalence and quality of long-term recovery support from substance abuse and addiction. These grants are intended to support the development, enhancement, expansion, and delivery of recovery support services (RSS) as well as promotion of and education about recovery"

(continued)

Table 4.3 (continued)

Grant program	Program description
Grants to Expand Substance Abuse Treatment Capacity in Family Treatment Drug Courts	"The purpose of this program is to expand and/or enhance substance use disorder (SUD) treatment services in existing family treatment drug courts, which use the family treatment drug court model in order to provide alcohol and drug treatment (including recovery support services, screening, assessment, case management, and program coordination) to parents with a SUD and/or co-occurring SUD and mental disorders who have had a dependency petition filed against them or are at risk of such filing. Services must address the needs of the family as a whole and include direct service provision to children (18 and under) of individuals served by this project"
The Substance Abuse and HIV Prevention Navigator Program for Racial/Ethnic Minorities Ages 13–24 Cooperative Agreement	"The purpose of this program is to provide services to those at highest risk for HIV and substance use disorders, especially racial/ethnic males ages 13–24 at risk for HIV/AIDS including males who have sex with other males (MSM). The program will place a particular emphasis on those individuals who are not in stable housing in communities with high incidence and prevalence rates of substance misuse and HIV infection. It will provide opportunities to enhance outreach to the population of focus and assist them in receiving HIV medical care"
Resiliency in Communities After Stress and Trauma	"The purpose of this program is to assist high-risk youth and families and promote resilience and equity in communities that have recently faced civil unrest through implementation of evidence-based, violence prevention, and community youth engagement programs, as well as linkages to trauma-informed behavioral health services. The goal of the ReCAST Program is for local community entities to work together in ways that lead to improved behavioral health, empowered community residents, reductions in trauma, and sustained community change"
Cooperative Agreements to Implement the National Strategy for Suicide Prevention	"The purpose of this program is to support states in implementing the 2012 National Strategy for Suicide Prevention (NSSP) goals and objectives focused on preventing suicide and suicide attempts among adults age 25 and older in order to reduce the overall suicide rate and number of suicides in the U.S. nationally"

4.5.2   National Alliance on Mental Illness

The National Alliance on Mental Illness or NAMI is a mental health organization created to help improve the lives of people suffering from mental illness. The goals of NAMI include educating and advocating on topics related to mental illness. Additionally, the organization works to promote awareness with events including NAMIWalks as well as offer help and support with the NAMI HelpLine. For colleges and universities, NAMI on Campus is a campus club that works to end the stigma associated with mental illness as well as help to make connections for services and needs for students on campus. NAMI offers a startup packet and support to create a club on campus for those interested.

As an example of a NAMI local office, NAMI New Orleans offers a prime example of a vibrant NAMI operation working in collaboration with community partners to advance its mission. NAMI New Orleans operates two offices in the greater New Orleans area and provides a variety of services for the community. Adults living with severe mental illness in the area can receive services like counseling, Community Psychiatric Support and Treatment (CPST), Permanent Supportive Housing Services, psychosocial rehabilitation skills training (PSR), and even a drop-in center.

> The Drop-In Center provides groups weekly as well as educational courses that last for 10 weeks regularly. These groups are run by peers trained by the NAMI Peer-to-Peer program. "The Peer-to-Peer program helps [an individual]:
>
> - Create a personalized relapse prevention plan
> - Learn how to interact with healthcare providers
> - Develop confidence for making decisions and reducing stress
> - Stay up-to-date on mental health research
> - Understand the impact of symptoms on the person's life
> - Access practical resources on how to maintain the journey toward recovery" (NAMI, 2017g)

Programs like these are important in that an individual with mental illness can receive support and help from others who understand their situation. Additionally, and importantly, individuals can learn to advocate for themselves in their own lives, especially in relation to medical needs. Ultimately, support and confidence can aid in the overall recovery and wellness for the person with mental illness.

In addition to services provided directly to the individuals in need in the community, NAMI also provides programming for family members and caretakers of those with mental illness. These programs can beneficial to understand the illness of a loved one, understand their role in recovery and wellness, help to reduce stigma and boost awareness, and finally aid in reduction of burnout and compassion fatigue. NAMI New Orleans provides Mental Health First Aid, Mental Healthcare Navigation Team, Family Education and Support, Peer Education and Support, Advocacy and Community Education, and Advance Directive for Mental Health Treatment.

The Family Education and Support programs vary from structured multi-week courses taught by trained professionals to the Survivors of Suicide Loss support group which "is a free peer-led support group for adults whose lives have been impacted by the loss of a loved one to suicide, whether recently or in the past" (NAMI New Orleans, 2017).

4.6   Example of Innovation in Available Resources and Emerging Technology: Mobile Health (mHealth)

The use of applications or apps by many has grown for all sorts of options. From shopping to language skills and everything in between, "there's an app for that." Now, there are also apps for therapy and treatment. Talkspace is a web-based treatment platform that can be used on a computer or cell phone. The process involves an initial assessment and then a matching process (not unlike online dating) to establish a positive relationship between therapist and potential client. Users can denote special needs like LGBTQ friendly or Veteran knowledge to assure their needs are met in future therapy session.

Though application and web-based treatment options are nontraditional, they do provide options and help for those who may not otherwise have access or not seek treatment. The use of electronic devices can make the argument of both a help and a hindrance since there have been many studies regarding the limits on screen time or being present rather than glued to a phone, but that is a different book entirely.

The American Psychiatric Association (APA) has taken notice of the use of technology in treatment and is working to ensure best practices are used. The APA provides a process for rating apps by professionals. As well as rating, professionals can use the app evaluation model on the APA's website to review and identify the best apps for their clients. The model is founded in the idea of "do no harm."

The four areas comprising the model (beyond gathering basic background information) are:

1. Safety/Privacy
2. Evidence (i.e., effectiveness)
3. Ease of Use
4. Interoperability (American Psychiatric Association, 2017).

4.7 A Canary in the Shaft: American Mental Health Troubles Seen Abroad

Unfortunately, the struggles to treat mental illness are more widespread than the United States, particularly when discussing the issues of justice-involved individuals with mental health issues. In Italy, for example, there were recent changes in government and funds which resulted in the closing of the forensic hospitals. This means that all individuals in the hospital that were previously being treated were either transferring to a regular hospital, put into a traditional jail/prison setting, or released. As a result, the health-care system, criminal justice system, and community are all affected. In 2015, Italy finally closed their six remaining forensic psychiatric hospitals (Barbui & Saraceno, 2015; Casacchia et al., 2015):

> In 2012, a new law (Law 9/2012) established that new residential facilities had to be developed to better meet the needs of providing intensive and high-quality mental healthcare to socially dangerous individuals with mental disorders under proper secure conditions. These small-scale facilities (no more than 20 individuals, up to 4 patients per bedroom) are intended to replace admissions to forensic psychiatric hospitals.... As expected, the new law has activated a heated debate among Italian mental health professionals. As a general point it should be emphasised that this reform has been approved without clear cut evidence of its cost-effectiveness. Similarly, the results of studies describing the outcomes of patients discharged from forensic psychiatric hospitals are unavailable, and no recent and reliable information on the clinical characteristics and care needs of forensic psychiatric patients have been collected.... [A]nother critical consideration is the extra burden that community services will face. Several facilities in Italy are presently understaffed and in the past few

years economic resources have been cut, to a varying degree, across the country. Additional resources will also be needed to increase the competence of mental health professionals working in community services in treating criminal offenders with mental disorders (Barbui & Saraceno, 2015, p. 445).

It appears that the American experience is not exclusive nor unique. As such, American students and professionals should be aware of other systems under stress and observe differences (and similarities) to other approaches to navigate these problems as a learning device. Further, growth from shared experiences works for mental health patients; why should it not be helpful for mental health professionals as well?

4.8   Conclusion

In the conversation about treatment, specifically for justice-involved individuals, there are both good news and bad news. There are new innovations and technology being created daily to aid in allowing access to treatment for persons who otherwise may not have had any help. Additionally, federal grant funding allows for counties, parishes, and states to incorporate successful models that have been proven to work but would not have been a possibility due to funding. That being said, there continues to be strife in the realm of treatment for many states. The point here is that individuals experiencing symptoms of mental illness need treatment, not unlike any other illness. If a person is in need of treatment, then why are they often incarcerated? The answer is broken system.

Those with severe mental illness are more likely to be homeless. If they are homeless, they may be out in public experiencing delusions and/or hallucinations. As mentioned before, the stigma and stereotype with mental illness lead the public and sometimes first responders (who may not be properly trained) to believe these individuals are violent or cause a public threat. In reality, most are not violent but are in dire need of help and care. Taking a person to jail who is hearing voices or is severely paranoid is not the answer. Jail will not help because it is not treatment. Not only that, if they are paranoid or in the midst of a delusion or hallucination being taken against their will only to be locked up will most likely escalate the situation. Imagine being locked away and not understanding why or fearing harm. This compromises the safety of the individual, the first responders, the public, and those inside the jail/prison system.

This brings back the conversation regarding jail and prison staff and their safety. Without treatment, illnesses get worse, and in this case those illnesses lead to further delusions or hallucinations. Often, this results in self-harm, possibly suicide. Then, consider those witnessing these acts and attempting to help. Incarceration does not cure mental illness.

Even further, the cost of incarcerating an individual comes into play. Keeping a person in jail or prison for days, weeks, months, or even years gets expensive. Alternatively, treatment can be provided and may be shorter and cost less.

Obviously, some violent crimes are the exception to the treatment instead of incarceration argument. There is a reality of those who commit horrible, violent crimes due to a mental illness, and incarceration is part of the sentence for those crimes.

Humanity should be considered in all situations. No one would ever think to lock up a person with diabetes or cancer, so why should bipolar disorder or schizophrenia be any different. Even consider nonpsychotic disorders like depression and anxiety. If a person experiencing clinical depression is incarcerated without treatment, how is that person expected to recover? If they are released, how can society expect success? Also, as mentioned before, these individuals tend to return time and time again to jail. Each time costs money, and each time does nothing to help the person with mental illness. Therefore, time and money are wasted, and the person's illness gets worse. Additionally, the person may seek medical attention as well, thus costing more money from the health-care system. This benefits no one including the taxpayer.

Changes should be made at all levels of interaction: local, state, and federal. On one side, there are taxpayers and government officials often discussing the fiscal side of the argument. The other side includes individuals with mental illness, their loved ones, and health professionals. It may appear to have a simple solution—send those with mental illness to treatment rather than jail or prison. It saves the local county/parish money, state, and federal government and helps the person. Ideally, that is simple, but the obstacles and barriers involved can be overwhelming, time-consuming, and shrouded with fear and misunderstanding often crippling the system and halting any change.

Many people know of someone with mental illness or a substance abuse problem. Whether it be a close friend or family member or a distant relative or coworker, these concerns do exist and are prevalent. Now, considering that person, do they not deserve treatment to help them recover?

First responders often struggle with the reality of the broken system as well. As discussed before, their job (and often identity) is to help others in need. Keeping that in mind, imagine the difficulty of repeated attempts to help individuals encountered on a regular basis. How does a first responder keep faith in the system? In their job? Further, the local/state/federal government? These situations all lead to burnout and mental health struggles for those on the front line, not to mention the growing frustration of the lack of help being provided to those in need. Visually seeing people deteriorate regularly cannot be easy.

Furthermore, for the individual inside the system, hope and positivity can be difficult to find. Fear of incarceration may be the sole reason for a person to avoid seeking help when needed, leading to hopelessness and, again, worsening symptoms. Without a proper support system, this fear may also lead to grave consequences with suicide. Add in the stigma of mental illness, substance abuse, and criminal history and the results are a trifecta of negativity. It can seem impossible to change or even begin steps to recover, sobriety, and wellness. Those in need of help may also not know the resources available to them or, even worse, may not have access to seek out said resources.

Thinking of loved ones, the importance of education and support is also essential here. Families can play a crucial role in helping a person change for the better after a mental illness crisis or even just a diagnosis. Also, those with substance abuse and criminal history are in dire need of education and support. Those who live with the individual in need can learn to understand the signs and symptoms of their illness(es). Learning these can aid in proactive measures to possibly prevent further issues or from an eruption of symptoms. Additionally, support after treatment can be beneficial to possibly prevent further issues.

References

Alcoholics Anonymous. (1981). *The twelve steps of Alcoholics Anonymous*. Retrieved October 27, 2017, from https://www.aa.org/assets/en_US/smf-121_en.pdf

American Psychiatric Association. (2017). *App evaluation model*. Retrieved October 27, 2017, from https://www.psychiatry.org/psychiatrists/practice/mental-health-apps/app-evaluation-model

Barbui, C., & Saraceno, B. (2015). Closing forensic psychiatric hospitals in Italy: A new revolution begins? *The British Journal of Psychiatry, 206*(6), 445–446.

Casacchia, M., Malavolta, M., Bianchini, V., Giusti, L., Di, V. M., Giosuè, P., et al. (2015). Closing forensic psychiatric hospitals in Italy: A new deal for mental health care? *Rivista di Psichiatria, 50*(5), 199–209.

Centers for Medicare and Medicaid Services. (2017). *Community mental health centers*. Retrieved October 31, 2017, from https://www.cms.gov/Medicare/Provider-Enrollment-and-Certification/CertificationandComplianc/CommunityHealthCenters.html

Fraze, T., Lewis, V. A., Rodriguez, H. P., & Fisher, E. S. (2016). Housing, transportation, and food: How ACOs seek to improve population health by addressing nonmedical needs of patients. *Health Affairs, 35*(11), 2109–2115.

Insel, T. (2010). *Turning the corner, not the key, in treatment of serious mental illness*. Retrieved October 25, 2017, from https://www.nimh.nih.gov/about/directors/thomas-insel/blog/2010/turning-the-corner-not-the-key-in-treatment-of-serious-mental-illness.shtml

Kaskutas, L. A. (2009). Alcoholics anonymous effectiveness: Faith meets science. *Journal of Addictive Diseases, 28*(2), 145–157.

Louisiana Department of Health. (2017). *Department of Health and Department of Corrections team up to provide health care coverage for newly released offenders*. Retrieved October 27, 2017, from http://new.dhh.louisiana.gov/index.cfm/newsroom/detail/4170

Minnesota Department of Human Services. (2017). *First episode psychosis*. Retrieved October 27, 2017, from https://mn.gov/dhs/people-we-serve/adults/health-care/mental-health/programs-services/first-episode-psychosis.jsp

National Academies of Sciences, Engineering, and Medicine. (2016). *Connecting patients to transportation: Incentives and return on investment*. Retrieved October 27, 2017, from https://www.ncbi.nlm.nih.gov/books/NBK402427/

National Alliance on Mental Illness. (2017a). *Mental health by the numbers*. Retrieved October 25, 2017, from https://www.nami.org/Learn-More/Mental-Health-By-the-Numbers

National Alliance on Mental Illness. (2017b). *Medicaid*. Retrieved October 27, 2017, from https://www.nami.org/Learn-More/Mental-Health-Public-Policy/Medicaid

National Alliance on Mental Illness. (2017c). *Dual diagnosis*. Retrieved October 27, 2017, from https://www.nami.org/Learn-More/Mental-Health-Conditions/Related-Conditions/Dual-Diagnosis

National Alliance on Mental Illness. (2017d). *Psychosocial treatments*. Retrieved October 27, 2017, from https://www.nami.org/Learn-More/Treatment/Psychosocial-Treatments

National Alliance on Mental Illness. (2017e). *Treatment settings*. Retrieved October 27, 2017, from https://www.nami.org/NAMI/media/NAMI-Media/Images/FactSheets/Treatment-Settings-FS.pdf

National Alliance on Mental Illness. (2017f). *Securing stable housing*. Retrieved October 27, 2017, from https://www.nami.org/Find-Support/Living-with-a-Mental-Health-Condition/Securing-Stable-Housing

National Alliance on Mental Illness. (2017g). *NAMI Peer-to-Peer*. Retrieved October 27, 2017, from https://www.nami.org/Find-Support/NAMI-Programs/NAMI-Peer-to-Peer

National Alliance on Mental Illness Minnesota. (2017). *Fact sheet: Assertive community treatment (ACT)*. Retrieved October 27, 2017, from http://www.namihelps.org/assets/PDFs/fact-sheets/General/Assertive-Community-Treatment.pdf

National Alliance on Mental Illness New Orleans. (2017). *Survivors of suicide loss support group (Uptown)*. Retrieved October 27, 2017, from https://namineworleans.org/event-registration/

National Alliance on Mental Illness St. Tammany. (2017). *Resources*. Retrieved October 25, 2017, from http://namisttammany.org/resources/

National Institute on Drug Abuse. (2017). *Principles of drug abuse treatment for criminal justice populations - A research-based guide*. Retrieved October 27, 2017, from https://www.drugabuse.gov/publications/principles-drug-abuse-treatment-criminal-justice-populations/legally-mandated-treatment-effective

Office of the National Coordinator for Health Information Technology. (2017). *Dashboard*. Retrieved October 27, 2017, from https://dashboard.healthit.gov

Palabindala, V., Pamarthy, A., & Jonnalagadda, N. R. (2016). Adoption of electronic health records and barriers. *Journal of Community Hospital Internal Medicine Perspectives, 6*(5). Retrieved October 27, 2017, from http://www.tandfonline.com/doi/full/10.3402/jchimp.v6.32643

Substance Abuse and Mental Health Services Administration. (2006). *Detoxification and substance abuse treatment. Treatment improvement protocol (TIP) Series, No. 45*. Retrieved October 27, 2017, from https://store.samhsa.gov/shin/content/SMA13-4131/SMA13-4131.pdf

Substance Abuse and Mental Health Services Administration. (2012). *People with mental health & substance use conditions: The core clinical features*. Retrieved October 27, 2017, from https://www.integration.samhsa.gov/clinical-practice/CIHS_Health_Homes_Core_Clinical_Features.pdf

Substance Abuse and Mental Health Services Administration. (2017). *Health IT for patients and families*. Retrieved October 27, 2017, from https://www.samhsa.gov/health-information-technology/patients-families

United States Department of Housing and Urban Development. (2017). *Public housing occupancy guidebook*. Retrieved October 27, 2017, from https://www.hud.gov/sites/documents/DOC_10760.PDF

United States Department of Health and Hospitals. (2017). HITECH Act Enforcement Interim Final Rule. Retrieved September 1, 2017, from https://www.hhs.gov/hipaa/for-professionals/special-topics/hitech-act-enforcement-interim-final-rule/index.html

Chapter 5
Jails

You never really understand a person until you consider things from his point of view…
until you climb into his skin and walk around in it.—Harper Lee

The fact that jails have become a key focal point for mental illness over the years is not inherently the central problem. This may be a semantical point, but it is an important one to think over. As discussed earlier, the history of caring for those with mental illness is fraught with horrors, stigma, abuse, and misunderstanding. Shifting the primary location of care for patients from the asylum to the communities they reside was quite intentional and, in part, driven by humanitarian interests. The perception of this shift is remarkable. What better way exists to "fix" a broken system than destroying it and freeing the tortured souls bound up in its clutches? Truly, these are almost identical interests that drove the creation of asylums in the first place just a generation before—recall our discussion of Dorothea Dix and her advocacy for these very reforms. While it is tempting to simply suggest that jails are no place for individuals with mental illness, the broader truth is that jails can perform a vital role in the continuum of treatment when tailored evidence-based programs are put into place. This brings us to *the* central problem: jails are utilized as the de facto focal point for mental illness largely without process, decisive action, and dedicated programming. Thus, shifting the responsibility of care effectively did little to solve the underlying issue of a broken continuum of care, with the operational word being *care*.

5.1 Know the Role

As a legal matter, the standard of care rests in how we have come to define a constitutionally acceptable level of care. What this boils down to, in most circumstances, is defining the absolute minimum level of care required to run a legally compliant jail. Yet, even this standard can be quite costly. For example, a Southwestern

Louisiana jail administrator speculated that her costs run upward to $100 per day to care for an individual with mental illness at this standard. In all actuality, this estimate runs on the cheaper end of the spectrum across the United States; for example, an often cited report in *the Miami Herald* estimated that care for individuals with mental illness in the Broward County, Florida jail is about $130 per day compared to the $80 for an "average" inmate back in 2007 (Miller & Fantz, 2007). A Vera Institute report updated in 2014 has compiled similar situations across the country. In Harris County (Houston), Texas, the annual expenditure for mental health care reached $24 million dollars per year. In Northeast Ohio, over half of a jail's medical budget was spent on psychotropic drugs alone (Vera Institute, 2014). Again, most of these tallies cover just the bare necessities as required by the constitution.

This institutional mentality is beginning to thaw as justice professionals are increasingly acknowledging the failing logic of providing short-term care that only covers basic needs. Largely driven by the desire to tamp down cost, justice administrators have recently sought out ways to adapt their forced role of primary mental health-care providers for an at-risk population by partnering diverse array of community stakeholders to formulate a stronger continuum of care (and dispersing the costs involved to a wider range of players). As this innovation is taking place, the vast majority of jurisdictions are slow to respond, if at all. Major court decisions have driven reform in the past, and even these pressures brought about change slowly.

5.1.1   Constitutionally Acceptable Level of Care: The Status Quo

The basis for defining a "legal" level of care began with litigating perceived protections of incarcerated persons under the Eighth Amendment—"Excessive bail shall not be required, nor excessive fines imposed, nor cruel and unusual punishments inflicted." In 1974, a prisoner in Texas named J.W. Gamble filed a civil rights action under 42 USC § 1983 by handwritten petition. While it seems that Gamble's primary objective was compensation for maltreatment, his case instead defined the first set of constitutional obligations of medical care for the incarcerated. Gamble's complaint described a back injury he sustained in 1973 while unloading a truck full of cotton bales as a part of his prison work duties. He continued to work but soon reported his discomfort to prison staff and was granted a pass to the medical unit at the facility. Gamble was evaluated by a medical assistant (with prescribing capabilities) for a hernia and was initially sent back to his cell. He continued to have problems and was able to go back to the medical unit—this time being seen by a nurse and a doctor. At this point, he obtained some medication for pain. The next day, he returned to the medical unit and was seen by another doctor, Dr. Astone, received a diagnosis of a lower back strain, and was placed on a treatment plan consisting of medication and cell restriction requiring Gamble to remain in his cell with the only exclusion of showering. A few days later, Dr. Astone extended this treatment plan after reevaluation and further ordered that Gamble be assigned to a bottom bunk (an order the prison staff did not enforce). This sort of treatment carried on throughout the month of November under Dr. Astone's care, seemingly without improvement.

It was at this point things seemed to shift for Gamble. On December 3, 1974, Dr. Astone removed Gamble's cell restrictions, which also approved him for light work, despite continued pain and discomfort. As staff assigned work duties to him, his complaints to supervisory staff landed him in segregated housing as punishment. This issue was heard by a disciplinary committee days later resulting in a recommendation to be seen by medical staff; but they insisted that he be seen by a different physician. Dr. Gray treated Gamble for high blood pressure and pain, prescriptions were lost and delayed, and he remained in segregation for the entire month. This treatment stretched into January and came to a head in February. At this point, Gamble reported chest pains and "blank outs," yet staff were slow to respond, taking all day on February 4th to move him from segregation to the medical unit. He was hospitalized that evening and diagnosed with an arrhythmia yet soon sent back to segregation. When his symptoms reappeared, staff refused to bring him back to the medical unit—Gamble asked several times on February 7 and 8, and he was turned down repeatedly. Finally, on February 9th, he was again treated for his heart condition, and he wrote his petition to the courts on February 11th.

Initially, the district court dismissed his petition as the presiding judge did not view his case to have a clear legal claim. Typically, a judge at this level is trained to evaluate if a plaintiff can argue concrete, tangible harms have occurred and have been clearly documented. The appeals court was not moved by this logic and reinstated the complaint based on their finding of an insufficient levels of medical treatment. Soon, the Supreme Court would weigh in with an 8 to 1 decision:

> We therefore conclude that deliberate indifference to serious medical needs of prisoners constitutes the "unnecessary and wanton infliction of pain," *Gregg v. Georgia, supra*, at 173 (joint opinion), proscribed by the Eighth Amendment. This is true whether the indifference is manifested by prison doctors in their response to the prisoner's needs [n10]or by prison guards in intentionally denying or delaying access to medical [p105] care[n11] or intentionally interfering with the treatment once prescribed. [n12] Regardless of how evidenced, deliberate indifference to a prisoner's serious illness or injury states a cause of action under § 1983.

On first glance, it seems as though the Court was moved by Gamble's handwritten petition. Perhaps Gamble was able to lay out a claim based on the repeated times he was denied care, or his accounts of how his prescriptions were lost, or when the prison staff interfered with his treatment when they put him back to work or punished him by sending him to a segregation unit. The truth is the case is much more complicated than it appears:

> This conclusion does not mean, however, that every claim by a prisoner that he has not received adequate medical treatment states a violation of the Eighth Amendment. An accident, although it may produce added anguish, is not on that basis alone to be characterized as wanton infliction of unnecessary pain....in the medical context, an inadvertent failure to provide adequate medical care cannot be said to constitute "an unnecessary and wanton

infliction of pain" or to be [p106] "repugnant to the conscience of mankind." Thus, a complaint that a physician has been negligent in diagnosing or treating a medical condition does not state a valid claim of medical mistreatment under the Eighth Amendment. Medical malpractice does not become a constitutional violation merely because the victim is a prisoner. In order to state a cognizable claim, a prisoner must allege acts or omissions sufficiently harmful to evidence deliberate indifference to serious medical needs. It is only such indifference that can offend "evolving standards of decency" in violation of the Eighth Amendment.

As it turns out, the Court believed the district court judge was correct in that Gamble did not have a § 1983 claim, at least against the medical director Dr. Gray. The majority opinion cited the repeated instances of treatment Gamble received by the prison medical staff—whether it was "good" treatment was not to be decided in this venue. Further, since the lower court of appeals' decision focused on the care of the physicians and medical staff under Dr. Gray, their decision outlining the lack of civil rights violations was limited to these individuals (particularly, absolving Dr. Gray). Instead of deciding the fate of the other litigants mentioned in the petition, like the warden of the prison and the Texas Department of Corrections leadership, the Supreme Court decided to push this back down to the lower courts to decide in light of their recent clarifications of the Eighth Amendment in this situation. The level of care may have amounted to malpractice, which would need to be litigated differently; however, the decision rendered that incarcerated persons were constitutionally protected against "wanton infliction of unnecessary pain." Gamble may have lost, but his case surely caused ripples in correctional medical care.

This was the legal foundation for all cases involving standards of medical care for incarcerated people that will follow; however, there has not been a landmark case on the level of Estelle v. Gamble to directly address mental health care for justice-involved individuals. One key exception exists from a stream of action in California. Advocates there took a different approach to address the emerging mental health deficiencies in jails and prisons beginning in the 1990s—focus on increasing sparseness of resources and personnel given an expanding incarceration population. It was these broadening deficiencies in adequate care that triggered § 1983 civil rights violations, infringing upon inmates' constitutional rights under the Eighth Amendment. The momentum for this conflict began to surge when a magistrate certified a class "consisting of 'all inmates with serious mental disorders who are now or who will in the future be confined within the California Department of Corrections'" (with limited exceptions) who together had volumes of stories of neglect and maltreatment. After years of litigation, this case—Coleman v. Wilson—was initially resolved in 1995 by appointing a special master to oversee a remediation plan to remedy the conditions in California prisons. Importantly, this special master was charged with holding the California Department of Corrections accountable for six components of mental health treatment to meet minimal constitutional requirements:

The six components are: (1) a systematic program for screening and evaluating inmates to identify those in need of mental health care; (2) a treatment program that involves more than segregation and close supervision of mentally ill inmates; (3) employment of a sufficient number of trained mental health professionals; (4) maintenance of accurate, complete and confidential mental health treatment records; (5) administration of psychotropic medication only with appropriate supervision and periodic evaluation; and (6) a basic program to identify, treat, and supervise inmates at risk for suicide. *Balla v. Idaho State Board of Corrections*, 595 F.Supp. 1558, 1577 (D.Idaho, 1984)

This case references precedent that originated out of Texas (*Ruiz v. Estelle, 503 F.Supp. 1265* (S.D.Tex.1980)), which was expanded upon further in a case against the Idaho Department of Corrections in 1984. These six components defining the minimal constitutional level of mental health care would eventually become further tested at the Federal District Court level when California failed several times to resolve Coleman v. Wilson under the appointed special master. This new case, Coleman v. Brown, sought to bring California into compliance with Coleman v. Wilson almost 10 years later in 2013. Yet again, a judge sided with the plaintiffs, arguing that California needed to continue to provide relief to the class of mentally ill inmates under the care of the California Department of Corrections.

These key features of legal precedents, as many others across the country, can also be found interwoven in the accreditation standards of the corrections industry. In fact, the evolution of best practices (again, geared to ensure a *minimal* array of services to be constitutionally acceptable) can be easily gleaned from each edition of industrial standards released by the American Correctional Association (ACA) and the National Commission on Correctional Health Care (NCCHC). For example, the ACA Performance-Based Standards for American Correctional Association (2001) mandate the following: round-the-clock emergency health care with on-site crisis intervention, emergency rooms or other appropriate health facilities, and on-call mental health professional services with an emergency health facility that is not located nearby (Standard 4-ACRS- 4C-03); a training program to be in place for *care worker* staff to recognize signs and symptoms of mental illness, substance use disorder, and intellectual disability (Standard 4-ACRS- 4C-04); mental health screening by trained professionals that covers mental health problems and suicide attempts/ideation, substance abuse, and direct observation of behaviors (Standard 4-ACRS- 4C-06); and a written suicide prevention and intervention program with dedicated training that covers all staff who supervise inmates. These standards have become commonplace throughout American corrections. Yet, given the fact that more individuals with mental illness remain untreated rather than receive treatment in jails should give us pause. Perhaps these standards provide a safety net for the most seriously ill; however, it appears that they are ineffective for the vulnerable population en masse.

5.1.2   Common Interactions

For generations now, vocations that care for individuals with mental illness have suffered from a lack of prestige, pay, desirability, and so on. Jobs within jails certainly fall in this category. A quick search for information on these jobs reveals high turnover, issues with burnout, and, at times, a lack of further career opportunities. Yet, as mentioned earlier, jails have become a critical focal point for mental health crises—roughly 15% of male and 30% of female jail inmates have a serious mental illness, and the vast majority do not receive any treatment (NAMI, 2017). Further, most correctional officers have little training in mental health and substance abuse awareness and treatment (Stohr, Self, & Lovrich, 1992). A majority of jails across the country thus heavily depend on their treatment staff to identify mental illness, develop a treatment plan, and help to ensure the six components of mental health care are provided to meet constitutional standards.

Jail correctional officers, in particular, play a critical role in promoting a healthy environment for both fellow staff and inmates. The recent stories brimming from the Orleans Parish Prison (the New Orleans jail ran by the Orleans Parish Sheriff's Office) and Riker's Island Prison Complex (the New York City jail ran by New York City Correction Department) offer allegories as to the serious behavioral health consequences of staffing issues among other organizational failures. For example, in New Orleans, just months after opening a state-of-the-art jail complex, the Orleans Parish Sheriff's Office reported 200 inmate-on-inmate altercations, 44 instances of use of force on inmates by state, 16 assaults on staff, 3 rapes, 29 inmates transferred to the hospital for injury or sickness, and 16 suicide attempts—all within the first 3 months (McCampbell et al. 2017; Sledge, 2017). In New York, tales of correctional staff retaliating against inmates who attempt suicide at Riker's Island have surfaced, depicting just how brutal the jail environment has become (Rayman, 2016). Both failing jails are now notorious for high turnover, leading to the stagnation of the critical changes needed to promote a safe and therapeutic environment. While these are extreme cases, it is important to note that line correctional officers are often only equipped to identify suicide risk by a matter of policy and receive little more training pertaining to mental health. Their jobs are wrought with low job satisfaction, little autonomy, and inadequate pay. Mental health seems to be a low priority for line officers who spend the most interface time with inmates, by far.

The key players involved in the postarrest phase of a potential justice-based intervention include jail intake and medical/treatment staff, line correctional officers, public defenders, prosecutors, and judges, with the heaviest burden on intake and medical/treatment staff to flag potential inmates for services and assistance. Robust research has only begun to evaluate the systemic breakdown in counties and parishes across the country to successfully capture mental illness and explore effective interventions. As such, we do not have a deep understanding of the everyday interactions of these key players and inmates with mental illness. Of particular importance here, the Stepping Up Initiative (2017) is the leading movement for change at the local level. This Initiative is a partnership of the National Association of Counties, the Council of State Governments Justice Center, and the American Psychiatric Association Foundation, which partnered to offer a structured guide, training, and seed funding to reduce the number of people with mental illness in jails beginning in 2015. As of this writing, 365 counties have passed resolutions through local leadership to join this initiative, the first step of which is to engage in a comprehensive system-wide evaluation of just how individuals with mental illness are processed and captured (or not captured) by the current system. The Initiative also serves to assist localities in building a diverse partnership of key stakeholders who have been deemed essential to creating successful models for change.

5.1.3   Common Problems

As the Stepping Up Initiative prepared to launch, its advertising campaign to counties and parishes identified the following commonplace problems in jails across the United States: (1) prevalence of serious mental illness was three to six times higher in jails relative to the general population, (2) three out of four of these individuals have co-occurring disorders, (3) once in jail, these individuals tend to experience longer stays in jail relative to individuals without mental illness, and (4) these individuals are at a much higher risk of recidivism upon release relative to individuals without mental illness (Council of State Governments Justice Center, 2014; Haneberg, Fabelo, Osher, & Thompson, 2017). Certainly, this list is not exhaustive, but it captures the failing logic of the current systems in place across the country—it depicts a system that has recurring failures as an intervention for people with mental illness. The analogy to a revolving door has become apt.

Perhaps the systemic failure is most punctuated by an examination of suicide ideation, attempts, and completions in jails; as indicated earlier in this text, the risk of suicide tends to be the highest in jails. According to the Bureau of Justice Statistics, suicides among jail inmates have been on the rise, with the most current rate being 46 per 100,000 inmates as of 2013 (Noonan, 2015). Compare this to a national average of roughly 12 per 100,000, the difference in jails is about four times higher than the general population (Centers for Disease Control and Prevention, 2017). Existing data on suicide ideation and attempts among jail inmates is scant and much older. However, the underlying patterns of crisis still emerge.

One of the first briefs coming from the Stepping Up Initiative leadership summarizes a growing body of knowledge on what, exactly, our failures are in the jail setting. It begins by outlining the changes that have occurred in services for individuals with mental illness over the last decade: a mass proliferation of specialized police response teams and programs, specialized programming to divert low-level offenders with mental illness from the mainstream justice system, broader use of specialty courts, and enhanced mental health services in jails to name a few. Even with these innovations in place, the brief describes four barriers preventing gains. First, and primarily, most locales suffer from the lack of adequate data to identify a targeted population and monitor it effectively. For example, having access to basic information such as the total number and identities of individuals with mental illness arrested and who currently in the local jail is important. Additional relevant information about this population is also crucial, such as the length of stay in jail, bond status, whether individuals have previously received treatment or are currently being treated, and the ability to follow rearrest. Without adequate data tools, developing a system-wide response to any underlying problem becomes problematic.

Second, many programs that are in place lack an evidence-based services, tools, and programming, and critically, "community-based behavioral health-care providers are rarely familiar with (or skilled in delivering) the approaches that need to be integrated into their treatment models to reduce the likelihood of someone offending" (Haneberg, Fabelo, Osher, & Thompson, 2017). Third, due to scarce resources, innovation has been small in scope and scale, thus blunting any ability to create sustained systemic changes. Finally, and related to the first barrier, many innovations have lacked adequate tracking to determine their impact. Did the initiatives reduce arrests for individuals with mental illness, reduce the length of time these individuals spend in jail, and/or increase treatment options, connections, and adherence to treatment regimes? These barriers translate into underdiagnosis/lack of diagnosis, continued exasperated behavioral problems, overpopulation through recidivism, and continued vulnerability for individuals with mental illness in potentially problematic and unhealthy jail environments.

The services offered to inmates within jails continue to be in line with constitutional minimums, yet change is afoot. Oftentimes, only one mental health professional is dedicated to provide services for an entire jail of hundreds of inmates. While prisons offer programs for education, vocational training, etc. that help with mental health and behavioral change, jails have consistently lacked the same breadth of scope of programs for inmates in many jurisdictions. Further, jail inmates usually serve a shorter sentence than those in prison; this lack of time does not afford the chance for long-term treatment services or programming. Thus, this highlights the importance of a collaboration between jails, courts, probation, and community players to shore up a continuum of care to break this cycle. This is exactly what the Stepping Up Initiative lays out.

5.1.4   Preventable Tragedies

Unfortunately, death of inmates inside jails and prisons are real possibilities. Even further, inmates with mental illness are more likely to suffer harm while incarcerated according to many studies. One report published by the University of Texas School of Law Civil Rights Clinic (2016) called "Preventable Tragedies" discusses the deaths of ten different inmates in county jails, all with mental health concerns—such as Terry Borum in Swisher County Jail, Gregory Cheek in Nueces County Jail, and Amy Lynn Cowling in Gregg County Jail. The first part of the report describes each of the deaths in personal detail to highlight the "cracks" in the county jail system in Texas and its real impact on human lives. An interesting point to note here is that each of these deaths took place under very different circumstances and in different county jails. These tragedies were all easily preventable in many ways. This report also goes on to provide 12 recommendations for Texas county jails based on national standards to help improve care for inmates with mental illness, which the authors truly believe would serve to prevent each of the tragedies listed in this study.

Similar recommendations were also provided by the Stanford School of Law in their study on mental health in jail inmates (more on this study in Chap. 7; Steinberg, Mills, & Romano, 2017).

Each of the stories provided in the "Preventable Tragedies" report sheds light on a different problem with the county jail system, specifically in Texas. Earlier in this text, the statistics on jail settings were discussed which included the elevated number of inmates, increasing number with mental health diagnoses, lack of funding, lack of access to care, etc. The trends that these statistics depict also are typical in Texas, and the evidence supporting this claim is provided with each case in this report. For example, the story of Terry Borum is alarming in that his severe alcoholism was known prior to his incarceration by jail staff and the Sheriff, but no action was taken to care for him until his case became an emergency situation. Terry had a history of depression that resulted in his alcoholism, and when a minor altercation led him to the county jail, his symptoms reached a breaking point. His past suicide attempt complicated his mental health history and should have been one of the first reasons to prioritize medical treatment to ensure his care was appropriate. As the report details the story, treatment did not happen at all, and after he went into delirium tremens that included hallucinations and seizures, he fell inside his jail cell causing a serious head injury. It was at this point that medical care was initialized and Borum was fully evaluated. Yet, it was too late; due to the lack of nutrition, the haphazard care provided, and the jail's unwillingness to use their medical care budget on Terry, he was not able to survive a survivable injury and died in a nearby hospital.

In another case within the "Preventable Tragedies" report, Gregory Cheek was arrested after breaking into a home and painting the walls blue and yellow. At the time of his arrest, he was covered in blue paint and suffering from delusions. Despite this, his intake assessment reported no medical issues, no mental health issues, and no medications prescribed at the time. Gregory was seen by the jail's psychiatrist who recommended he be transferred to the state hospital on more than one occasion. Additionally, a magistrate judge ordered that Gregory be transferred to the state hospital, but none of these instructions were followed. After suffering the beginning signs of hypothermia, Gregory died in jail from a bacterial infection that was left untreated. A review of his case after his death reveals that the jail psychiatrist ignored reports from the medical staff to follow up on Gregory's medication while inadequate medical care and follow-up attention was paid to a worsening physical condition. It turns out that Gregory succumbed to Waterhouse-Friderichsen syndrome—a severe bacterial infection of the adrenal glands causing gland failure and bleeding. In this case, neither Gregory's physical nor mental health was attended to, which can be surprising to some as his mental health symptoms were severe and readily recognizable, as was his signs of his failing physical health, specifically his rapid weight loss and chronic hyperthermia in days nearing his death.

Amy Lynn Cowling's story was similar to Terry Borum above in that her death is attributed to the complications of withdrawal. Yet in Cowling's case, several prescriptions meant to treat her mental health illnesses (Seroquel and Xanax) and substance use disorder (methadone) were discontinued due to the Gregg County Jail's strict policy on drugs in the jail. While the jail's physician would have ordered an alternative course of medical treatment to fit the jail's policy and keep Amy's treatment from slipping, she never had the chance to see the doctor. The reason—the doctor only makes visits to the jail on Wednesdays and Amy was booked on a Friday. After her medication was discontinued, Amy's physical and mental health rapidly decompensated, and she was moved to an isolation cell with orders to be closely watched. Yet, the correctional officers on watch that evening decided to falsify the observation logs and could not account for why Amy was found unresponsive on the day she died.

These stories are just three of the many across the country of individuals with mental illness dying in county jails. The stories of Terry and Gregory are different, but both show the results of improper care while incarcerated. Terry's illness was known to jail officials, but they chose to ignore his needs as well as use the budget of the jail as an excuse not to seek medical treatment. In Gregory's case, he was initially treated as though he was perfectly healthy and later evaluated. Upon evaluation, the mental health professionals and even a judge decided he needed more treatment than the jail could offer, but no one chose to uphold the orders. It seems like a comedy of errors has led to the deaths of these ten people—Terry Borum, a 53-year-old grandfather who lived by and maintained traditional country values; Gregory Cheek, a young artist and surfer, husband and father to a young girl; and Amy Lynn Cowling, a 33-year-old mother of three who was in recovery for her opioid addiction.

The stories of deaths in county jails are alarming and unsettling, and they happen with a frequency that surely can be reduced. Yet, this seems difficult when considering the level of care inherent in what is deemed as constitutionally acceptable. The authors offer the following areas of improvement to aid in reform while maintaining this very same standard: (1) increase diversion from jail for low-risk individuals with mental illness, (2) improve screening and assessment tools to ensure adequate care and informed decision-making, (3) arm the judiciary with the results of screening and assessment to aid in diversion, whenever appropriate, (4) evaluate and refine suicide prevention programs with partnerships that include mental health professionals, (5) increase and strengthen collaborations with mental health professionals and local agencies, (6) ensure the ability to continue medication treatment regimens with appropriate medications or their alternatives, (7) develop and update medical detoxification programming, (8) consider adding peer support specialists, (9) improve monitoring programs and ensure that jail staff are accountable for monitoring inmates with mental health concerns, (10) reduce the use of restraints and isolation cells, and (11) limit the use of force and consider the use of force only as a last resort. While these steps are a good start for jail administrators, these recommendations remain quite inward-looking and fail to address some of the broader concerns that impact the jail that are outside of its control. The following section addresses some of the most promising approaches in recent years to address the issues the "Preventable Tragedies" report unearths.

5.2 Evidence-Based Solutions

The state of the art for local, system-wide reform has deftly been outlined by the Stepping Up Initiative materials, to be customized to each location through local partnerships all focused on providing better care for individuals with mental illness (Haneberg et al. 2017). The initial call to action outlines six steps to structure progress: (1) assemble a team of local leadership across multiple agencies and key stakeholders and decision-makers throughout the community committed to change, (2) invest in an ability to identify individuals with mental illness and gauge their risk of recidivism and further identify the needs of these individuals, (3) assess treatment and service capacity in the local area, (4) create a plan with measurable outcomes, (5) implement an approach with a scientific research design to ensure quality assurance and accountability of each partnership, and (6) track the progress using data and make data-informed decisions to ensure continued success. Each step along the way, any interested county/parish partnership can access a large resource pool supported by the National Alliance on Mental Illness, Major County Sheriffs' Association, National Association of County Behavioral Health & Developmental Disability Directors, National Association of State and Drug Abuse Directors, National Association of State Mental Health Directors, National Council on Behavioral Health, National Sheriffs' Association, and Policy Research Associates, among many more.

The first step provides the backbone of change. It requires a wide range of stakeholders to "put skin in the game" to address the problems of justice-involved mental health individuals. Typically, each entity signs onto a memorandum of understanding defining its commitment to this team, its role, and its responsibilities. Primarily, this gets all of the key players in the same room to begin discussing strengths and weaknesses, resources and gaps, and problems and solutions. A key advantage of having these partnerships is that it helps to avoid blind spots in planning; each partner brings a unique perspective and experiences to aid in building a strategy to problem solve.

5.2.1 Step Two: Latest Generation Assessment and Screening Tools and Data Capacity

After assembling a team, many locales realize that their tools for identifying individuals with mental illness being processed through the justice system are old and outdated and perform poorly, and jails are often at the center of this process. Further, the team may also realize that their local jails do not have a definition of mental illness and serious mental illness consistent with the state and/or local health officials' definitions—a serious issue if these jails are the primary centers for mental health screening for the area. This lack of definition would critically pose problems when trying to connect individuals to care in the community for follow-up care. Following

Table 5.1 Evidence-based screening tools, adapted from SAMHSA

Mental disorders	Substance use disorders	Co-occurring disorders	Motivation and readiness	Trauma history and PTSD	Suicide risk
Brief Jail Mental Health Screen (BJMHS)	Texas Christian University Drug Screen-V (TCUDS-V)	Mini International Neuropsychiatric Interview Screen (MINI-Screen)	Texas Christian Motivation Form (TCU-MotForm)	Trauma History Screen (THS)	Interpersonal Needs Questionnaire (INQ) combined with Acquired Capacity for Suicide Scale (ACSS)
Correctional Mental Health Screen (CMHS-F or CHHS-M)	Simple Screening Instrument (SSI)	BJMHS combined with TCUDS-V	University of Rhode Island Change Assessment Scale-M (URICA-M)	Life-Stressor Checklist (LSC-R)	Beck Scale for Suicide Ideation (BSS)
Mental Health Screening Form-III (MHSF-III)	Alcohol, Smoking, and Substance Involvement Screening Test (ASSIST)	CMHS-F or CMHS-M combined with TCUDS-V		Life Events Checklist for DSM-V combined with Post-traumatic Stress Disorder Checklist for DSM-V (PCL-5)	Adult Suicidal Ideation Questionnaire (ASIQ)

the establishment of a consistent definition of mental illness across the local system (including substance use disorders), the team can move on to select validated screening tools for mental illness and substance use disorders to proficiently flag individuals with potential mental illness and substance abuse disorders that fit this definition (see Table 5.1). Subsequent to screening, any flagged concerns must be further evaluated by mental health professionals using validated and reliable assessment techniques. Just like the instruments embedded into the population surveys of jail and prison inmates that are used to identify individuals with mental illness, the tools described in Table 5.1 provide reliable and accurate information about potential mental health and substance use disorder diagnoses. In fact, these tools were designed to be given by any trained personnel, not just mental health professionals or sworn officers.

Importantly, screening and assessment do not equate to a diagnosis or diagnoses that can, in turn, inform treatment. All flagged individuals must then be seen by a mental health professional to confirm or refute the screening result and, if appropriate, begin an individualized treatment plan. Many times, the mental health professional assessment is done after release, thus requiring communication and data sharing between the jail and community mental health partners. Or, as mentioned earlier, initial mental health assessments may require follow-ups to continue to define and/or refine diagnoses. In that, meaning not all diagnoses are black or white—there often exists gray area. For some, diagnosis requires time and more than one evaluation or a second option for another doctor. For others, mental illness develops slowly over time, so it may not be an easy diagnosis right away, or a change may need to be made. Either way, the screening and assessment tools described in Table 5.1 can be performed expeditiously, with the intent that it can easily be integrated with jail intake.

Further, latest generation risk and need assessment tools provide users with the ability to prioritize treatment for individuals who, after screening, are identified as high risk and high need. In other words:

> With mounting research that demonstrates the value of science-based tools to predict a person's likelihood of reoffending, criminal justice practitioners are increasingly using these tools to focus limited resources on the people who are most likely to reoffend. At the same time, mental health and substance use practitioners are trying to prioritize their scarce treatment resources for people with the most serious behavioral health needs....when [a] person is assessed as being at moderate to high risk of reoffending, connection to treatment is an even higher priority, along with interventions such as supervision and cognitive behavioral therapy to reduce the risk of recidivism. (Haneberg et al. 2017)

Thus, having a well-defined screening and assessment process, equipped with the latest generation actuarial tools (many of which are in the public domain), introduces vast improvements in the efficiency of mental illness interventions. This makes a broad catchment system possible and is the foundation for change while preserving precious resources for optimal results. While the ideal goal for each locale would be to provide services for each individual with a mental health diagnosis, a realistic goal would be to provide an individualized treatment plan for each individual while providing direct services for those with the highest risk and needs.

Having such a process also enables local partnerships to monitor change. For example, while planning its local Stepping Up Initiatives, the partnerships in Bexar County, Texas (e.g., San Antonio) realized they did not have a reliable accurate count of just how many individuals in the Bexar County Jail have mental illness on any given day. Their solution was to explore and establish a universal screening process for mental illness together as a partnership. Other important baseline data may be sought during this planning stage, such as length of stay, connectivity to treatment after release, and a reliable method to measure recidivism. All of these metrics rely on the ability to accurately and reliably identify individuals with mental illness and need to be put into place to measure successes and inefficiencies in the system being put into place.

The Stepping Up Initiative literature identifies four key data tools that need to be constructed for optimal success: (1) a tool to track the number of people with mental illness (and/or serious mental illness) passing through intake at the jail (e.g., being booked); (2) a tool that tracks the length of stay of all individuals, with the ability to compare the length of stay of those with mental illness (and/or serious mental illness) to the overall average or, more importantly, to individuals without mental illness; (3) a tool that tracks connections to treatment, in particular, *successful* connections to treatment; and (4) a tool that tracks recidivism based on an accepted definition by the team. A reflection on these data tools suggests that jail staff and leadership shoulder the effort to create and maintain these resources; in the team context, any barriers the jail leadership may face in development and maintenance of these tools can, indeed, be troubleshooted by the team in good faith. However, the jail remains a core conduit of change.

5.2.2   *Defining a Sequential Intercept Model and Notating Gaps in Services*

A tool that has promulgated in counties/parishes considering change is the Sequential Intercept Model. Initially developed by Munetz and Griffin (2006), the Sequential Intercept Model is a visualization of the flow of individuals with mental illness into and out of the criminal justice system, beginning with law enforcement and first responder contact and entry into jail, and follows each of the various pathways of criminal justice processing through eventual release and termination of justice involvement (Griffin, Heilbrun, Mulvey, DeMatteo, & Schubert, 2015). These models are customized to each locality, with the emphasis of finding what Munetz and Griffin call points of interception at which an intervention can be developed for qualifying individuals; these intervention points commonly occur at initial contact with first responders, at initial detention and preliminary hearings, during a stay in jail, interface with the courts (e.g., public defenders, prosecutors, and judges), or upon psychiatric evaluation, at reentry back into the community, and with interface with community corrections (e.g., probation and parole officers). As this is a visual tool, an example can be found with Fig. 5.1.

The Stepping Up Initiative literature states that local teams should look beyond the Sequential Intercept Model and include an exhaustive community model for mental health crisis. This extra step will allow for proactive measures to be taken to potentially intervene before justice involvement even begins. After each point of interception has been defined, teams can then evaluate local resources available to intervene at each point, identify the training necessary for the players involved at point to effectively intervene, perhaps identify additional personnel who can make intervention possible, and so on. For example, if a law enforcement agency has the capacity to train its officers to differentiate potential misdemeanor cases involving individuals experiencing potential mental health symptoms (see above), then there stands a chance to divert potential mental health consumers out of the criminal justice system before criminal processing begins. In this case, the intervention involves not only players in the criminal justice system but providers in the community that can work cases brought to them by law enforcement while ensuring public safety.

In other words, the Sequential Intercept Model, or a broader, detailed process analysis, gives the ability to map out failures or inefficiencies in the system that

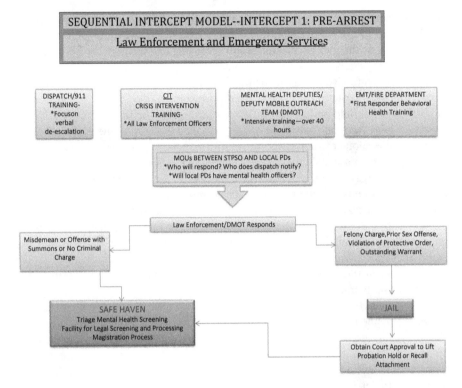

Fig. 5.1 The refined Sequential Intercept Model, Pre-Arrest, for the 22nd Judicial District Court of Louisiana and its local partners (Courtesy of Judge Peter G. Garcia and Diane Dicke)

require priority attention by the team. Here is an example—a Stepping Up Initiative team discovered that a large number of individuals with serious mental illness were being processed for probation revocations due to technical violations and new crimes. Upon this discovery, the team (including representatives from probation) identified that did not have any specialized probation supervision services available for individuals with severe mental illness and high risk of recidivism. Solutions can be designed, installed, measured, and further refined, if necessary.

5.2.3 Prioritize and Implement New Policies, Practices, and Improvements and Then Track Progress

After a complete introspection of local needs, strengths, and gaps, the team can begin prioritizing improvements to the local system. For jails, emphasis is typically placed on ensuring successful reentry back into the community as well as connectivity to treatment and/or court programs customized for individuals with mental illness (specifically, customized for different types of individuals based on risk and need). As mentioned earlier, jails shoulder the burden of developing and maintaining the data tools to inform decision-making in a data-driven way and—most importantly—serve as the hub for mental health screening and assessment. These initiatives often are identified as an immediate goal by the group; the Stepping Up Initiative literature also recommends for each locale to prioritize further goals into short-term and long-term categories, based on an agreed-upon logic (e.g., need and/ or initiatives that hold promise for broad impacts). After the foundational tools and processes have been put into place during the planning period, the team is free to work with one another to determine its priorities; recommendations are available by the Stepping Up partnerships; however, determinations should be driven by local decision-making. It is likely that one or a few parties on the team will take lead on one of several chosen initiatives, perhaps forming subcommittees for each task/ implementation plan. Thus, regular progress updates should occur as a team that includes robust evaluation components to determine impact and to identify room for improvement and quality assurance. Strong communication and partnerships are key to success.

Finally, each initiative *must* be monitored to track progress. For example, the team may ask, is training needed? If so, was the training successful? To determine success, the team may partner with a local university and/or researcher to study the knowledge gained from training and/or ability to successfully put training into use. This may require a pretest, posttest design—giving trainees an exam before they are trained and upon successful completion of training to determine knowledge gained—and/or it may require observation of trainees after successful completion of training to determine whether someone who received training is using the skills and knowledge gained in their jobs. Each evaluation should be customized to the location, its partners, the situation, and so on. However, the key point here is that each initiative should be devised in a way that allows for adequate evaluation with a robust research design to ensure wise investment of funds and optimal success.

5.3   Bureau of Justice Assistance: A Source of Support

The Bureau of Justice Assistance, a child agency within the United States Department of Justice (Office of Justice Programs), has been the leading funding agency to support Stepping Up Initiatives across the country. Key funding streams for jail initiatives include opportunities under the Second Chance Act such as Targeting Adults with Co-occurring Substance Abuse and Mental Health Disorders, Adult Mentoring, and Adult Offender Reentry Demonstration, as well as opportunities under the Mentally Ill Offender Treatment and Crime Reduction Reauthorization and Improvement Act of 2008, primarily the Justice and Mental Health Collaboration Program. Historically, these funding streams have aided jails in adopting, piloting, and troubleshooting screening assessment tools and processes, provided training, and have aided local partnerships in developing and adopting *evidence-based* programs and services with the intent that these initiatives are sustainable if deemed successful.

5.4 National Registry of Evidence-Based Programs and Practices and CrimeSolutions.gov

The National Registry of Evidence-Based Programs and Practices, or NREPP, is an extremely useful resource created in 1997 by SAMHSA: "The purpose of NREPP is to help people learn more about available evidence-based programs and practices and determine which of these may best meet their needs. NREPP is one way SAMHSA is working to improve access to information on evaluated interventions and reduce the lag time between creation of scientific knowledge and its practical application in the field" (SAMHSA, 2017). In other words, the NREPP repository provides practitioners with a list of scientifically vetted programs and services (as well as programs/services not quite making the cut) to serve as a guide for potential solutions for initiatives calling for mental health and substance use interventions. To accomplish this, the NREPP has provided independent assessments, by certified assessors, of the existing research on each intervention since its inception. Each assessment is designed to generate easy-to-use ratings (currently being: effective, promising, ineffective, and inconclusive) of various components of the intervention to summarize the volumes of research examined an assessment team. In July of 2017, the NREPP hosted 466 interventions, with the ability to narrow potential programs/services by easy-to-use criteria based on the target population to receive this program/service.

For example, a jail professional can use the NREPP search tools to look for interventions specific setting, in this case, correctional facilities—which narrows down the field to ten reviewed interventions as of July 2017. One of these interventions, Trauma Affect Regulation: Guide for Education and Treatment (TARGET), is cleanly summarized in an easy-to-read Program Snapshot (see Fig. 5.2). Upon a quick glance, any NREPP end user can determine that TARGET has been proven effective in treating anxiety disorders and symptoms as well as trauma- and stress-related disorders and symptoms, improving coping behaviors, improving general functioning and well-being, and helping individuals who internalize their problems. Yet, TARGET has been proven ineffective in allaying depression and depressive symptoms as well as improves self-concept but shows promise in assisting with self-regulation and social connectedness. If end users wish to wade through the research reviewed for each rating provided, easy-to-follow links are provided to enable a deeper assessment. Within minutes, any team seeking high-quality, scientifically proven programming and services to best serve their clients can rely on the information found within the NREPP to begin the selection process with confidence.

Similar to the NREPP, CrimeSolutions.gov, developed by the National Institute of Justice and launched in mid-2011, offers repository of independently assessed programs and practices to aid in informed initiative development and implementation—just with exclusive focus on programs with justice-involved individuals and with a slightly more simplistic *overall* rating scale (e.g., effective, promising, and no effects, with only one finding per program and practice; National Institute of

Trauma Affect Regulation: Guide for Education and Treatment (TARGET)

Program Description

Trauma Affect Regulation: Guide for Education and Therapy (TARGET) is an educational and psychotherapeutic intervention for adults, adolescents, and families that is designed to prevent and treat traumatic stress disorders; co-occurring addictive, affective, personality, or psychotic disorders; and adjustment disorders related to other types of stressors.

The program comprises a seven-step sequence of skills based on a psychobiological metamodel, the FREEDOM Steps. This model enables participants to recognize, understand, and gain control of stress reactions by enhancing their adaptive capacities for emotion regulation, mental focusing, executive function, mindfulness, and interpersonal engagement and interaction. The purpose of this skill sequence is to offer a systematic approach to processing current life experiences and trauma- or stressor-related symptoms without intensive trauma-memory processing; however, it can also be used to enhance trauma-memory processing and narrative reconstruction. Steps are grouped to allow participants to 1) learn and practice skills with the therapist; and 2) rehearse and apply the skills to anticipate, prevent, and manage symptoms that can arise in real-life situations.

There is also a manualized protocol for delivering brief (4-session; T4) and time-limited (10- to14-session) versions of the program, which can be provided as individual or group psychotherapy within a variety of settings. TARGET has been adapted to be gender-specific, culturally responsive, and attuned to the needs of youths and adults who have experienced specific types of trauma, including childhood trauma, sexual trauma, domestic violence, community violence, sexual-identity-related trauma, or military trauma.

⊘ **Evaluation Findings by Outcome**

Program Snapshot

Evidence Ratings
- Anxiety Disorders and Symptoms
- Coping
- General Functioning and Well-Being
- Internalizing Problems
- Trauma- and Stress-Related Disorders and Symptoms
- ⊗ Depression and Depressive Symptoms
- Self-Regulation
- Social Connectedness
- ⊗ Self-Concept

Program Contact
Julian Ford, Ph.D.
Professor of Psychiatry and Law,
University of Connecticut
263 Farmington Avenue, Farmington CT

Fig. 5.2 National Registry of Evidence-Based Practices; results displaying the summary of Trauma Affect Regulation: Guide for Education and Treatment (TARGET)

Justice, 2017). As of July of 2017, 471 programs (e.g., "a specific set of activities carried out according to guidelines to achieve a defined purpose") and 58 practices (e.g., "a general category of programs, strategies, or procedures that share similar characteristics with regard to the issues they address and how they address them") have been assessed by CrimeSolutions.gov. Diving deeper, if an end user were to search for specific programs tailored specifically to individuals with mental illness in correctional facilities (excluding substance use disorder), CrimeSolutions.gov displays just four promising programs and no practices for review (as of July 2017). At this time, the vast majority of jail-based programs reviewed relating to mental health are substance use disorder-specific, with 1 effective program (Project BUILD), 12 promising ones, and 8 with no effects found. Likewise, jail-based practices relating to mental health *only* exist for substance use disorders, with two effective practices (Incarceration-based Therapeutic Communities for Adults and Motivational Interviewing), two promising ones, and three with no effects.

Thus, a great deal of work needs to be done to explore meaningful interventions in jails and within partnerships with jails. Part of the point of the Stepping Up Initiative is for counties/parishes to take bold steps to implement initiatives that can build on our collective knowledge of what works, what is promising, and what is flat out ineffective or counterproductive. As of this writing, more than 600 awards have been given by the Bureau of Justice Assistance under the Second Chance Act programs and 168 awards under the Justice and Mental Health Collaboration Program; many of these funded projects will aid in furthering our knowledge, which will expand the information found in the NREPP and CrimeSolutions.gov.

5.5   The Role of Jails in the Future

The original core intent of jails are twofold: (1) to *strategically* hold individuals in confinement awaiting trial, with public safety as the chief concern when considering decisions to detain, and (2) as a sentencing option for minor offenses that do not require prison time. For a litany of reasons but primarily due to the lack of evidence-based data tools, jails have not been able to aid in strategically holding individuals who pose a public safety risk while helping to release individuals who do not. Further, jails do not have the capacity or have limited capacity to offer the necessary services to help individuals with mental illness, which will remain to be the case in the foreseeable future. Jail professionals are increasingly accepting their roles within a broader partnership of local community stakeholders to best serve individuals with mental illness, with key emphasis remaining on services rendered in the community. This ideal, to deliver care in the least restrictive environment, has become renewed with an understanding that jails are a critical catchment point to *begin* or *restart* behavioral health interventions.

Therefore, jails of the future will need be better connected with community and agency partnerships, particularly relating to shared communication and critical data sharing. Jails will become a primary referral service for individuals, with an emphasis on connecting individuals with evidence-based care tailored to their needs. Jail professionals will take the lead on identifying the vast majority of individuals needing care in these improved local catchment systems. Therefore, they will become a major player and have a central for implementing change. Individuals who have historically needed care and have been cycling through the justice system due to lack of care, being underserved, or just receiving services proven to have no evidence to effect change will begin to get the care they deserve.

5.5.1   Drain the Jail: Customized Specialty Courts

One intervention option for jails is to establish a partnership with the local criminal court in the creation of a mental health court, particularly if individuals with mental illness tend to have longer jail stays relative to those without mental illness. Mental health courts, which will be expanded on in the next chapter, allow for individuals with mental illness to be released from jail into a program supervised by a team—typically, a judge, case manager, treatment provider, probation officer, prosecutor, and defense attorney. The court then takes lead in connecting their clients with appropriate evidence-based treatment; monitors progress, treatment compliance, and setbacks; and ensures public safety.

The jail continues to be a key partner in two primary ways. First, jail professionals continue to take in identifying individuals who may have mental illness to be potential clients. Ideally, this should be accomplished through validated screening and assessment tools; however, if the jail simply does not have the resources to upgrade their data tools, mental health court case managers can be trained to go into jails to provide these services to identify potential clients. If the latter work flow is chosen, the jail-court partnership may invest in training of key staff to better identify signs and symptoms of mental illness (e.g., Mental Health First Aid) in order to assist case managers in identifying individuals to be screened and assessed as often individual case managers will not have the capacity to review every individual booked into jail. While not ideal, it is a step in the right direction in the absence of a central screening and assessment process.

Second, jails often serve as a behavior modification tool for mental health courts. Specifically, these programs commonly employ jail sanctions for noncompliance with program rules or treatment protocols, with this sanction type being the most punitive short of dismissal from the program. Typically, this happens when a client fails a drug screen, repeatedly misses treatment sessions, and so on. There is a stream of research that attempts to estimate the number of days jail sanctions should last for positive change in light of noncompliance; it should be noted that too lengthy of a stay can backfire and cause problems, so great care must be taken in partnership with the jail to ensure the success of this measure.

5.5.2 Avoid the Jail: Safe Haven

Instead of intercepting individuals as they pass through jail, and perhaps, as described above, partner with the court as a primary referral source, an initial catchment point could be set up with first responders to capture individuals with potential mental illness before they go to jail. In other words, for individuals who are having a mental health crisis but may not be engaging in illegal behavior, first responders should have a resource available to them to affect an intervention. A model called Safe Haven, developed in San Antonio, serves as a leading model across the country for this very situation. Safe Haven has been developed to be a centralized hub and shelter for the care of individuals in crisis, with staffing by key agencies and personnel most apt to help—mental health professionals (including substance use), housing specialists, law enforcement (including probation and parole), and education and career development professionals, among others.

While intended to serve the homeless, a Safe Haven can offer screening and assessment with referral out to services just like a jail can, yet at an earlier point of intercept (e.g., before arrest or hospitalization) is imminent. Much more coverage on this model will be offered in the chapter on community-based services. Jails should often be included as a partner in these projects as data sharing can become critical. For example, if an individual released from jail and ends up homeless, any effort to connect this individual to treatment or any screening and assessment performed by the jail may be extremely valuable to a Safe Haven.

5.5.3   Use the Jail: Expand Available Services, Case Management, and Use of Reentry Plan

Jails with resources may have the ability to adopt evidence-based programs and services to act on the findings of screening and assessment immediately. This becomes important for inmates serving time in a jail. In fact, recent research suggests that individualized treatment that begins prior to release and continues into aftercare post-release is most likely to be successful (Travis & Visher, 2005; Osher, 2006; Osher, 2007). As such, jail reentry programs will continue to grow and proliferate in the upcoming years.

Seeking Safety is one such program designed for individuals (men and women) with post-traumatic stress disorder symptoms or diagnosis co-occurring with substance use disorder (Najavits, 2001). This flexible program is designed to provide clients with effective coping skills and psychoeducation. To do so, the program focuses on defining safety as one's primary goal in one's relationships, thinking patterns, behaviors, and emotions while addressing PTSD symptoms along with substance use simultaneously. The Hampton Roads Regional Jail in Portsmouth, Virginia, is currently piloting this program with local funding with hope to expand on its evidence-based in the local area through external grant funding. Many jails across the country are engaging in similar strategies as they search for a pool of funding to rely on to sustain these initiatives.

Holistic reentry programs designed to treating substance use disorder, not specifically mental illness, are much more commonplace and routinely funded. One excellent example is the Allegheny County Jail-Based Reentry Specialist Program. This program begins in the jail with 5 or more months of programming that includes case management, education (literacy and GED classes, tutoring, basic education, and pre-apprenticeship training), structured job readiness classes, relapse prevention, cognitive behavioral therapy, and gender-specific drug treatment for substance use disorder, housing support services, parenting classes, and much more. Upon release, clients can receive up to 12 additional months of programming, with many of the same offerings available in the community. This model is becoming increasingly popular, and jails are increasingly working with community partners to ensure the continuity of programming and services upon release. At some point in the near future, this model will be customized for individuals with mental illness to provide services for individuals that must serve time in jail and who may not be a good fit for alternative programs available, such as diversion or mental health court.

5.5.4   Out-of-the-(Pizza)-Box Innovations

Chicago's Cook County Jail is using a new and innovate approach to fund programming within the jail (Babwin, 2017; Janssen, 2017). Rather than using taxpayer dollars to fund their version of a work release program called "Recipe for Change," they have turned to an internal solution. The inmates at Cook County Jail are creating and selling pizzas inside the jail. According to media interviews, jail staff are using the pizza system as a means to treat inmates humanely while affording inmates an opportunity to learn skills that may be helpful upon release from jail. Additionally, this pizza program is used as a behavior incentive. If any inmate is involved in disruptive behavior, they are immediately transferred out to Division 11 cell block where the Recipe for Change program is housed, thus resulting in the loss of pizza privileges.

Participating inmates attend classes 5 days each week, just like many other jail culinary program. Classes are taught on different topics related to the foodservice industry, such as food safety and sanitation, as well as preparation techniques and cooking skills. There is a set menu daily, which always includes a pizza that uses fresh ingredients from the nearby Cook County Sheriff's garden (Freeman, 2017).

Sheriff Tom Dart suggests that this program has already begun to show an immediate positive impact on inmates. The plan in the future is to obtain a food truck so that the pizzas can be sold to a nearby courthouse, creating additional revenue to self-fund this training program. The Recipe for Change program is just one small step in positivity within the jail system and the community. Jail inmates are finding a bit of humanity among good food. Upon return to their community, their skills in the kitchen are transferable. Yet, it should be noted that it seems as though the program lacks an evidence-based for broad impact. The out-of-the-box revenue generation concept of the program can fund solutions to resolve this gap. At times, solutions such as these are easier to come by as taxpayers are often wary of increasing their burden.

5.6   Conclusion

In the United States, our jail system continues to be a large provider of mental health services. This fact is both alarming and concerning in that there is a need to have those services be both adequate and documented. Budget cuts and funding concerns have led to understaffing and overcrowding in most local jails. Additionally, recidivism and lack of alternative resources in community only help to fuel the fire of increased inmates and struggles. Slowly, communities are coming together to work toward a better way to handle these issues for those in their area. In later chapters, some of those resources will be discussed with the hopes of bringing to light success stories. Those success stories can continue to the process of creating change.

As it stands now, there is a lack of adequate research on the jail system and how inmates are treated both physically and mentally. Specifically, there is a lack of baseline knowledge about training of correctional officers from one state to another, much less within the counties/parishes in each state. This is significant because this lack of information does not allow for proper comparisons. Without proper comparisons, there is no baseline evidence to support positive or negative outcomes. Thus, improvement becomes nearly impossible, particularly jails within major cities like Los Angeles and New York that have documented problems with mental health services. If there does not exist standardized information on training of corrections officers, how would a researcher be able to compare? If officers in both California and New York were required to have a specific certificate, research could be done to establish success or failure. Additionally, comparisons could be made to say that certain trains or methods work better than others, thus improving the system as a whole. All in all, these changes could allow for a more comprehensive approach to overcoming obstacles within the jail system and the treatment of those incarcerated.

Moving on, as discussed many times with recidivism, typically a person who is incarcerated without programming to help in change, will return to jail or prison. Going along with that thought, it could be safe to say that those in these jail systems may very well enter the prison system eventually. Why is this important? Research about short-term stays within the jail system could lead to significant information as it relates to the prison system. Therefore, having states work together for better standards or even just within a state system could vastly change outlooks for the criminal justice system of the United States.

Another note regarding the lack of research, if a community has no information on the number of individuals with mental illness within their jail system, then there would be no initiative to treat those individuals. Often these jails have known that there were individuals within the system with mental health, but no knowledge was known of the extent of the number. Luckily, this has prompted some communities to take action.

References

28 F.Supp.3d 1068 - COLEMAN v. BROWN, *United States District Court, E.D. California*.

42 U.S.C. § 1983. Civil action for deprivation of rights.

503 F.Supp. 1265. Ruiz v. Estelle, United States District Court, S.D Texas.

933e F.Supp. 954 - COLEMAN v. WILSON, *United States District Court, E.D. California*.

American Correctional Association. (2001). *Performance-based standards for adult community residential services*. American Correctional Association: Lanham, MD.

Babwin, D. (2017). Chicago inmates can order fancy Italian pizza made in jail. *US News*. Retrieved June 1, 2017, from https://www.usnews.com/news/best-states/illinois/articles/2017-05-26/chicago-inmates-can-order-fancy-italian-pizza-made-in-jail

Center for Disease Control and Prevention. (2017). *National suicide statistics*. Retrieved June 1, 2017, from https://www.cdc.gov/violenceprevention/suicide/statistics/

Council of State Governments Justice Center. (2014). *Stepping up: A national initiative to reduce the number of people with mental illnesses in jails*. Retrieved June 1, 2017, from https://csgjusticecenter.org/wp-content/uploads/2014/12/SteppingUpInitiative.pdf

Estelle v. Gamble. 429 US 97.

Freeman, S. (2017). A Chicago chef is rehabilitating inmates one pizza at a time. *Vice*. Retrieved June 1, 2017, from https://munchies.vice.com/en_us/article/53q3ba/a-chicago-chef-is-rehabilitating-inmates-one-pizza-at-a-time

Griffin, P. A., Heilbrun, K., Mulvey, E. P., DeMatteo, D., & Schubert, C. A. (Eds.). (2015). *The Sequential Intercept Model and criminal justice: Promoting community alternatives for individuals with serious mental illness*. New York: Oxford University Press.

Haneberg, R., Fabelo, T, Osher, F., & Thompson, M. (2017). *Reducing the number of people with mental illnesses in jail: Six questions county leaders need to ask.* Retrieved June 1, 2017, from https://stepuptogether.org/wp-content/uploads/2017/01/Reducing-the-Number-of-People-with-Mental-Illnesses-in-Jail_Six-Questions.pdf

Idaho, D. (1984). *Balla v. Idaho State Board of Corrections*, United States District Court. 595 F.Supp. 1558, 1577.

Janssen, K. (2017). Cook County jail inmates can order hot pizza delivered to their cells. *Chicago Tribune.* Retrieved June 1, 2017, from http://www.chicagotribune.com/news/chicagoinc/ct-pizza-in-jail-0510-chicago-inc-20170509-story.html

McCampbell, S.W., Grenawitzke, H.E., Patterson, R.F., Greifinger, R.B., Frasier, M.L., Hardyman, P.L., et al. (2017). *Report No. 7 of the independent monitors.* Retrieved July 15, 2017, from http://www.nolajailmonitors.org/uploads/3/7/5/7/37578255/_7_compliance_report.pdf

Miller, C.M. & Fantz, A. (2007, November 15). Special "psych" jails planned. *Miami Herald.*

Munetz, M. R., & Griffin, P. A. (2006). Use of the sequential intercept model as an approach to decriminalization of people with serious mental illness. *Psychiatric Services, 57*(4), 544–549.

Najavits, L. M. (2001). *Seeking safety: A treatment manual for PTSD and substance abuse.* New York: Guilford Press.

National Alliance on Mental Illness. (2017). *Jailing people with mental illness.* Retrieved June 1, 2017, from https://www.nami.org/Learn-More/Public-Policy/Jailing-People-with-Mental-Illness

National Institute of Justice. (2017). *Crime solutions.* Retrieved June 1, 2017, from https://www.crimesolutions.gov

Noonan, M. (2015). *Mortality in local jails and state prisons, 2000-2013 - Statistical tables.* Washington, DC: Bureau of Justice Statistics. Retrieved June 1, 2017, from https://www.bjs.gov/content/pub/pdf/mljsp0013st.pdf

Osher, F. C. (2006). *Integrating mental health and substance abuse services for justice-involved persons with co-occurring disorders.* Delmar, NY: National GAINS Center.

Osher, F. C. (2007). Short-term strategies to improve reentry of jail populations: Expanding and implementing the APIC model. *American Jails.* Retrieved June 1, 2017, from https://www.bja.gov/Publications/APIC_Model.pdf

Rayman, G. (2016). Rikers inmate moved to isolation cell after suicide attempt. *New York Daily News.* Retrieved June 1, 2017, from http://www.nydailynews.com/new-york/rikers-inmate-moved-isolation-cell-suicide-attempt-article-1.2531720

Sledge, M. (2017). Report: New Orleans jail has 'regressed' under new administrator, with 'unacceptable' violence. *The New Orleans Advocate.* Retrieved June 1, 2017, from http://www.theadvocate.com/new_orleans/news/courts/article_d281246a-3059-11e7-9c76-abc1dd0205eb.html

Steinberg, D., Mills, D., & Romano, M. (2015). When did prisons become acceptable mental healthcare facilities? Stanford Law School. Retrieved June 1, 2017, from https://law.stanford.edu/wp-content/uploads/sites/default/files/publication/863745/doc/slspublic/Report_v12.pdf

Stepping Up Initiative. (2017). *Stepping up: A national initiative to reduce the number of people with mental illnesses in jails.* Retrieved June 1, 2017, from https://stepuptogether.org/

Stohr, M. K., Self, R. L., & Lovrich, N. P. (1992). Staff turnover in new generation jails: An investigation of its causes and prevention. *Journal of Criminal Justice, 20*(5), 455–478.

Substance Abuse and Mental Health Services Administration. (2017). *National registry of evidence-based programs and practices.* Retrieved June 1, 2017, from http://nrepp.samhsa.gov/landing.aspx

Travis, J., & Visher, C. (Eds.). (2005). *Prisoner reentry and crime in America.* New York: Cambridge University Press.

University of Texas School of Law Civil Rights Clinic. (2016). *Preventable tragedies: How to reduce mental health-related deaths in Texas jails.* Retrieved June 1, 2017, from https://law.utexas.edu/wp-content/uploads/sites/11/2016/11/2016-11-CVRC-Preventable-Tragedies.pdf

Vera Institute. (2014). *On life support: Public health in the age of mass incarceration.* Retrieved June 1, 2017, from https://www.vera.org/publications/on-life-support-public-health-in-the-age-of-mass-incarceration

Chapter 6
Court Programs

The dawn of widespread court intervention for mental health concerns truly began with the drug court concept developed in Dade (now Miami-Dade) County, Florida, at the conclusion of the 1980s in direct response to Miami's infamous drug scene. The darker aspects of popular culture depictions of drugs impact on Miami—*Scarface*, *Cocaine Cowboys*, and *Miami Vice*, to name a few—were in plain view on a daily basis for local judges, public defenders, and prosecutors. Specifically, these key players grew wary of witnessing the same offenders appear before the court under the same or incredibly similar circumstances, sparking the concept of drug court (Goldkamp & Weiland, 1993). Later named a problem-solving court, specialty court, or therapeutic court, the innovation of drug court centers on its holistic approach of combining aspects of treatment, providing general care by leveraging community resources (e.g., housing, health care, food banks, transportation, etc.), and judicial oversight to enable its participants a chance to break the drug-crime-criminal justice pattern in their lives (Carey, Mackin, & Finigan, 2012). In years to come, this concept was reinforced and fine-tuned with emerging evidence-based practices to ensure the lasting success and pro-social gains of participants, and a vast array of research would be published to support the successes of a fully operational drug court steeped in evidence-based practices (Gottfredson, Najaka, & Kearley, 2003; Rossman & Zweig, 2012; Wilson, Mitchell, & MacKenzie, 2006). Soon, this model would be redeveloped to cater to individuals with the mental health-(drugs)-crime-criminal justice pattern in their lives—called mental health court or behavioral health court. These specialty courts lie at the forefront of local court innovations to intervene on behalf of individuals with mental illness being processed by the criminal justice system.

© Springer International Publishing AG, part of Springer Nature 2018
J. Hector, D. Khey, *Criminal Justice and Mental Health*,
https://doi.org/10.1007/978-3-319-76442-9_6

6.1   Know the Role-Drug Court

According to the National Institute of Justice (2017), there are 1558 adult drug courts and 409 juvenile drug courts in operation as of June 2015, with at least one in operation in each of the United States. While variability in the program exists, the core operation in each appears to be consistent. This core begins with defining the appropriate target population to serve, which, in this case, should be adults or juveniles (not both) with a known substance use disorder (Eckholm, 2008). To ensure that this target population is indeed being targeted by the program, evidence-based screening and assessment tools *must* be adopted. A notable criticism of drug courts is that, historically, programs have generally defined eligible participants as nonviolent, probation-eligible individuals who have committed a drug offense or a drug-related offense, which may widen the criminal justice net to include individuals without a substance use problem (Drug Policy Alliance, 2011). In doing so, much of the previous research may have been overly optimistic in their rates of success. Follow-up research continues to support the success of drug court when (1) validated screening and assessment tools are in place and when (2) evidence-based programming with success in the target population is used. However, it is difficult to determine just how many of the 1558 adult drug courts and 409 juvenile drug courts operate with fidelity to these two prerequisites for success.

Generally speaking, prospective drug court *clients* must enter a guilty plea to their charges if determined to be eligible for the program. The drug court team—consisting of a presiding judge, case manager, prosecutor, defense attorney, treatment professional, and probation officer—will consider each client for admittance on a case-by-case basis. The program itself is set up in phases, which begin at a high intensity of programming and hands-on participation and eventually eases until independence can be established (Adult Drug Court Research to Practice Initiative, 2017). For example, Phase 1 often requires an intensive weekly schedule of mandatory drug treatment hours that may include counseling, intensive outpatient (IOP) drug treatment, several sessions of group therapy (likely, Alcoholics Anonymous or Narcotics Anonymous), and routine randomized drug screening. It also includes a weekly status meeting with the judge and the drug court team to monitor progress, reward compliance and success, attend to potential emerging problems, and meaningfully correct any relapse, noncompliance, or misbehavior. As a client is successful in the program, each requirement of the program eases—less time spent in treatment, lower number of group therapy meetings required (although additional attendance is still encouraged), fewer status meetings in court each month, and less frequent drug testing. In all, drug courts typically have three to five phases which can last 12, 18, or 24 months with an added aftercare phase to aid in a prosocial, drug- and crime-free lifestyle (Lowenkamp, Holsinger, & Latessa, 2005).

As this program has matured, the National Association of Drug Court Professionals has been key in promulgating best practices and standards for the continued optimal success of drug courts. Its seminal "Ten Key Components of Drug Courts," published over a year ago, establishes the core elements indicative of successful programs after years of introspection and research (see Table 6.1).

Table 6.1 Ten key components of drug court (National Association of Drug Court Professionals, 2017)

Key Components
1. Drug courts integrate alcohol and other drug treatment services with justice system case processing
2. Using a nonadversarial approach, prosecution and defense counsel promote public safety while protecting participants' due process rights
3. Eligible participants are identified early and promptly placed in the drug court program
4. Drug courts provide access to a continuum of alcohol, drug, and other related treatment and rehabilitation services
5. Abstinence is monitored by frequent alcohol and other drug testing
6. A coordinated strategy governs drug court responses to participants' compliance
7. Ongoing judicial interaction with each drug court participant is essential
8. Monitoring and evaluation measure the achievement of program goals and gauge effectiveness
9. Continuing interdisciplinary education promotes effective drug court planning, implementation, and operations
10. Forging partnerships among drug courts, public agencies, and community-based organizations generate local support and enhances drug court program effectiveness

The overall successes of a well-run drug court, based on whether or not these courts can stay true to these ten key components, are substantial. Reductions of crime range from 8 to 26 percent, cost savings have been estimated at $2 to $27 dollars per every dollar invested into drug court, and drug court participants are consistently more likely to reduce drug use relative to non-participants.

6.1.1   Drug Court Adaptations for Special Populations

As soon as criminal justice practitioners realized the promise of drug courts, forward thinkers began to adapt the core structure of drug court to other target populations that become commonly involved with the criminal justice system (Brennan, Battaglia, & Jones, 2011; Festinger, Dugosh, & Marlow, 2015; Halper, 2014; Marlowe 2010; Morse et al. 2014; Tiger, 2012). In June 2015, the National Association of Drug Court Professionals recognized and tabulated the following therapeutic courts:

Family court (also known as family preservation court, designed to aid a drug dependent mother, father, or both in maintaining custody of their children and healing familial strains and dissolution due to drug abuse—312)
Veterans court (designed to focus on the special needs of former military members, often by addressing traumatic experiences of combat—313)
Sobriety court (also known as DUI or DWI court, designed specifically for alcoholism in conjunction with driving under the influence—284)
Tribal court (designed to focus on American Indians—138)

Mental health court (also called co-occurring or behavioral health court, designed to
   focus primarily on mental health diagnoses with secondary focus on substance
   use disorder—*366 reported by the GAINS Center*)
Reentry court (designed to focus on the experiences common to individuals returning to the community from incarceration—29)
Campus courts (also known as back on TRAC, designed to focus on college
   students—3)

Each customization often taps additional team members with expertise in the
targeted "special" population to ensure success. For example, for a veterans court,
the team may expressly search for case managers, probation officers, and treatment
professionals with a military background to aid in better understanding client behaviors and to have better success in building better rapport for best outcomes. Further,
former military members in recovery may serve as better peer support specialists
and/or mentors with veterans court clients than those without military experience.
These differences can assist clients in tamping down feelings of isolation and any
"us versus them" sentiment compared to enduring a traditional drug court experience. The same arguments can be made for tribal court and campus court. Research
on these adaptations are ongoing, but show promise in effecting change for each
targeted population.

6.1.2   Mental Health Courts

According to a Bureau of Justice Assistance report in 2000, mental health court was
pioneered in four very different jurisdictions, beginning in Broward County (Fort
Lauderdale), Florida, King County (Seattle), Washington, Anchorage, Alaska, and
San Bernardino, California. In each of these jurisdictions, the mental health court
team commonly faced defendants with issues related to homelessness, persistent
lapses of the community mental health-care system, jail overcrowding, and unabated
drug abuse. To address these issues, the traditional drug court program was equipped
with treatment, including psychiatric and counseling services, geared for co-
occurring disorders, stronger ties to housing assistance, and team members familiar
with mental health disorders and individuals with mental illness.

Additionally, drug courts are, by and large, steeped in an abstinence-based orientation. Mental health courts, by necessity, must alter this long-standing tradition to
accept required medication regimes to treat clients' underlying mental illness.
Often, these therapeutic courts work with treatment professionals to find medications that may minimize substance use disorder symptomatology. For example, clients diagnosed with anxiety disorders may have historically been treated with
medications known to be commonly abused, such as Xanax. In the context of mental
health court, if a client has a pattern of substance use disorder co-occurring with an
anxiety disorder, the mental health court team may work with treatment providers
to find the treatment protocol for this case. Commonly, final treatment decisions
remain with treatment providers.

Another key difference exists when comparing traditional drug courts and mental health court as it pertains to defining and measuring success. For drug court clients, success is easier to conceive—pro-social drug- and crime-free living, as indicated by clients passing drug tests, successfully complying and completing treatment, paying all restitution and fees, and so on (Bureau of Justice Assistance, 2000). Mental health court clients, on the other hand, strive for optimal functionality given their lifelong mental health diagnoses, and this level of functioning will vary from client to client. Thus, success will vary across mental health court client. With this in mind, outcome studies have shown promising reductions in recidivism and violence (McNiel & Binder, 2007; Moore & Hiday, 2006).

The proliferation of mental health courts has also created a demand for a customized set of key components derived from the drug court model (Council of State Governments Justice Center, 2007; summarized in Table 6.2). Just like drug court, these components guide the creation, implementation, and continued success of mental health courts and provide a foundation for a standardized orientation.

6.1.3 The 22nd Judicial District Behavioral Health Court of Louisiana

The Behavioral Health Court (BHC) in the 22nd Judicial District Court of Louisiana (Covington), only one of three in the state, was designed as a win-win for stakeholders and clients alike. For clients, individuals receive both professional drug treatment and mental health services while remaining in the community in lieu of potential incarceration with little chance of receiving anywhere near this level of care, with the goal of treatment continuation. For stakeholders, rehabilitation presents an opportunity to disrupt established drug-crime trajectories; its success thus holds the key to produce increases in local public safety and vast cost savings to the local justice and health-care system.

The BHC program began in November of 2011 with each member of the BHC team volunteering their time during the lunch hour. Led by District Judge Peter Garcia, BHC partnered with the local National Alliance on Mental Illness outpost and the Florida Parishes Human Services Authority to offer linkages to community services such as housing, transportation, co-occurring group therapy, food assistance, and assistance in obtaining public benefits, as well as mental health and substance use treatment services. While Judge Garcia and his team were building capacity to provide the best care possible for current and future clients, the State of Louisiana had moved forward with a plan to privatize mental health services and divest a large portion of public funds to aid this effort. This resulted in a widespread closure of local, state-run behavioral health clinics and hospitals, leaving the criminal justice system as the only likely source of mental health care. This action further weakened the ability of the Florida Parishes Human Services Authority to provide optimal care for individuals with co-occurring disorders. At this time, Louisiana ranks 43rd out of the 50 states for per capita expenditures on mental health; the

Table 6.2 Ten key components, or "essential elements," of mental health court (Bureau of Justice Assistance, 2007)

Key Components
1. Planning and Administration: A broad-based group of stakeholders representing the criminal justice, mental health, substance abuse treatment, and related systems, and the community guides the planning and administration of the court
2. Target Population: Eligibility criteria address public safety and consider a community's treatment capacity in addition to the availability of alternatives to pretrial detention for defendants with mental illness. Eligibility criteria also take into account the relationship between mental illness and a defendant's offenses while allowing the individual circumstances of each case to be considered
3. Timely Participant Identification and Linkage to Services: Participants are identified, referred, and accepted into mental health courts and then linked to community-based service providers as quickly as possible
4. Terms of Participation: Terms of participation are clear, promote public safety, facilitate the defendant's engagement in treatment, are individualized to correspond to the level of risk that the defendant presents to the community, and provide for positive legal outcomes for those individuals who successfully complete the program
5. Informed Choice: Defendants fully understand the program requirements before agreeing to participate in a mental health court. They are provided legal counsel to inform this decision and subsequent decisions about program involvement. Procedures exist in the mental health court to address, in a timely fashion, concerns about a defendant's competency whenever they arise
6. Treatment Supports and Services: Mental health courts connect participants to comprehensive and individualized supports and services in the community. They strive to use—and increase the availability of—treatment and services that are evidence-based
7. Confidentiality: Health and legal information should be shared in a way that protects potential participants' confidentiality rights as mental health consumers and their constitutional rights as defendants. Information gathered as part of the participants' court-ordered treatment program or services should be safeguarded in the event that participants are returned to traditional court processing
8. Court Team: A team of criminal justice and mental health staff and service and treatment providers receives special, ongoing training and helps mental health court participants achieve treatment and criminal justice goals by regularly reviewing and revising the court process
9. Monitoring Adherence to Court Requirements: Criminal justice and mental health staff collaboratively monitor participants' adherence to court conditions, offer individualized graduated incentives and sanctions, and modify treatment as necessary to promote public safety and participants' recovery
10. Sustainability: Data are collected and analyzed to demonstrate the impact of the mental health court, its performance is assessed periodically (and procedures are modified accordingly), court processes are institutionalized, and support for the court in the community is cultivated and expanded

Florida Parishes Human Services Authority further receives less funding per capita than most of its sister districts, leaving the 22nd Judicial District Court vulnerable citizens even more vulnerable (Miller & Khey, 2016).

Since 2014, BHC has expanded its operations with the benefit of a joint grant program offered by SAMHSA and the Bureau of Justice Assistance, giving the program the ability to increase its case management capacity, further invest in evidence-based practices (such as trauma-informed care and Assertive Community Treatment), and offer protections of its clients against the weakening state of the local mental health system. While the outcome studies focusing on potential reduced hospitalizations, reductions in arrest and reconviction, and reductions in drug use, Miller and Khey (2016) published the results of a thorough process evaluation to determine whether BHC was operating as proposed, with true evidence-based services in place. Overall, Miller and Khey found a strong professional orientation of the services being delivered to BHC clients, particularly those within the direct control of the court. The broad weakening of the local mental health-care system, on the other hand, seemed to produce counterproductive effects on the treatment quality available to some clients. Specifically, therapeutic sessions provided by local practitioners appeared to only offer social support rather than engage in any known form of therapy, such as cognitive behavioral therapy or dialectic behavioral therapy. As a result, BHC leadership worked with its local partners to deepen its ability to offer such services to current and future clients.

Counterproductive forces to reform, such as the problems resulting from a weakened mental health-care system as noted above, are likely *more* common when the target population is individuals with mental illness or with co-occurring disorders. Further, this is even more likely the case in jurisdictions that need these types of innovation the most. Anecdotally speaking, such issues may explain why the pace the expansion of other types of specialty courts have outpaced mental health courts: only 70 mental health courts are in existence today, with one formal and two informal versions in Louisiana *not* included in that total (and for a state that desperately needs relief). In addition to the growing research supporting the efficacy of mental health courts, the human stories behind the numbers can be quite astounding:

A mental health advocate in the 22nd Judicial District BHC recalls a success story – That was [client x], case study #1. He absolutely refused to go to self-help groups, like AA. Had a strong desire to function independently and lived on his own in Abita Springs. He had a long history of difficulty with communicating, organization problems, and always seemed to have an unhealthy living situation. We found out at one point his house didn't have heat and we were able to buy him a floor heater. He also neglected his physical health, then he started doing better and got prescription glasses. [As he participated in BHC], he became a leader in the AA community and even started running groups. He even came back to BHC years later to try and help out some one he met in AA. Prior to BHC, [client x] had 37 charges from 1988 through 2012, which include simple battery, aggravated battery, resisting arrest, domestic abuse, driving with a suspended license, possession of marijuana, driving while intoxicated (over four convictions), and much more. Since he was accepted into BHC, he had no new criminal charges, became a model client, and just 'got it.' (Khey, unpublished research)

The recent policy shifts to accept Medicaid expansion in 31 states, and Washington DC has aided to shield the mental health court target population from a weak local mental health system of care. With the help from a mental health court team, clients often find themselves able to navigate the system and connect with needed services, particularly when receiving Medicaid assistance. It provides more avenues for covered treatment provision and opens up a menu of available services that can aid in healthy outcomes. For example, in the 22nd Judicial District BHC, it is estimated that just more than half of the program's participants benefited from Medicaid and Medicaid expansion. This issue becomes critical as our national leaders debate the future of Medicaid and Medicaid expansion.

6.2   Older Initiatives: Mental Health Court Precursors

Before mental health court, court intervention relating to mental illness occurred infrequently through civil commitments, competency hearings, not guilty by reason of insanity (NGBRI) pleas, or when defendants challenge criminal justice processing through their attorneys (often, public defenders) for reasons related to their mental state (at the time or during the time of the offense). Primarily due to jail overcrowding and heavy court caseloads, local criminal justice systems searched for alternatives and improvements in justice processing, largely led by the courts on criminal justice task forces across the country (Bureau of Justice Assistance, 2000). Yet, court-centered innovation to serve individuals with mental illness began in the 1960s with the use of diversion (Matthews, 1970). For example, both the cities of Chicago and New York court systems heavily relied on partnerships with the mental health-care system. In fact, the Chicago system maintained an embedded partnership—the Psychiatric Institute—to directly handle misdemeanor referrals from the court on site and, further, offer an inpatient facility immediately next to the jail for felony case referrals. One of the primary goals of the Institute was to offer the court alternatives to criminal justice sanctions, whenever possible (particularly when considering public safety in its calculus). The possible recommendations were much like what mental health court offers today—outpatient treatment and referrals to drug and alcohol treatment. One divergence from mental health court, however, was that this system often recommended civil commitment as a viable alternative for the court to weigh in its decision-making. Meanwhile, the New York system was set up to allow for local police to directly divert individuals with potential mental health concerns directly to local hospitals. From this point, the hospitals had a direct line of communication with the courts to continue criminal processing and assist in planning alternatives, whenever possible, for both misdemeanor and felony cases.

While these interconnected systems of care faded away with deinstitutionalization, diversion persisted in some ways. For example, Steadman, Morris, and Dennis (1995) profiled diversion programs for individual with mental illness and found 230 out of 685 jail systems surveyed had linkages to such diversion programs, many of which had linkages to the local courts. In fact, several key similarities to mental health emerged from the successful programs reviewed. For example, one program featured an interdisciplinary team of ten staff members to work intensively with 100 clients at a time. This project is further aided by "key players" that include judges, a local mental health director, public defenders, district attorneys, probation officers, and a supervisor of services in the local jail.

Research on these innovations needs improvement (Schneider, 2010). While there seems to be many good ideas for court intervention, the only one with a significant (and current) evidence base remains to be mental health courts. Thus, mental health courts are seen as *the* diversion tool for the courts for this target population. In fact, the Treatment Advocacy Center released a report entitled "Mental Health Diversion Practices: A Survey of the States," which attempts to estimate the percentage of populations served by two sources of diversion—mental health courts and crisis intervention teams (CIT, see Chap. 3; Stettin, Frese, & Lamb, 2013). Their findings can be found in Table 6.3. What we have learned from these past experiences is that a team-based effort often lends to optimal results. The added value of judicial oversight often lends an enforcement mechanism for accountability, both for key stakeholders and justice-involved individuals.

6.3   A Note on Veterans Treatment Courts

One of the most recent adaptations of drug court—veterans treatment court—is more closely aligned with mental health court due to its primary focus on trauma related to military service and/or combat. This may include post-traumatic stress disorder, traumatic brain injury, and military sexual trauma. Recent data suggests that one in five veterans experiences mental health disorder symptomatology or cognitive impairment, and one in sex veterans deployed in Operation Enduring Freedom and Operation Iraqi Freedom can be diagnosed with substance use disorder (Tanielian, Jaycox, Schell, Marshall, Burnam, Eibner, Karney, Meredith, Ringel, & Vaiana, 2008). Yet, the most powerful reason why to hold a unique and separate veterans treatment court aside from either drug court or mental health court lies in the story that first inspired the idea:

> One day, a Vietnam veteran appeared before Judge (Robert) Russell (in drug court in Buffalo, New York). He had not been making his treatment appointments, and he refused to communicate with the court team or his treatment providers. As the judge tried to engage him, he remained unresponsive, his eyes on the floor. In a moment of exasperation, Judge Russell called two members of his court to the bench. Hank and Jack were also Vietnam veterans, so the judge asked that they spend some time with the gentleman, veteran to veteran. An hour later, when Judge Russell called the case again, the man approached the front of the courtroom, stood at parade rest, and looked the judge in the eye. The judge then asked him if he was ready to accept the support and treatment that were being offered to him through the court. He immediately responded, "Yes, sir." That was the spark…. (Justice for Vets, 2017)

Veterans treatment court is designed to tap into the military culture and structure to benefit its clients. It leverages military training that often instills brotherhood and strong camaraderie to support the recovery of a veteran with mental illness and/or substance use disorder. Further, expertise is brought into veterans treatment courts to aid in navigating the exclusive benefits available to veterans for their past military service through the Veterans Health Administration, Veterans Benefits Administration, the State Department of Veterans Affairs, and local veteran

Table 6.3 Treatment Advocacy's Center grades of states' diversion practices

State	% served by a mental health court	% served by CIT	Average % of population served	Grade
D.C.	100%	100%	100%	A+
Utah	85%	97%	91%	A+
Florida	67%	97%	82%	A
California	78%	79%	79%	A
Ohio	63%	88%	76%	A
Connecticut	100%	37%	69%	B+
Illinois	78%	59%	69%	B+
Idaho	76%	58%	67%	B+
Nevada	88%	37%	63%	B
Washington	62%	63%	63%	B
Colorado	35%	86%	61%	B
Georgia	49%	70%	60%	B
Maine	34%	83%	59%	B
New Mexico	63%	50%	57%	B
North Carolina	24%	87%	56%	B
Arizona	21%	84%	53%	B-
Minnesota	31%	70%	51%	B-
Delaware	100%	0%	50%	B-
Oklahoma	59%	40%	50%	B-
Pennsylvania	60%	40%	50%	B-
Oregon	54%	38%	46%	C+
Kentucky	28%	61%	45%	C+
Virginia	6%	70%	38%	C
Texas	44%	27%	36%	C
Wisconsin	11%	60%	36%	C
Kansas	18%	49%	34%	C-
Tennessee	16%	51%	34%	C-
Indiana	25%	37%	31%	C-
Maryland	30%	31%	31%	C-
New Hampshire	40%	19%	30%	C-
North Dakota	22%	34%	28%	D
Michigan	48%	3%	26%	D
Wyoming	0%	52%	26%	D
Montana	17%	30%	24%	D
Louisiana	8%	38%	23%	D
New Jersey	7%	33%	20%	D
South Carolina	27%	10%	19%	F
Vermont	35%	1%	18%	F
Alabama	34%	0%	17%	F
South Dakota	0%	29%	15%	F
Iowa	8%	13%	11%	F
Massachusetts	13%	3%	8%	F
Mississippi	2%	13%	8%	F
Arkansas	10%	0%	5%	F

State	%	%	%	Grade
Missouri	51%	38%	45%	C+
Alaska	44%	44%	44%	C
Hawaii	70%	12%	41%	C
Nebraska	42%	40%	41%	C
New York	75%	5%	40%	C
West Virginia	9%	0%	5%	F
Rhode Island	0%	0%	0%	F
Nat'l Average	48%	49%	49%	C+

service organizations. For example, veterans may benefit from general health care, substance abuse treatment, group therapy, transportation, peer mentoring by a veteran in recovery, transportation services, housing services, and much more. Often, veterans treatment courts seek to offer connectivity to all of these benefits in one place with individualized case management services to ensure that no one slips through the cracks.

With almost a decade of development, veterans treatment courts are beginning to develop an evidence base of their own. Most recently, Knudsen and Wingenfeld (2016) determined that a well-run veterans treatment court significantly decreased PTSD symptoms, improved client treatment orientation, promoted sleep, aided in improved family relations, decreased substance use, reduced depression, supported emotional well-being, and helped with perceived overall energy. Only nine of the 86 participants were rearrested in twelve months. These findings are indeed promising, yet they lack scientific rigor. To address this, the National Institute of Justice has commissioned a rigorous, multisite evaluation of veterans treatment courts with initial findings to be published in the next two to three years.

6.4   The Future of Mental Health Courts

While veteran treatment courts benefit from having the firm support of the Federal government through different aspects of the US Department of Veterans Affairs, mental health courts and their local partners often have to shoulder the cost of the specialty court and the requisite array of services. For example, a newly initiated veterans court in southeastern Louisiana estimates its costs as $50,000 for a case manager's salary and benefits, $40,000 per annum in treatment costs not covered by Veterans Affairs, $8000 in drug screen and confirmation to ensure compliance, and $2000 in operating costs, supplies, and incidentals, for a total of roughly $100,000 per year to comfortably operate this type of specialty court. Many jurisdictions use state-allocated funds and/or court funds generated by fees generated by adjudications to cover these costs.

We are at an interesting crossroad relating to mental health courts. In the current political climate, veterans treatment courts are well positioned to reap both direct and indirect benefits through reinvestment in the US Department of Veterans Affairs. Yet, mental health courts are showing signs of stress. A review of media accounts offer anecdotal evidence of potential problems on the horizon: in Delaware, a panel is recommending to unify the state's specialty courts instead of keeping them separate (Reyes, 2017); in Flint, the Genesee Health System was facing a budget crises which is threatening mental health court services (Pierret 2016); in South Dakota, the state legislature did not fund a request to create its first mental health court due to fiscal concerns (Walker, 2017). Critically, the fate of Medicaid will prove to be central to the viability of mental health courts across the country. As a relatable illustration, the GAINS Center reviewed a common issue currently faced by all specialty courts, including (and particularly) mental health courts—the impact of having public benefits terminated or suspended when a person is incarcerated. As clients are waiting to have their benefits reinstated, they often face insurmountable problems trying to make ends meet, finding timely care, gaining access to medication, and so on (GAINS Center, 1999). If Medicaid were significantly curtailed or eliminated, very real possibilities being considered by the 115th US Congress with tacit backing of President Trump, a significant burden would be shifted to localities and states to be able to provide care to mental health clients and the wider target population.

Yet, the bipartisan Twenty-First Century Cures Act takes Federal leadership on mental health (and mental health courts) in a positive direction. It reauthorizes the Comprehensive Justice and Mental Health Act to continue to provide grant funding for mental health courts and innovative research in this domain. Additionally, the legislation enables improvements in data monitoring. This will allow for us to more effectively monitor any change in policy with greater precision, which will further allow for us to seek corrective action for any political shift that has unintended consequences. There appears to be significant momentum for criminal justice reform, including for individuals with mental illness and co-occurring disorders. It seems likely, then, that progress will continue, despite countervailing forces—the result of which may produce stifled progress, but progress nonetheless.

6.5   A Key Weakness in the Court's Role: Revocation

In the *Journal of the American Academy of Psychiatry and Law*, an article titled *Mental Illness and Revocation of Restricted Probation* discusses the court case of William Burke versus the State of Montana (Kambam & Guyer, 2006). In this lawsuit, William Burke appealed the ruling set forth that he violated his probation, but instead his behavior was related to his mental health diagnosis. William Burke was sentenced to seven years by Cascade County with the Department of Corrections after a robbery charge. He served four years in prison in February 2004 and then was set to serve the remaining three years of his term on probation. In May of 2004, Burke's probation officer "filed a Report of Violation, alleging that Burke had violated eight different conditions of his probation." Due to this, a warrant was issued for his arrest, and when he appeared in court, Burke requested a mental health evaluation. "Dr. Michael Scolatti, a licensed clinical psychologist, performed an evaluation of Burke and rendered a diagnosis of antisocial personality disorder, borderline intellectual functioning, bipolar disorder with psychotic features, and attention deficit/hyperactivity disorder (ADHD). Furthermore, he reported that Burke's bipolar disorder and ADHD were 'relatively severe disorders that require medication' and illnesses that would significantly compromise his ability to conform to the law. He opined that Burke should be placed at the state hospital." A request was made by Burke's law team to have him serve the remainder of his sentence in a state psychiatric hospital to receive treatment rather than incarceration. Unfortunately, the court ruled that Burke's behavior and mental illness did not play a part in whether he was able to commit the violations that were alleged. Burke was then sent back to prison to serve out the rest of time on his original sentence.

Example of a callout:

The Supreme Court of Montana affirmed the Disposition Order of the district court, finding no abuse of discretion in the sentencing of the defendant to prison, the expert psychological testimony concerning his mental illness notwithstanding. The supreme court cited Mont. Code Ann. § 46-18-203(7)(a)(iii), which sets out the sentencing alternatives and discretionary prerogatives of the trial judge attached to probation revocation. The supreme court found that the sentencing imposed by the trial judge was in conformity with the statute

---

A related sentencing statute, Mont. Code Ann. § 46-14-311 (2005), requires that, following a finding of guilty or a plea of guilty made by a defendant, consideration by the trial judge of a defendant's claim of mental disease or defect or developmental disability during sentencing must occur. The statute states: Whenever a defendant ... claims that ... the defendant was suffering from a mental disease or defect or developmental disability that rendered the defendant unable to appreciate the criminality of the defendant's behavior or to conform the defendant's behavior to the requirements of the law, the sentencing court shall consider any relevant evidence presented at the trial and shall require additional evidence that it considers necessary for the determination of the issue, including examination of the defendant and a report of the examination

---

Although Burke challenged one finding of fact under this statute, the state supreme court disagreed, concluding that Burke had not demonstrated that the district court "acted arbitrarily without employment of conscientious judgment or exceeded the bounds of reason, resulting in substantial injustice." The state supreme court cited the provision of wide latitude in sentencing and held that the trial judge had given adequate consideration of the various relevant sentencing factors. The supreme court noted that the trial judge had taken into account the testimony of the psychologist (Scolatti), Burke's need for mental health care, his prognosis for treatment and his risk to reoffend violently, observations that the Montana State Prison has a mental health treatment program, and various sentencing options other than prison. Furthermore, the state supreme court noted that Scolatti had testified that despite Burke's mental illnesses, Scolatti could not specify what role these illnesses played in his probation violations nor would he testify that to a medical certainty, Burke's mental illnesses caused him to violate the conditions of his probation. As for the capacity to conform to the law, Scolatti, while noting some volitional impairment, testified that the defendant "still has some volitional choice of whether or not to commit a crime." The supreme court took note of the expert's testimony on volitional capacity as further indication that the trial judge had not abused his sentencing discretion in imposing a prison term, despite evidence that the defendant had some mental illnesses

---

The supreme court noted that the law in Montana is not settled on the question of whether a defendant may invoke the provisions of Mont. Code Ann. § 46-14-311 (2005), at a revocation hearing, or whether the consideration which must be afforded to evidence of mental illness at sentencing applies only to sentencing at the original trial proceedings and is unavailable to defendants at probation revocation hearings and sentencing dispositions. Since the supreme court could uphold the trial court's sentencing solely on the provision of Mont. Code Ann. § 46-18-203(7)(a)(iii), it noted the trial judge need not have (even though he had) taken into account any mental health evidence that defendant proffered under Mont. Code Ann. § 46-14-311 (2005)

This is a case of little precedential weight and few moving parts; no constitutional issues are raised. It involves the application of three state statutes and one hapless defendant and speaks to the considerable latitude in discretion afforded to the trial judge in probation revocation hearings and sentencing procedures. Here, the defendant contested only one judicial finding of fact of the sentencing judge: that the defendant had the volitional capacity to avoid committing acts that violated the terms of his probation. The standard of appellate review is high: was there an abuse of discretion?

Implicit in the trial judge's findings and the state supreme court's affirmation is a certain discounting of the weight afforded to expert psychological testimony, even when called for by statute, admitted by the judge, and spared rebuttal by the opposing party (in this instance, the state). When defendants in Montana are charged with violation of the conditions of their probation, a Revocation Hearing is held before a judge and the standard of proof is a preponderance of the evidence. Once a violation is found (in the present case, the defendant came to admit to five violations), the trial judge is given great latitude in sentencing, (Mont. Code Ann. § 46-18-203)

Because the defendant raised the issue of his mental illness in the sentencing procedure, the judge allowed expert testimony concerning the defendant's volitional capacity and his treatment needs into evidence (Mont. Code Ann. § 46-14-311). The expert testified that the defendant was mentally ill and volitionally compromised and would best be served by being remanded to the state's mental hospital, an option available to the judge in his sentencing discretion. The trial judge weighed the expert testimony, concluded that the defendant had a modicum of volition in his violation of probation and sentenced him to serve his full probationary term (four years) in state prison, as permitted as a statutory exercise of judicial discretion (Mont. Code Ann. § 46-14-312). A wavering of certainty by the expert on the volitional question was cited by the judge, as were the uncertain benefits of psychological treatment and the potential dangerousness of the defendant

6.6 Conclusion

Court programs have been around for a number of years but are expanding and diversifying to better serve communities and justice-involved individuals. Luckily, with the help of dedicated individuals, some of these court programs are beginning to show signs of true success. These successes are both beneficial for those involved in the program but also their communities and our country as a whole. These small "breaths of life" are the life support needed to resurrect a failing system. There is hope that change can happen and those in need can receive not only the services needed but also the chance to regain their lives as productive members of society.

Two key court innovations are mental health courts (also known as behavioral health courts) and veterans treatment courts. These adaptations of drug courts (also known as specialty courts) are developing an evidence-based and a proven track record of success. While the evidence is promising, some jurisdictions struggle with funding to keep these programs running under optimal conditions or even running at all. Veterans treatment courts have an advantage in that Veterans Affairs and government benefits due to US veterans shoulder much of the cost (e.g., treatment cost) of the program. Thus, in the near future, veterans treatment court is likely to expand at a faster rate relative to mental health courts despite the fact that both certainly target the same symptomatology.

On a final note, much more research needs to be done in the area of court innovations, particularly as a resource to interventions that can occur before criminal justice processing can begin. In other words, as law enforcement and community partners work to divert eligible individuals away from the criminal justice system, court players (including judges) may have an opportunity to offer resources and legitimacy that no other partner can. Specialty courts seem to be the beginning of court participation in mental health innovations, and much more development should be expected in this arena in the near future.

References

Adult Drug Court Research to Practice Initiative. (2017). Retrieved June 1, 2017, from http://www.research2practice.org

Brennan, P, Battaglia, M., & Jones, G. (Producers). (2011 – current). *Last Shot with Judge Gunn. (Television Series).* Fayetteville, AK: Trifecta Entertainment. Retrieved from http://lastshot-judgegunn.com/

Bureau of Justice Assistance. (2000). *Emerging judicial strategies for the mentally ill in the criminal caseload: Mental health courts in Fort Lauderdale, Seattle, San Bernardino, and Anchorage.* Retrieved July 10, 2017, from https://www.ncjrs.gov/pdffiles1/bja/182504.pdf

Bureau of Justice Assistance. (2007). *Improving responses to people with mental illnesses: The essential elements of a mental health court.* Retrieved July 1, 2017, from https://www.bja.gov/publications/mhc_essential_elements.pdf

Carey, S. M., Mackin, J. R., & Finigan, M. W. (2012). What works? The ten key components of drug court: Research-based best practices. *Drug Court Review, 8*(1), 6–42.

Council of State Governments Justice Center. (2007). *Improving responses to people with mental illness: The essential elements of a mental health court.* Retrieved June 1, 2017, from https://www.bja.gov/publications/mhc_essential_elements.pdf

Drug Policy Alliance. (2011). *Drug courts are not the answer: Toward a health-centered approach to drug use.* Retrieved June 1, 2017, from https://www.drugpolicy.org/docUploads/Drug_Courts_Are_Not_the_Answer_Final2.pdf

Eckholm, E. (2008). *Courts give addicts a chance to straighten out.* The New York Times, Retrieved June 1, 2017, from http://www.nytimes.com/2008/10/15/us/15drugs.html

Festinger, D. S., Dugosh, K. L., & Marlowe, D. (2015). Improving outcomes for low-risk/low-need drug court clients: Life in the fast lane. *Drug & Alcohol Dependence, 146,* e276.

GAINS Center (1999). *Medicaid benefits for jail detainees with co-occurring mental health and substance use disorders.* Prepared by Sherman, R. Delmar, NY: The National GAINS Center for People with Co-Occurring Disorders in the Criminal Justice System. Retrieved June 1, 2017, from http://www.prainc.com/gains/publications/medicaid.htm

Goldkamp, J. S., & Weiland, D. (1993). *Assessing the impact of Dade County's felony drug court: Final report.* Washington, DC: US Department of Justice, Office of Justice Programs, National Institute of Justice. Retrieved June 1, 2017, from https://www.ncjrs.gov/pdffiles1/Digitization/144524NCJRS.pdf

Gottfredson, D. C., Najaka, S. S., & Kearley, B. (2003). Effectiveness of drug treatment courts: Evidence from a randomized trial. *Criminology & Public Policy, 2*(2), 171–196.

Halper, E. (2014). *Drug courts, meant to aid addicts, now a battlefield of pot politics.* LA Times. http://www.latimes.com/nation/la-na-drug-court-20140727-story.html

Justice for Vets. (2017). Retrieved June 1, 2017, from https://justiceforvets.org/

Kambam, P., & Guyer, M. (2006). Mental illness and revocation of restricted probation. *Journal of the American Academy of Psychiatry and the Law Online, 35*(1), 120–122.

Knudsen, K. J., & Wingenfeld, S. (2016). A specialized treatment court for veterans with trauma exposure: Implications for the field. *Community Mental Health Journal, 52*(2), 127–135.

Lowenkamp, C. T., Holsinger, A. M., & Latessa, E. J. (2005). Are drug courts effective? A meta-analytic review. *Journal of Community Corrections, Fall, 5,* 28.

Marlowe, D. B. (2010). *Research update on adult drug courts.* Retrieved June 1, 2017, from http://www.nadcp.org/sites/default/files/nadcp/Research%20Update%20on%20Adult%20Drug%20Courts%20-%20NADCP_1.pdf

Matthews, A. R. (1970). *Mental Disability and the Criminal Justice System.* Chicago: American Bar Foundation.

McNiel, D. E., & Binder, R. L. (2007). Effectiveness of a mental health court in reducing criminal recidivism and violence. *American Journal of Psychiatry, 164*(9), 1395–1403.

Miller, J. M., & Khey, D. N. (2016). An implementation and process evaluation of the louisiana 22nd judicial district's behavioral health court. *American Journal of Criminal Justice, 41*(1), 124–135.

Moore, M. E., & Hiday, V. A. (2006). Mental health court outcomes: A comparison of re-arrest and re-arrest severity between mental health court and traditional court participants. *Law and human behavior, 30*(6), 659–674.

Morse, D. S., Cerulli, C., Bedell, P., Wilson, J. L., Thomas, K., Mittal, M., et al. (2014). Meeting health and psychological needs of women in drug treatment court. *Journal of Substance Abuse Treatment, 46*(2), 150–157.

National Association of Drug Court Professionals. (2017). http://www.nadcp.org

National Institute of Justice. (2017). *Drug courts.* Retrieved June 1, 2017, from https://www.nij.gov/topics/courts/drug-courts/Pages/welcome.aspx

Pierret, A. (2016). *Mental health court upset with potential cuts.* Retrieved June 1, 2017, from http://www.abc12.com/content/news/Mental-Health-Court-upset-with-potential-cuts-398980391.html

Reyes, J. M. (2017). *Drug, mental health courts merged in New Castle County.* Retrieved June 1, 2017, from http://www.delawareonline.com/story/news/local/2017/04/24/drug-mental-health-courts-merged-new-castle-county/100840368/

Rossman, S. B., & Zweig, J. M. (2012). *The multisite adult drug court evaluation.* Retrieved June 1, 2017, from http://www.nadcp.org/sites/default/files/nadcp/Multisite%20Adult%20Drug%20Court%20Evaluation%20-%20NADCP.pdf

Schneider, R. D. (2010). Mental health courts and diversion programs: A global survey. *International Journal of Law and Psychiatry, 33*(4), 201–206.

Steadman, H. J., Morris, S. M., & Dennis, D. L. (1995). The diversion of mentally ill persons from jails to community-based services: A profile of programs. *American Journal of Public Health, 85*(12), 1630–1635.

Stettin, B., Frese, F. J., & Lamb, H. R. (2013). *Mental health diversion practices: A survey of the states.* Arlington, VA: Treatment Advocacy Center.

Tanielian, T., Jaycox, L.H., Schell, T.L., Marshall, G.N., Burnam, M.A., Eibner, C., Karney, B., Meredith, L.S., Ringel, J.S., & Vaiana, M.E. (2008). *Invisible wounds of war: Summary and recommendations for addressing psychological and cognitive injuries.* Santa Monica, CA: RAND Corporation.

Tiger, R. (2012). *Judging Addicts: Drug Courts and Coercion in the Justice System.* New York: New York University Press.

Walker, M. (2017). Mental health court money left out of state budget. *Argus Leader.* Retrieved June 1, 2017, from http://www.argusleader.com/story/news/crime/2017/05/02/mental-health-court-money-left-out-state-budget/101041622/

Wilson, D. B., Mitchell, O., & MacKenzie, D. L. (2006). A systematic review of drug court effects on recidivism. *Journal of Experimental Criminology, 2*(4), 459–487.

Chapter 7
Prison

What we've got here is failure to communicate. Some men you just can't reach. So you get what we had here last week, which is the way he wants it. Well, he gets it. I don't like it any more than you men.—Captain, Cool Hand Luke (Carroll & Rosenberg, 1967)

Prisons present a complex array of problems relating to mental health. Perhaps most notably, the prison environment is quintessentially *iatrogenic*—that is, the "treatment" for substance abuse and mental illness now comes commonly in the form of incarceration, and this treatment by incarceration is related to further sickness. In other words, the American prison environment is the antithesis of a therapeutic community. Argumentatively, this has resulted in part from a combination result of a recent "no-frills" movement (Finn, 1996) and a growing scarceness of resources. Regardless, prison is often awash in contraband (e.g., alcohol and drugs) and trauma-inducing situations (e.g., physical and sexual violence, administrative segregation and isolation, and missing the death of loved ones in the free world while incarcerated). The data provided in earlier sections of this text presented the daunting statistics behind these issues: just over half of state prisoners have a mental health problem; only one-third of state inmates with a mental illness receive treatment for their illness in prison; and a smaller proportion receives professional mental health therapy for their symptoms. It appears that change is occurring most slowly for prisons than any other segment of the criminal justice system, primarily due to persistent budgetary constraints dating back to at least 1998 (National Center on Addiction and Substance Abuse, 1998).

7.1 Know the Role

The seminal guide on substance abuse treatment in the criminal justice system disseminated by SAMHSA offers a handy section on treatment issues specific to prison (SAMHSA, 2014). While it relates to substance use and abuse, its content easily applies to broadly treatment issues in prison. In its prison section, the guide spends a great deal of time discussing the issues of inmate culture. It explains that, compared to jail inmates, those in prison are more likely to learn to adopt prison cultural mores as a means of survival. This path to an inmate identity is also honed by the pressures of the institution and by the common interactions between inmates with one another and with prison staff. Of particular importance, "there are many more people who are accustomed to the setting and who take the attitude that it is 'no big deal' [in prisons, as opposed to jails]....The hardened demeanor and 'macho' attitude adopted as part of the inmate culture can discourage offenders from participating in treatment...as [it] is a sign of 'weakness.'...[For example,] inmates who enroll in treatment are often characterized by other prisoners as too weak to 'handle their drugs' in the community" (SAMHSA, 2014, p. 193).

Thus, there often is a unique and complex dynamic in prisons that presents countervailing forces relating to mental health: (1) the prison environment is laden with the potential to develop mental health symptoms in otherwise healthy adults and, further, puts individuals with mental health diagnoses (particularly those with co-occurring disorders) at great risk of decompensating and falling deeper into their disease, and (2) the stigma of seeking help often becomes intensified in this setting, lending to a significant barrier to treatment. These forces become particularly significant when realizing that, after initial intake and medical screening and assessment, follow-up typically happens only when necessary—for example, upon a mental health crisis, overdose, contraband violation, or the like. Truly, in this setting, squeaky wheels (especially the loud ones) will get attended to, yet many prisoners become adept at hiding any signs that may raise suspicion that they need help. And further, if prison administrators sought to provide care to everyone who needs it, the cost of adequate care would quickly bankrupt all prison operations.

With this in mind, a prominent subsection in the guide is entitled "What treatment services can *reasonably* be provided in the prison setting" (emphasis added). The ideal program being advocated for is a "true" therapeutic community (TC) inside of the prison setting with complete segregation from the general population 24 h and 7 days a week for optimal success. TCs feature the integration of work (and/or educational or vocational programming), professional counseling, and a healthy (e.g., pro-social) community environment. Oftentimes, prison administrators must compromise by offering as many components of the TC as possible given the resources available. In many cases, TCs are composed of individuals who remain in general population who receive a schedule of programming to attend, which features the components of a TC—counseling, education classes, group therapy sessions, and so on. Further, self-help programming has become extremely popular in this framework due to its simplicity to set up and the few resources required to sustain them.

Yet, is it reasonable to assume that as long as prisons offer an array of services (such as these mentioned above) to their inmate population, regardless if they are driven to use them or not, that prisons are fulfilling their constitutional duties of inmate care? With often scarce resources and remote distancing from the community-based care system that can support jails and other forms of justice involvement (e.g., community corrections), the answer to "what treatment services can reasonably be provided in a prison setting?" is a pressing one.

7.1.1 Reaffirming Minimal Mental Health Care: The Epicenter (California) and the New Frontier (Alabama)

In May 2017, experts at the Stanford Law School teamed up with a California State Senator to publish a study entitled "When did prisons become acceptable mental healthcare facilities?" (Steinberg et al., 2015). This work begins by focusing on the rapid increase of mentally ill people in the California prison system after deinstitutionalization and then brings to light the current conditions of incarceration for individuals with mental illness, which specifically tend to result in longer sentences than those who have not been diagnosed with a mental illness. Steinberg et al. (2015) offer some glim statistics about the California State Prison System to drive their points home: as of 2017, 45% of inmates had been treated for *severe* mental illness in the past year (vastly more by proportion than other states as indicated by the data provided earlier in this text); the number of prison inmates with mental illness has doubled in the 15 years prior to the report's release (since 2000); and the average sentence for burglary is 30% longer for an individual with a mental health diagnosis compared to the average sentence for defendants without mental illness who are convicted of the same crime, leading the sentencing disparities among other crime types (e.g., robbery, assault, assault with a weapon, child molestation, second-degree murder, weapon charges, and drug sales—much like as seen within jails). Criminal justice reform in California was intended, in part, to ameliorate these issues—especially in light of *Coleman v. Wilson*. Yet, behavioral health disparities continue in California as evidenced by the number of inmates with mental illness gaining relief under new resentencing laws (e.g., Proposition 36) relative to inmates without mental health problems; that is, individuals with a mental health diagnosis have recently been denied resentencing relief relative to those who do not have a diagnosis.

These issues highlight the enduring nature of seeding institutional change. California has been at the forefront of a paradigm shift for prisoners with mental illness since 1994 with the formation of the California Department of Corrections and Rehabilitation Mental Health Services Delivery System (2009; see Table 7.1). Despite years of effort, defining model policies and procedures and promulgating them throughout the prison system, and engaging in best practices, significant slippage is still commonplace. For example, in the most recent complaint in *Coleman v. Brown* (2017)—which was originally filed as *Coleman v. Wilson* as discussed earlier in this text—the Department of Corrections was found to have not provided prompt care for inmates experiencing life-threatening psychiatric crises. Small and Pickoff-White (2017) offer additional details in their expose on the facts of the case; according to their investigative journalist accounting on the matter, over 25% of individuals needing critical care for life-threatening mental health crises experienced longer than a 24-h wait in February of 2017. Further, some inmates were placed on a waitlist, resulting in death in extreme cases. With the federal judge in this most recent flare up of *Coleman v. Brown* deciding in favor of the defendants, as a matter of law, this means that the bar for the minimal constitutional level of care in California has been reified by the standards set forth in Table 7.1.

Table 7.1 Summary of California Department of Corrections and Rehabilitation mental health program

Primary component	Program description
Crisis intervention	"A crisis is defined as a sudden or rapid onset or exacerbation of symptoms of mental illness, which may include suicidality or other aberrant behavior which requires immediate intervention. Crisis intervention is provided at all institutions to inmate suffering from a situational crisis or an acute episode of mental disorder. The first step in providing crisis intervention is adequate training for all institutional staff in the recognition of mental health crisis symptoms, a plan for immediate staff response, and procedures for referral to clinical staff. Custody and clinical staff cooperation is critical to ensure that an inmate in a mental health crisis is treated as soon as possible"
Comprehensive services	"The MHSDS (Mental Health Services Delivery System) offers comprehensive services and a continuum of treatment for all required levels of care. In addition to standardized screening and evaluation, all levels of care found in a county mental health system are represented in the CDCR MHSDS programs. All levels of care include treatment services provided by multiple clinical disciplines, and development and update of treatment plans by an Interdisciplinary Treatment Team (IDTT), which includes appropriate custody staff involvement"
Decentralized services	"Mental health services are geographically decentralized by making basic services widely available. All levels of care, except inpatient hospitalization, are available at most geographically-defined Service Areas. Case management and crisis intervention are provided at all institutions"
Clinical and administrative oversight	"In coordination with each institution, the CDCR Division of Correctional Health Care Services (DCHCS) and Division of Adult Institutions will continue to update standardized program policy and develop a system for monitoring delivery of program services. The CDCR shall develop an annual review schedule. A systemwide automated tracking and records system continues to evolve to support administrative and clinical oversight"
Standardized screening	"Access to mental health services is enhanced for all inmates through standardized screening of all admissions at Reception Centers. Standardized screening ensures that all inmates have equal and reliable access to services. The data generated by standardized screening provides the CDCR with necessary information to improve the assessment of mental health service needs. If screening reveals indicators of mental disorder, such as prior psychiatric hospitalization, current psychotropic medication, suicidality or seriously maladaptive behaviors, follow-up evaluation by a clinician shall determine the immediate treatment needs of the inmate. Early identification of an inmate's mental health needs will provide an appropriate level of treatment and promote individual functioning within the clinically least restrictive environment consistent with the safety and security needs of both the inmate-patient and the institution. Avoiding the utilization of more expensive services will aid in budget containment"

(continued)

Table 7.1 (continued)

Primary component	Program description
Prerelease planning	"This component of service, in conjunction with the Correctional Counselor's preparation of the CDCR 611, Release Program Study, focuses on preparing the seriously mentally disordered inmate-patient for parole. Its objective is to maximize the individual's potential for successful linkage and transition to the Parole Outpatient Clinic, or, if required, to inpatient services in the community or the Mentally Disordered Offender Program operated at the DMH facilities. In the case of paroling inmate-patients, this includes facilitating the work of the Parole and Community Services Division's Transitional Case Management Program"

Table 7.2 Summary of Steinburg, Mills, and Romano's three modest but significant proposals

Reform the way we sentence the mentally ill	• Take mental health into account at sentencing • Use the *preponderance of evidence* burden of proof when determining whether a defendant's crime was likely committed as a result of his/her mental illness – If proof positive, provide non-prison/noncustodial sentences, whenever possible, for nonserious and nonviolent offenses Note: the cost of such treatment is far less than the cost of incarceration
Provide meaningful treatment in prison	• Sentencing judge should be able to order treatment in the terms and condition of an offender's incarceration • Create an oversight court (consisting of judges and mental health professionals) to review cases to ensure proper and adequate services are being rendered to each inmate • Court continues to provide meaningful oversight of treatment throughout incarceration
Continue meaningful treatment after prison	• Provide evaluation before release of potential mental health needs in the community • Refer releasees to mental health centers with full access to health and treatment records

These revelations have disheartened many but continue to drive reformers to press for possible solutions for change. While California has consistently been working in good faith toward improvements in their system, Steinberg, Mills, and Romano describe "three modest but significant proposals" to give the state some momentum to realize some *real* gains in improvement. First, "reform the way we sentence the mentally ill," discusses taking a different look at crimes that are non-violent and nonserious that may have been committed as a result of the person's mental illness. Rather than incarceration, a judge could then sentence the person to treatment which is much more cost-effective. Second, prisons must begin to provide *meaningful* treatment for inmates while they are incarcerated. Last, treatment should continue to the point of release, during release, and must connect with meaningful treatment in the community (Table 7.2).

To accomplish these aims, Steinberg, Mills, and Romano identify that California will still need to invest greatly in additional infrastructure, such as mental health case managers for parolees, transitional housing for inmates returning back to the community, and expanded alternatives like mental health court (see Chap. 6). These investments, it should be noted, should arguably save the public money in the long run as the cost of incarceration tends to be the most exorbitant relative to any alternative. Yet, the radical component of Steinberg, Mills, and Romano's proposition—judicial oversight of the mental health services of prison inmates—may just be the missing ingredient California needs for lasting change.

Judicial oversight is not new. Traditionally, this comes in the form of federal consent decrees, which places prison facilities into receivership of the court—meaning that the oversight of operations rests with judges and/or the individuals they designate. This has happened with Louisiana's prisons in 1969 and with California's prisons as described above. Consent decrees have historically been wrought with political conflict and have pitted local administrators against their external overseers in a plainly adversarial approach. Steinberg, Mills, and Romano's special Mental Health Prison Oversight Court may hold a distinct advantage over consent decrees if this model can approach oversight in a non-adversarial way. That is, instead of a top-down approach to ensure oversight and compliance, a team-based approach that includes correctional, mental health, and legal professionals (all led by a judge) in shaping decision-making may prove beneficial.

While California has been at the forefront of these issues, Alabama's prisons have only begun this cycle by revealing its institutional failures to serve individuals with mental illness in the case *Braggs et al., v. Dunn* (2017). At the conclusion of the dramatic trial, Federal Judge Myron H. Thompson issued a 302-page ruling featuring an order for immediate- and long-term relief of the violation of Eighth Amendment rights of a class comprised of mentally ill inmates and to the Alabama Disabilities Advocacy Program. Specifically, Judge Thompson found that the defendants were at fault for:

> (1) Failing to identify prisoners with serious mental-health needs and to classify their needs properly; (2) Failing to provide individualized treatment plans to prisoners with serious mental-health needs; (3) Failing to provide psychotherapy by qualified and properly supervised mental-health staff and with adequate frequency and sound confidentiality; (4) Providing insufficient out-of-cell time and treatment to those who need residential treatment; and failing to provide hospital-level care to those who need it; (5) Failing to identify suicide risks adequately and providing inadequate treatment and monitoring to those who are suicidal, engaging in self-harm, or otherwise undergoing a mental-health crisis; (6) Imposing disciplinary sanctions on mentally ill prisoners for symptoms of their mental illness, and imposing disciplinary sanctions without regard for the impact of sanctions on prisoners' mental health; and (7) Placing seriously mentally ill prisoners in segregation without extenuating circumstances and for prolonged periods of time; placing prisoners with serious mental-health needs in segregation without adequate consideration of the impact on mental health; and providing inadequate treatment and monitoring in segregation.

Further, Judge Thompson carefully articulated the "abundant evidence presented in support of the Eighth Amendment claim" throughout his decision. Starting with the basics, Judge Thompson opined on the scope of the Alabama Department of Corrections population—about 19,500 men and women spread across 15 major facilities (one for women). Of this total population, evidence presented at trial suggested an approximate mental health caseload of 3400 inmates actively receiving some form of mental health treatment. A wealth of data from the Alabama Department of Corrections and its private (for-profit) mental health-care provider, MHM Correctional Services, Inc., would unveil minimal resources dedicated to providing mental health care when considering this level of need. Alabama's two mental health units providing treatment for its most severely ill have 346 male residential treatment beds and 30 stabilization unit beds (for acute mental health crises) and 30 female residential treatment beds and 8 stabilization unit beds for women—suggesting that the entire Alabama prison system can professionally handle only 38 mental health crises at any given time. Further, Alabama Department of Corrections only retains one governmental employee in a leadership position with mental health expertise; all other mental healthcare functions reside with the contracted service provider.

MHM Correctional Services, Inc., provided the following information to the court about their current staffing across the entire system: the Alabama contract includes a medical director (psychiatrist), mid-level managers (quality improvement manager and chief psychologist), 45 full-time mental health professional counselors/social workers, 4 psychiatrists and 8 certified registered nurse practitioners (who are qualified to diagnose, prescribe medication, and provide psychotherapy), 3 psychologists, and 3 registered nurses who supervise 40 licensed practical nurses (LPNs conduct mental health intake and monitor medication compliance and side effects). The testimony in conjunction with these scant resources led Judge Thompson to conclude that the low prevalence rates of mental illness in Alabama's prisons relative to other states were not due to high-quality mental health care in Alabama's prisons or that Alabama's prisons simply had fewer mentally ill inmates than other states. Many cases seemed to be slipping through the cracks at intake (poor supervision of minimally trained front-line staff) and evidence suggested that referrals for evaluation and treatment were often neglected. When mental illness is identified correctly, evidence suggested that follow-up care was haphazard with delays or cancellations of professional counseling largely due to a shortage of counselors or the correctional staff required to ensure safety. For inmates with severe mental illness, Judge Thompson found that the specialized mental health units operated as large segregation units with little evidence of counseling, programming, or time allotted for inmates to spend out of their cells. If hospitalization was deemed medically necessary, the Department of Corrections simply did not provide this level of care.

At trial, the Commissioner of the Alabama Department of Corrections candidly offered an explanation for these conditions—that the system is struggling with overcrowding in conjunction with understaffing. The dangerous effects of these shortcomings were on full display in court for 7 weeks. The trail began with a rousing start. A prisoner named Jamie Wallace shared painful testimony with the court, whose personal prison story was fraught with multiple suicide attempts with visible scars to show for it at trial. Mr. Wallace struggled to detail his experiences of not receiving any help from the system to the point when Judge Thompson had to order a recess and to continue testimony in chambers. After his story was detailed for the record, Judge Thompson excused Mr. Wallace and immediately ordered both sets of attorneys to provide him with a report on Mr. Wallace's mental condition and what was being done about it. In a twist, Mr. Wallace would hang himself 10 days later, thus laying bare the exact basis of the litigation at hand—the system was not just failing, it was in failure.

Highlights of the system failures that were detailed in the weeks after Mr. Wallace's testimony were jarring. For example, Judge Thompson described that correctional staff tended to "gamble" with prisoners lives as they did not have a good method of determining suicidality and had such few suicide-watch cells to work with. Further, the suicide-watch cells available were far from suicide-proof: visibility was poor for direct monitoring, cells still included places where one could tie off ligatures, and dangerous items that could easily aid in self-injury were still easily available. In fact, before the trial could conclude, another inmate (not related to the trial) had committed suicide adding to the steep uptick of prison suicides that has occurred in the last 2 years:

> [A]s explained earlier, the court had a close encounter with one of the tragic consequences of inadequate mental-health care during the trial. Over the course of the trial, two prisoners committed suicide, one of whom was named plaintiff Jamie Wallace. Prior to his suicide, defendants' expert, Dr. Patterson, concluded based on a review of Wallace's medical records that the care he received was inadequate. Dr. Haney, a correctional mental-health care expert, met Wallace months before his death, while he was housed in a residential treatment unit, and in his report expressed serious concerns about the care he was receiving. Wallace's case was emblematic of multiple systemic deficiencies. Wallace testified, and his records reflected, that mental-health staff did not provide much in the way of consistent psycho-therapeutic treatment, which is distinct from medications administered by nurses and cursory 'check ins' with staff. MHM clinicians recommended that he be transferred to a mental-health hospital, but ADOC failed to do so. His psychiatrist at the time of this death testified that the medically appropriate combination of supervised out-of-cell time and close monitoring when he was in his cell was unavailable due to a shortage of correctional officers. As a result, Wallace was left alone for days in an isolated cell in a treatment unit, where he had enough time to tie a sheet unnoticed; because his cell was not suicide-proof, he was able to find a tie-off point from which to hang himself.

From all accounts, American prison systems are often at a near or full crisis of mental health services, and this segment of the criminal justice system seems least able to promote change. While California has seen decades of progressive reform, many of these reforms have not been fully actualized primarily due to what has come to be a repeated mantra—resources and money. The story of the California and of Alabama will, no doubt, repeat itself in the future with other straining and failing systems—often being sparked by litigation. Each case will only serve to reinforce new standards to be promulgated across the county.

7.1.2 The Common Affront: Locking Someone in Ad Seg

As alluded to in the case of Alabama above, prisons often maintain controversial facilities called administrative segregation, often called "ad seg" or solitary confinement. These facilities are used in instances when an inmate is violent or has some behavioral issues as punishment, for behavior modification, or, primarily, for security reasons (e.g., an inmate is too dangerous for general population). In an article in the *National Prison Project Journal*, social psychologist Haney (1993; see also, Haney, 2003) describes the effects of administrative segregation as "psychologically destructive" and shown to produce social withdrawal, violence, and self-mutilation behaviors and suicidal ideation, leading to what he would later term a "social death." Individuals with preexisting mental illness are, in fact, at a greater risk of negative consequences (Haney, 2003). A comprehensive review of the literature confirms this; Smith (2006) finds evidence to support that solitary confinement impacts many prisoners negatively and substantially so. These impacts are moderated by duration of confinement, environmental factors, and characteristics of the prisoner. Yet, the negative impact endures for many.

Administrative segregation often involves an inmate being locked up for, at times, 23 h a day. Any recreational time outside of this cell is often suspended, or if it is allowed, it is often of a minimal duration. Imagine that scenario, being locked in a tiny cell for 23 h a day for days or weeks at a time. Additionally, many of the items an inmate may have in general population are not allowed or taken away when put into administrative segregation. Until recently, California prison was said to have used administrative segregation more so than any other state prison system—that is, until litigation forced its ways. In 2015, *Ashker v. Brown* was settled with promises to minimize the use of solitary housing units (nearly 3000 cells at that time) and put into place policies to ensure its proper use. It now seems that Alabama may be at the brink of needing similar intervention.

What is clear is that the use of administrative segregation provides fertile ground for litigation. Of particular note, Supreme Court Justice Anthony Kennedy made clear mention of his concerns with solitary confinement in a separate opinion on a case questioning the procedural rules of a criminal trial of a death row inmate:

> In response to a question, respondent's counsel advised the Court that, since being sentenced to death in 1989, Ayala has served the great majority of his more than 25 years in custody in "administrative segregation" or, as it is better known, solitary confinement....if his solitary confinement follows the usual pattern, it is likely respondent has been held for all or most of the past 20 years or more in a windowless cell no larger than a typical parking spot for 23 hours a day; and in the one hour when he leaves it, he likely is allowed little or no opportunity for conversation or interaction with anyone....It is estimated that 25,000 inmates in the United States are currently serving their sentence in whole or substantial part in solitary confinement, many regardless of their conduct in prison.
>
> The human toll wrought by extended terms of isolation long has been understood, and questioned, by writers and commenters. Eighteenth-century British prison reformer John Howard wrote "that criminals who had affected an air of boldness during their trial, and appeared quite unconcerned at the pronouncing sentence upon them, were struck with horror and shed tears when brought to these darksome solitary abodes." In literature, Charles Dickens recounted the toil of Dr. Manette, whose 18 years of isolation in One Hundred and Five North Tower, caused him, even years after his release, to lapse in and out of mindless state with almost no awareness or appreciation for time or his surroundings....Yet despite scholarly discussion and some commentary from other sources, the condition in which prisoners are kept simply has not been a matter of public inquiry or interest. To be sure, cases on prison procedures and conditions do reach the courts. See e.g., *Brown v. Plata*.... Sentencing judges, moreover, devote considerable time and thought to their task. There is no accepted mechanism, however, for them to take into account, when sentencing a defendant, whether the time in prison will be or should be served in solitary. So in many cases, it

is as if a judge had no choice but to say: "In imposing this capital sentence, the court is well aware that during the many years you will serve in prison before your execution, the penal system has a solitary confinement regime that will bring you to the edge of madness, perhaps to madness itself." Even if the law were to condone or permit this added punishment, so stark an outcome out not to be the result of society's simple unawareness or indifference....Over 150 years ago, Dostoyevsky wrote, "The degree of civilization in a society can be judged by entering its prisons." There is truth to this in our own time. (*Davis v. Ayala, 135 S.Ct. 2187, 2205*, 2015)

Thus, administrative segregation has been vaulted to the epicenter for mental health advocacy in recent years. Expect increased litigation forcing this issue, beginning in Alabama. Earlier efforts have resulted in settlements, not a summary judgment, which lacks the authority of case law. This absence of case may soon change as keenly noted by Justice Kennedy. While the Supreme Court has yet to hear a case specific to administrative segregation, the time for its review is becoming imminent.

7.1.3   A Local Case Study: Boston

The Boston Globe (2016) published an article in late 2016 discussing the perils of the criminal justice system in Massachusetts for individuals with mental illness and substance abuse. The article uses the story of an inmate Nick Lynch to discuss the struggles experienced by an incarcerated person in Boston. The year before, approximately 15,000 inmates were released from prisons and jails in Massachusetts. As with many of these stories, the problems worsen, and here more than half of those released inmates had a history of addiction, and more than one-third suffered from mental illness. This is not unlike many other states with inmates being released with diagnoses of one or both mental illness and/or substance abuse. Even more complicated, these diagnoses increase the likelihood of them being incarcerated again within 3 years.

The article brings up another great point stating, "The prison environment itself is a major obstacle to treatment: In a culture ruled by aggression and fear, the trust and openness required for therapy are exponentially harder to achieve." This statement is somewhat the epitome of the dilemma of crime and mental health. If prison is not the ideal environment for treatment and treatment is obviously needed, then why is the person being incarcerated? This is almost the exact same question posed by Steinberg, Mills, and Romano in California.

Further, as mentioned before, individuals are leaving prisons and jails in Massachusetts without the proper tools needed to be successful in society. Without medication, counseling, and support, those with mental illness and substance abuse issues are more likely to return to jail/prison. As one could imagine, the cost of incarceration can be expensive. Therefore, the idea of reducing recidivism would be beneficial to states and their Department of Corrections. In Massachusetts, the state would save $50,000 by lessening incarceration by just one inmate. This begs the question—what is the state doing to help released inmates? In Massachusetts, unfortunately, not much it seems. According to numbers from the state itself, more than 90% of the 6000 inmates who are estimated to have mental illness and released from prisons or jails received "little or no help" from the Department of Mental Health when trying to find treatment in the community.

Recently, the state has begun cutting the budget for mental health within the criminal justice system. This has largely come from reducing prescriptions provided to inmates by 35% between the years 2010 and 2015. The reduction of prescriptions can obviously be problematic for many reasons. The first group that was impacted was those receiving treatment for ADHD (attention-deficit hyperactive disorder); many others are slated to lose access to necessary treatment in the near future if these trends continue. The politics of prisons seem to be guided by crisis, as in until mental health reaches a critical mass; many systems seem to copasetic with the minimum effort needed to remain under the radar.

7.2 Example Progressive Programming and Program Elements

A change that has developed as a result of the increasing rates of incarceration and the already overcrowded prison systems is unique prison programming. Different states have been developing new way to fight recidivism and help inmates prepare for success outside of prison. These programs can receive some skepticism and resistance; some also have not yet developed to produce conclusive results. The good news, not unlike entrepreneurship, with creativity come success. The odds are that at least some of these particular programs will result in success.

7.2.1 Pen Pals, Inc.

As discussed earlier, a diverse array of innovations and alternative programming have occurred in recent years to address mental health issues in prison settings. Many of these alternatives seek to develop vocational and life skills as well as lessen the impact of the prison setting to inspire hope. From this movement, animal care programs have emerged to help inmates in this capacity. Although many programs of this nature exist across the country (and in many others), Pen Pals was developed out of a major natural disaster—Hurricane Katrina—which caused many animals to be without care as families evacuated their devastated homes. Dixon Correctional Institute (DCI), in Louisiana, is a medium-sized, medium-security prison that first of its kind to house a full animal shelter and clinic called Pen Pals.

In addition, Pen Pals features a fully operational clinic inside of the prison. Thus, not only can the rescued animals receive care and training from trustee inmates, they can also receive the medical care they need without having to be transported off-site. This serves to provide the trustees with an immersion experience of operating an animal shelter in the free world with the added mental health benefits of caring for animals in this capacity. Most importantly, Pen Pals continues to serve an important function for the local region as a no-kill shelter and is likely to receive more difficult cases than many shelters in the free world—an inept analogy to how some prisoners view their own lives or, at least, have done so in the past.

PEN PALS, INC. ANIMAL SHELTER AND ADOPTION CENTER

A NONPROFIT ORGANIZATION

ADOPTION GUARANTEED

TAX ID # 80-0646300

In 2005 Hurricane Katrina hit the state of Louisiana as a category 5 storm with maximum force. A conservative estimate reveals that over 50,000 animals were abandoned by their owners in New Orleans as they fled to safety. While their intentions were to return within days to retrieve their beloved pets, the animals were left trapped in homes or chained to fences, braving toxic waters, and 105-degree heat with no food or water. Hours became days as they waited to be rescued and reunited with their owners.

Rescuers were understaffed and overwhelmed by the scope of the problem and the time-critical nature of their effort. But motivated by compassion, relief came in the form of these few dedicated volunteers. Along with those volunteers, the Louisiana Department of Public Safety and Corrections, Dixon Correctional Institute (DCI) assisted by housing many of these abandoned animals. A makeshift animal clinic was set up, and inmates were trained in caring for animals of all types, shapes, and sizes. A vision was born out of tragedy.

In response to the events of this tragic and horrific situation, an agreement was made between the Humane Society of the United States (HSUS), the Louisiana State University School of Veterinary Medicine, and DCI, to establish a permanent and emergency temporary animal shelter on the grounds of the prison. The HSUS obtained a grant in the amount of $600,000 to fund the construction of the facilities. The permanent animal clinic (better known as Pen Pals, Inc., Dog and Cat Shelter and Adoption Center) provides comprehensive training for future veterinarians and promotes the rehabilitation of those incarcerated who are trained to assist.

Our belief is that tragedies will happen, but Pen Pals Inc. will be there with food and a leash in hand.

7.3 Pop Culture and Prison, New Links to Awareness

In addition to celebrities and other influential people, the mainstream media has taken to discussing the criminal justice system and mental health. Podcasts, television, as well as magazines and newspapers are covering the subjects to shed light on the system, including the flaws.

One of the more popular and raw television shows is *Lockup* on MSNBC. *Lockup* brings cameras into jails and prisons across the country to show the reality behind the bars. This reality includes interviews and insight from everyone involved from the wardens, corrections officers, support staff, and even inmates. The show has traveled to different areas and levels of prisons to show how things vary at each institution. Additionally, *Lockup* has specialty episodes to tackle some unique outliers like First Timers which covers individuals who are serving their first sentence in prison or jail, Special Investigation which covers the juvenile justice system, and Women Behind Bars which follows women in the system.

Despite the somewhat negative nature of the television show, the positive consequences are also very present. Each episode digs into the stories behind the inmates that make them human, rather than just a number. Background information, history, as well as interviews from staff and inmates create an overall picture of the tragedies that brought the person to jail or prison. This knowledge can be positive in that it helps to show the truth behind incarceration. Additionally, making the individual seem human allows for the compassion and empathy needed in some cases to aid in the rehabilitation of that person.

Lockup also provides footage and insight into the lives of mentally ill inmates. In the episode entitled Inside Wabash Valley Correctional Facility, the production staff interviews an inmate by the name of Joe Carr who is serving an 8-year sentence for robbery in this facility in Indiana. In this episode, the prison's psychologist is also interviewed where she discusses "shoe" or Special Housing Unit (SHU). At other facilities, this may be called administrative segregation. The brief interview with the psychologist and inmate paint the picture that mentally ill inmates are often put into the SHU after harming themselves. In Joe Carr's case, he swallowed ink pens in one incident and cut his leg open in another. He goes on to describe the feelings he experienced while cutting himself "when you're going through one of them phases, you don't even feel the pain...you don't even know you're doing it." Joe also describes his feelings of anger and using the acts of harming himself to "feel better." Joe was put into the SHU for hurting himself from we describe as being antisocial. After serving his time in the SHU, he was then put back into general population at the prison but describes the repeating cycle of self-harm. After several cycles of going to the SHU for harming himself, and then returning to general population with no success, Joe was then evaluated and diagnosed with bipolar disorder and transferred to the residential treatment unit (RTU). The interview concludes with Joe's own perspective about life after prison when he states "this is all you know...you're used to what, a population of 1200 people. Then, they turn you back into society of billions of people. Are you ready for it?"

The episode of Lockup featuring Joe Carr is just one of many that feature a person in the criminal justice system who is mentally ill. On a societal level, this leads to questions and controversy. What amount of harm is done to the individual for the repeated cycle of self-harm and punishment in the SHU? For those discussing the fiscal consequences, his repeated acts of self-harm resulted in many medical exams, most of which resulted in surgeries. How much of a burden does that put on the system? How could the burden and harm on the inmate be avoided? How could the burden on the system be avoided as well?

Another example of the portrayal of the criminal justice system and mentally ill inmates involves the controversy behind the 10-episode Netflix original *Making a Murderer*. *Making a Murderer* is dubbed a "real-life thriller" by Netflix and a true crime documentary by other sources. This series was filmed over a 10-year period following Steven Avery, a man who had been recently released from prison after serving 18 years for rape. At the beginning of the series, he had just been released after being exonerated with DNA evidence from his original 32-year charge. Despite this happy outlook, the series quickly takes a turn to Steven then being accused of murder. He, along with his nephew, Brendan Dassey, was arrested for the rape and murder of Teresa Halbach and sentenced to life in prison.

The controversy infiltrates this story in many ways including police corruption, evidence tampering, and questionable ethics. As it relates here, the mental health of both men, Steven Avery and Brendan Dassey, was called into question. As this book is being written, there is still development in this case bringing to light relevant issues regarding the treatment of individuals with mental health concerns by the system. It appears that we are at a moment in which coverage of mental health issues is beginning to increase across platforms, medium, and by source.

7.4   Out-of-the-Box Innovations

There are some positive trends in regard to prisons in other parts of the world. In recent years, The Netherlands has seen such a decline in crime that they have actually been closing their prisons. The stereotype in the United States is that prisoners serve "hard time" while in prison and they will be remorseful of the crimes they committed. The assumption is that the tough times of prison create a situation in which the person learns to not want to return to prison. It is somewhat of a behavior modification process. If the conditions inside prison are worse than outside or home, the idea is that a person who commits crimes would then not want to return to prison. The person would then want to do all possible to avoid another sentence, like changing their behaviors and no longer committing crime. The problem with this assumption and argument is that it just does not work in America. If this were the case, most prisons would be useless and empty at this point. The view of using prison as a form of punishment has really only led to an increase of inmates currently in prison as well as an increase in those that return for repeated offenses.

Prisons around the world are trying different approaches within their prisons to show the possibility that the alternative to "hard time" works better to combat recidivism. Rather than using a prison and sentence as punishment, other countries are working toward a prison sentence as a time for change and reform where the person can learn other skills to use after time served as well as maintain their support system with family and their mental health. In Suomenlinna Prison, often referred to as the "open prison," inmates in Finland do not see barbed wire and large fences around the grounds of the prison. The prison director Tapio Iinatti describes the thought process behind the way this prison is set up: "The main idea here is to prepare the inmates for release into the community. It doesn't make sense for an inmate to be in a closed prison for, say, 6 years and to suddenly enter civilian life. We also offer rehabilitation for people who have had problems related to alcohol, drugs or mental illness. And in any case, it's not so easy to be here."

Another prison described as using a humane approach is Halden Prison in Norway. Halden Fengsel has been dubbed "the world's most humane maximum-security prison." This nickname was given for many reasons including the lack of a security fence. Halden does not have the typical razor wire, electric, or tall fence surrounding, and yet prisoners have not tried to escape. Much like Finland, Norway looks at the time inside the prison as preparation for life outside, and there are both no life sentences and death penalties. This is a stark contrast to most American prisons, including that the maximum sentence for crimes is 21 years. The Norwegian Correctional Service has the motto "better out than in" to say that they ensure a person leaves prison improved. In order to do this, the government uses resources to provide a social support system, a job, and housing. Additionally, Norway provides education, health care, and a pension for all citizens. The interesting part of this is that at the time of this article in 2015, Norway spent about $93,000 per inmate per year on incarceration as compared to $31,000 in the United States. Taking this into consideration, the United States incarcerates on average 700 people per 100,000, while Norway is about 75 per 100,000. The United States could save nearly $45 billion per year if they were to also take on this practice.

> Norway banned capital punishment for civilians in 1902, and life sentences were abolished in 1981. But Norwegian prisons operated much like their American counterparts until 1998. That was the year Norway's Ministry of Justice reassessed the Correctional Service's goals and methods, putting the explicit focus on rehabilitating prisoners through education, job training and therapy. A second wave of change in 2007 made a priority of reintegration, with a special emphasis on helping inmates find housing and work with a steady income before they are even released. Halden was the first prison built after this overhaul, and so rehabilitation became the underpinning of its design process. Every aspect of the facility was designed to ease psychological pressures, mitigate conflict and minimize interpersonal conflict.

It seems that cost is *the* impetus for change in the United States. In times of recession, the pressure to change seems to reach a tipping point. While there appear to be some radically progressive policies in countries such as Norway, it seems that there may be room to learn from other countries' willingness to spend money lavishly on rehabilitative practices. In other words, countries such as Norway may offer the United States the ability to learn which rehabilitative processes and programs are promising, for which target population, and be able to consider cost-effectiveness before investing.

7.5   Conclusion

Prisons tend to get the least amount of attention in regard their mental health practices. When considering that near 95% of the American prison population will return back to the community at some point, this lack of attention is slowing changing. Currently, administrative segregation and intake are notable exceptions—there has been an array of interest in these two issues in recent years that have a growing research base. Many other facets of inmate mental health remain unclear, ill-defined with aging data, and are given tacit attention relative to jail inmate and jail inmate reentry, in particular.

While research activity and programs begin to grow, it seems that litigation will continue to define the critical issues that prison administrators will need to address into the near and distant future. Expect an increase in litigation in the upcoming years to continue to refine the definition of constitutionally accepted levels of care in prisons, particularly as it relates to administrative segregation.

References

Ashker v. Brown. 4:09-CV-05696. United States District Court, N.D. California.
Boston Globe. (2016). *There may be no worse place for the mentally ill people to receive treatment than prison*. Retrieved June 1, 2017, from https://apps.bostonglobe.com/spotlight/the-desperate-and-the-dead/series/prisons/
Braggs v. Dunn. 2:14CV601-MHT. United States District Court, M.D. Alabama.
California Department of Corrections and Rehabilitation. (2009). *Mental health services delivery system*. Retrieved June 1, 2017, from http://www.cdcr.ca.gov/DHCS/docs/Mental%20Health%20Program%20Guide.pdf
Carroll, G. & Rosenberg, S. (1967). *Cool Hand Luke [Motion Picture]*. USA: Warner Bros.
Coleman v. Brown. 938 F.Supp.2d 955.
Coleman v. Wilson. 912 F.Supp. 1282.
Davis v. Ayala. 135 S.Ct. 2187, 2205.
Finn, P. (1996). No-frills prisons and jails: A movement in flux. *Federal Probation, 60*(3), 35–44.
Haney, C. (1993). Infamous punishment: The psychological consequences of isolation. *National Prison Project Journal, 8*(2):3–7.
Haney, C. (2003). *The psychological impact of incarceration: Implications for post-prison adjustment. Prisoners once removed: The impact of incarceration and reentry on children, families, and communities*. Retrieved June 1, 2017, from http://webarchive.urban.org/UploadedPDF/410624_PyschologicalImpact.pdf
National Center on Addiction and Substance Abuse. (1998). Addiction treatment in prison will reduce crime, save billions of tax dollars, says CASA report. *News Briefs*. Retrieved January 3, 2017, from www.ndsn.org/jan98/prisons1.html
Steinberg, D., Mills, D., & Romano, M. (2015). When did prisons become acceptable mental healthcare facilities? *Stanford Law School*. Retrieved June 1, 2017, from https://law.stanford.edu/wp-content/uploads/sites/default/files/publication/863745/doc/slspublic/Report_v12.pdf
Small, J., & Pickoff-White, L. (2017). Judge threatens to fine California prisons for delayed mental health treatment. *KQED*. Retrieved June 1, 2017, from https://ww2.kqed.org/news/2017/04/20/judge-threatens-to-fine-california-prisons-for-delayed-mental-health-treatment/
Smith, P. S. (2006). The effects of solitary confinement on prison inmates: A brief history and review of the literature. *Crime and justice, 34*(1), 441–528.
Substance Abuse and Mental Health Services Administration. (2014). *Treatment improvement protocol 44: Substance abuse treatment for adults in the criminal justice system*. Retrieved June 1, 2017, from https://www.ncbi.nlm.nih.gov/books/NBK64137/pdf/Bookshelf_NBK64137.pdf

Chapter 8
Release and Reentry

> You may not control all the events that happen to you, but you can decide not to be reduced by them.—Maya Angelou

Reentering society can be one of the most difficult obstacles a justice-involved person can face in their lifetime. All facets of one's life change instantly upon release from prison. The controlled environment of a prison facility allows an inmate to create a routine and have stability in relationships and daily activities. A person behind bars knows exactly when the next phone call to a loved one will take place, the next meal, activity time, etc. These things are no longer regular, or controllable, on the outside in society. Often times, individuals struggle in the chaos that exists outside the prison walls. The best chance for success involves planning and preparing for those changes and learning coping skills to handle them in a healthy manner. Unfortunately, this is not always realistic on many levels. The most comprehensive evaluation of prisoner (e.g., excludes jail inmate) recidivism available reveals that 30.4% of prisoners return to prison within a year, 43.3% return in 2 years, 49.7% return in 3 years, 52.9% return in 4 years, and 55.1%—over half—return in 5 years (Durose, Cooper, & Snyder, 2014). If one simply looks at prisoners being arrested after release, many of which require stays in jail as arrestees await criminal justice processing, the statistics are even bleaker: 43.4% are arrested within a year, 59.5% within 2 years, 67.8% within 3 years, 73.0% in 4 years, and 76.6% in 5 years. Further, a large proportion of individuals rearrested after release from prison are drawn back into the criminal justice system (including jails and diversion programs), typically through a sanction by the court and/or by probation/parole violations and revocations. Ultimately, the plan to reduce contact with the criminal justice system exists within the transition planning before, in the moment of, and after release from incarceration, with the courts and probation/parole being key players in the reentry movement. This needs to include both jails and prisons, but importantly, it needs to include a mental health element more substantial than just attending to substance abuse treatment issues.

J. Hector, D. Khey, *Criminal Justice and Mental Health*,
https://doi.org/10.1007/978-3-319-76442-9_8

8.1   They're Back! But They Aren't Poltergeist: Stigma Revisited

Think about reentry akin to many common "phases" of one's life span—the transition from high school to college (e.g., emerging adulthood), the transition from college to the work force (e.g., adulthood), the transition of living with a spouse and/or parenthood, etc. Now, think about how complex these transition periods would be after a significant negative stretch in a person's life. Leaving jail or prison and going back to "the real world," and even leaving a substance abuse treatment facility or mental health setting, is often daunting. All of these transitions can be wrought with anxiety-provoking situations, such as the fear of the unknown or, simply, the fear of failure and of the implications of such. This time frame creates a very vulnerable space for many people—feelings of uncertainty and pressure seem omnipresent in an already unstable time.

The key problem to success is revealed when one realizes that this tricky transition period is often complicated by past and current experiences of trauma. One well-done study on prevalence rates of trauma experienced by male prisoners details the extent of this issue—44.7% inmates were exposed to physical trauma as a minor, 31.5% as an adult, and 25.1% as both a minor and as an adult. These rates exclude sexual trauma—10.9% of inmates were exposed to sexual trauma as a minor, 4.5% as an adult, and 3.7% as both a minor and adult (Wolff & Shi, 2012). One last rate to keep in mind, those who have experienced both physical and sexual trauma—9.6% of inmates experienced both as a minor. The prevalence rates of trauma exposure are even more staggering for incarcerated women. For both men and women, the vast majority of these experiences remain untreated, and many men remain undiagnosed to the mental illnesses these traumatic experiences can have a role in triggering. Now, imagine entering an important transitional period in your life with these confounding issues weighing on you.

The vast majority of people going to prison are nonviolent and are inevitably going to come back to the community—and many do not tend to come back "better" at this time. Reentry is a *normal* event as 100 million American adults (about one-third of working age adults) are cataloged in state criminal history systems versus roughly 69 million American adults 25 and older having bachelor's degrees; and 6.6% of Americans born in 2001 are estimated to serve time in a prison at some point in their lives (BJA, 2014; Bonczar, 2003; Ryan & Bauman, 2016). Many more Americans have experienced incarceration in their lifetimes, either jail or prison—the exact amount remains unknown as available jail data is unable to reveal this figure. The point is that while reentry is normal in the sense that it is common, the label of being an ex-offender remains potently stigmatic. This label potentially intensifies with complications of mental health. American criminal justice is revising its approach as a result. Yet, those with mental illness are likely to have continued problems as the capacity to deal with high-risk individuals begins to grow and expand.

Maruna and LeBel (2003) aptly discuss the role of stigma in the reentry context as the criminal justice system begins to reshape the paradigm of corrections to (re-) include social services. In this new approach they call the strengths-based paradigm, Maruna and LeBel point out that criminal justice practitioners are pushed to ask what positive contributions inmates can offer instead of the old question of what deficits people in the system may have:

> In the reentry context, the strengths *narrative* begins with the assumption that ex-convicts are stigmatized persons, and implicitly that this stigma (and not some internal dangerousness or deficit) is at the core of what makes ex-convicts likely to re-offend....[This push towards criminal involvement] is clearly based on a labeling/social exclusion story - on which, of course, the very idea of "reintegration" is also premised. Johnson (2002, p. 319) writes, 'released prisoners find themselves "in" but not "of" the larger society' and 'suffer from a presumption of moral contamination.' To combat this social exclusion, the strengths paradigm calls for opportunities for ex-convicts to make amends, demonstrate their value and potential, and make positive contributions to their communities. (Maruna & LeBel, 2003, p. 97; also quoting Johnson, 2002)

It is through these opportunities of contributing to society that can begin the de-labeling process for stigmatized people, part of what Maruna calls "making good" (Maruna, 2001). The us in the us-versus-them paradigm can begin publicly recertifying and reclassifying an individual as returning back into the group, in a very tribal sense. This reciprocal relationship can offer the stigmatized person hope while also showing the public that the ex-offender is worthy of support and investment as they reintegrate back into the community (Maruna & LeBel, 2003).

8.2   How Are We Dealing with It?

Generally speaking, there are three broad approaches to reentry: (1) jail to community reentry, (2) prison to community reentry, and (3) reentry court. Before explaining each approach, it is first important to note here that the existing literature on what works in reentry converge on this point: holistic services designed to address individual offender needs that begin prior to release and continue in an aftercare situation are most apt to be successful (Wolf, 2011; Lowenkamp, Latessa, & Holsinger, 2006; Osher, 2006; Osher, 2007; Petersilia, 2004; Pearson & Lipton, 1999; Travis & Visher, 2005). This consistent finding is, in part, driving previously isolated and siloed pieces of the criminal justice and mental health systems to begin collaborations and seek broader partnerships. If a true continuum of care is to be devised to ensure successful reentry (e.g., not returning back to prison, encouraging pro-social and healthy lifestyles, and self-sufficiency), communication and coordination is paramount.

One of the first tasks of these emerging partnerships often becomes trying to figure out how to maximize returns on extremely limited resources. The validated risk and need screening and assessment tools described in Chap. 5 become critical to accomplish this goal. When used properly, these tools not only match which evidence-based programs and services will help each individual returning back to the community; they can help prioritize available resources—particularly the most intensive (and often the most costly) ones—to those who are at most in critical need. Yet, the goal for each approach should be to begin services as early on, as well as during the transition back to the community, and continue these services to ensure successful reintegration.

8.2.1   Jail to Community Reentry

Jail-based reentry can often be tricky due to the short amount of time jail professionals have to work with. Improvement in mental health outcomes can only be realized through an ability to track data on inmate connectivity to services, whether in jail or back in the community. Without such data, it may be impossible to detect the moments people fall through the cracks of the system, often only to inevitably return to an emergency room, the jail, or the medical examiner or coroner's office. In 2008, Jeff Mellow and colleagues authored an extensive *Toolkit for Reentry* for jail administrators, which continues to offer terrific structure for reentry for jail inmates depending on length of stay in jail and level of risk and need. These best practices have not changed much since, and many jails are striving to improve. Changes are occurring slowly as the focus on jail administrators continues to be to provide a constitutional jail—as a result, many of these improvements may be construed as above and beyond instead of standard practice at this time.

The toolkit begins by describing four discrete tracks, or paths, of jail inmates. Track one refers to the easiest swath of jail inmates, those with low needs and/or have a very short stay ahead of them in jail. These individuals should receive easy-to-use resource guide to assist them in the reentry process. Services such as help finding housing, employment, substance abuse treatment and support, legal aid, and so on should be included and presented on a basic reading level. While the ideal goal of jails should be to screen and assess everyone coming through booking, it may not be possible to do so in every case depending on timing of release, personnel available to screen and assess, and volume of individuals going through the booking process. To enhance the ability to capture individuals needing services in this track, jail administrators may provide training to their booking staff to give them a keener eye of identifying signs and symptoms of mental illness and substance abuse. Additionally, these inmates should receive information on available government benefits, especially Medicaid, as Medicaid is often the primary provider of mental health and substance abuse treatment for vulnerable individuals. In a perfect world, data systems would be set up to allow each individual to be tracked from jail and into the local treatment system (and vice versa). While achieving this ideal may be daunting, it does not have to be. For example, some treatment providers in the New Orleans metropolitan area have linked up with local jails to receive an electronic roster of individuals being booked through the jail on a daily basis. While arduous, providers have tasked staff with monitoring these rosters for "frequent flyers" or known clients to be able to intervene quickly and provide transitional care as promptly as possible.

Track two is tailored to inmates with medium needs or to those who may just have a longer stay (but have not been identified as high needs). These individuals are able to be successfully screened and assessed. If they are identified as low needs, they are referred to Track one to receive helpful information and resource guides. On faith, it is assumed that these individuals have the wherewithal to guide their own path forward, often with success. At minimum, there is no (or minimal) indication of the potential barriers to successful reentry as revealed by screening and assessment. Inmates in Track two should also receive all of the helpful resource materials, but further, they should also receive an individualized reentry plan to give some structure of activities for these individuals returning back to the community. The best practice here is for jail practitioners to create these reentry plans *in collaboration with* the inmates. Together, staff and inmates can discuss issues with family relationships, housing, health care, mental health, substance abuse needs, and so on. At the end of this process, each inmate will receive an easy-to-follow self-guided plan to aid in their transition back into the community. Appointments with community service providers may be necessary; however, it will be up to each Track two inmate to ensure these appointments are made on their own. At times, some assistance is provided; however, follow-up by jail staff is rare as it is seen as unnecessary. Again, this is where data tools become critical in case local partnerships find that many people in Track two are not getting the services they need after they are released from jail. An ideal reentry plan should, at minimum, address the domains below in Table 8.1.

Track three inmates are those whose risk and needs assessment scores place them as high needs, but not necessarily high risk. In these cases, jail staff are instructed to replicate Track two services while increasing care by coordinating services in the community and having outside partners begin to collaborate on services as early as possible after release. Here, appointments are made prior to release and follow-ups are done to ensure connectivity to services. Track four inmates are those who are high risk and high needs; due to their obvious need for priority, jail staff and community partners often collaborate to begin services while incarcerated, as early as possible, and as intensive as possible. These individuals require immediate access to services, whenever possible with vigilant supervision to ensure compliance and the best chances of success. These individuals should receive concierge-like services to connect them with potential benefits or resources that can aid in their reentry, particularly Medicaid and health care. Further, best practices dictate that a case manager be assigned to them, at minimum, immediately upon release.

While these tracks offer guidance to jail administrators, it is important to recognize that these tracks intend to only offer broad structure to ideal concepts of handling reentry in the industry. In other words, it is intended that these tracks are modified and customized for each jail to match and meet its needs (specifically, the needs of its inmates and target populations). The *Reentry Toolkit* also offers several examples of jurisdictions that have made these customizations: Travis County, Texas; New York City, New York; Davidson County, Tennessee; Essex County, New Jersey; Montgomery County, Maryland; and so on.

Table 8.1 Domains to be addressed by written reentry plans (Mellow, Mukamal, LoBuglio, Solomon, & Osborne, 2008)

Domain	Description
Mental health care	Attend to the proximal and distal mental health concerns; includes substance abuse
Medical care	Attend to the proximal and distal physical health concerns; includes tuberculosis, hepatitis, and HIV screening and care
Medications	Ensure continuity of prescription drugs
Appointments	Ensure that appointments/referrals with service providers in the community are made, reminders are created, and follow-ups occur
Housing	Devise a housing plan in partnership with the returning individual, ensure its viability, and evaluate the potential stability it can offer
Employment	Connect the returning individual to an employment opportunity and/or employment services specialists; alternatively, or in addition, connect the returning individual to education/vocational development specialists
Substance/alcohol abuse	Directly connect returning individuals with resources in the community to support recovery and continued sobriety
Health care/benefits	Offer services or a referral to services that can offer health benefit enrollment assistance, primarily Medicaid
Income/benefits	Offer services or a referral to services that can offer government benefit enrollment assistance such as disability, food stamps, etc.
Food/clothing	Offer services or a referral to services that offer food pantries, free or low-cost clothing, and similar assistance
Transportation	Connect returning individuals to low-cost and no-cost transportation options in the community
Identification/driver's license	Partner with local agencies responsible for government identification and be able to provide returning individuals with an official form of ID; try to aid in restoring driver's license privileges, whenever possible
Life skills	Train returning individuals in life skills such as budgeting, parenting, etc.
Family/children	Offer aid and education in regard to child support compliance, family reunification, and so on
Emergency contacts	Arm returning individuals with a list of emergency contacts in the community in case they need emergency assistance
Referral services/court dates	Connect returning individuals with local agencies for potential services/care as well as inform him/her of impending court dates and obligations
Summary, jail-based services provided	Provide an easy-to-read summary of all of the services, treatment, and care given to an individual while in jail as a reference and to aid the future provision of care

8.2.1.1 An Example of an Early Adopter: Hampden County Sheriff's Department

A prime example of a multifaceted, jail-based reentry program fully integrated in a wider, comprehensive public and mental health system lies in Ludlow, Massachusetts (Solomon, Osborne, LoBuglio, Mellow, & Mukamal, 2008). This story of Hampden County begins in the early 1990s when a concern was raised by the local health clinic professionals when they reflected on their data of missed appointments—it turns out that many patients' missing appointments simply could not make it in because they were held up somewhere else. That somewhere else happened to often be the local jail ran by the Hampden County Sheriff. In the wake of these concerns, the sheriff at the time directed his staff to allow health-care provider entry into the jail in order to provide care—care that was not present in any substantial capacity before this point. Coordination of efforts and justice-mental health (and public health) collaboration was initiated. Shortly after these provider partners started working in the jail, they further realized that a majority of the clients they were seeing day in and day out all were returning to four ZIP codes. With this in mind, the local partnerships sought to target these four ZIP codes by contracting services with the existing community centers there, thereby establishing a reliable continuity of care from incarceration into release.

In 2015, the Hampden County Sheriff's Department reported that continued development of these systems with local partners, now called the After Incarceration Support Systems (AISS), has been utilized by over 17,500 clients. Interestingly, the vast majority of individuals seen by AISS are participating voluntarily, substantially more than individuals on probation and parole—this insinuates a level of success. Beyond insinuation, local analysis shows a substantial reduction of recidivism. These results should also be attributed to the systemic changes to jail policies and procedures to optimize the opportunities of connecting inmates with the services that they need. Upon introspection, jail administration realized that about 90% of their inmates were abusing some form of substance, 87% were male, 40% were under 30 years old, 57% were minorities, 73% were unemployed when they were arrested, 48% did not have a high school diploma or its equivalent, 40% have a mental health problem(s), 55% reported that they did not have positive family support, and about 40% did not have a stable home to return to. Over the years, the jail has perfected its solution; to address these problems, the jail has built the capacity to deploy several evidence-based screening and assessment tools (e.g., Level of Service Inventory (LSI-R), Texas Christian University Drug Screen (TCUDS—a tool in the public domain), the CAGE Assessment, the Clinical Institute Withdrawal Assessment for Alcohol Scale (CIWA-AR), and the Clinical Opiate Withdrawal Scale (COWS)), offer withdrawal protocols, provide treatment services for all levels of risk and need internally or via its partners, and have conceived their role differently, steeped in a public health model:

> In Hampden County (Massachusetts), the sheriff's department has developed classification matrices for violent offenders, nonviolent offenders, and those serving mandatory sentences that chart out their time at each security level by sentence length. For example, a nonviolent

offender serving 18 months who complies with his reentry plan and demonstrates excellent institutional conduct will spend 10 days at medium security, 1 month at minimum security, 2 months at secure prerelease, and the balance (or less) on day reporting (living at home and reporting regularly to the day reporting center). The department's matrices are adjusted regularly on the basis of population levels at the facility and prove to be an effective tool to prevent jail overcrowding and to place individuals at security levels that will allow them to work and receive community-based treatment prior to release. Thus, the classification needs of the institution and the reentry needs of individuals are both served by this process. (Solomon et al., 2008, p. 31)

Further, the collaboration has led to the development of a reentry crown of the local system—the AISS One-Stop Reentry Center—perfectly located for broad community impact in the Mason Square neighborhood. At this center, case manager aids in connecting individuals with intensive "wrap" services, all provided on-site by its community partners. These services include early recovery support, health and mental health services, psychiatric services, parenting groups for men and women, male violence interventions, targeted health care for homeless individuals, intensive outpatient services, job support groups, per-led support groups, writing groups (for women), food bank services and assistance with the SNAP application process, anger management, housing support, educational services, employment services, employment retention support, mentorship, resource and support group for sex offenders, support groups in Spanish, and a women's only support group. With all of these services, in addition to other sites of support such as the Substance Abuse Unit inside of the Hampden County Jail, the substance abuse services for women at the Western Massachusetts Regional Women's Correctional Center, and the Western Massachusetts Correctional Alcohol Center (which also specializes in opioid treatment as 65% of individuals in this setting have histories of opioid abuse), individuals across the risk and needs spectrum are almost certain to receive tailored services that so critically begin during incarceration and stick with the ideal of treating an individual in the least restrictive setting, in this case, as soon as possible (Fig. 8.1).

These innovations have spread across the country: San Bernardino, Snohomish County, New York City, Suffolk County, Montgomery County, Atlantic County, Norfolk County, Douglas County (OR), Miami-Dade County (FL), Maricopa County (AZ), Westchester County (NY), and Essex County offer stellar examples of how others are finding solutions that work best for the local community.

8.2.2   Prison to Community Reentry

Due to the massive numbers of individuals already in prison of which an estimated 95% are bound to return back into the community at some point, prisons are increasing their capacity to install robust reentry programming before release as well. Prisoners may face considerably more challenges simply due to the length of their stay away from society. Pro-social relationships (e.g., family) may further be strained, financial obligations may falter (e.g., forcing a repossession of a car), debts may loom, and issues with reinstating a driver's license may grow complicated (e.g.,

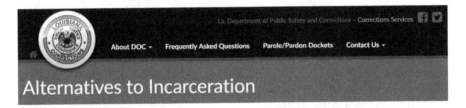

Fig. 8.1 Infographic on Day Reporting Centers in Louisiana, courtesy of the Louisiana Department of Public Safety and Corrections

outstanding traffic tickets may force heavy fines or further legal trouble). Additionally, inmates with health conditions may not receive optimal care behind bars and/or prison may place them at increased risk of contracting blood–borne pathogens, human immunodeficiency virus, hepatitis, syphilis, gonorrhea, chlamydia, and tuberculosis; they will, however, receive a level of care protected by the constitution (Bick, 2007).

In light of these challenges, the robust reentry processes described for inmates returning from jail must be further refined to be able to produce successful results. This can become daunting given the sheer relative volume of individuals on schedule to be released across the country. Some correctional leaders are also exploring options for an enhanced, step-down release that features the removal of inmates from a prison setting and places them into other facilities that may offer the sort of reentry process installed at the Hampden County Jail. That is, with excellent conduct and lower security risk (e.g., risk and need), inmates may benefit from more independence and freedom while still incarcerated in the form of minimum security housing, work release, and perhaps even release back to the community with day reporting requirements (and, most likely, an electronic monitoring bracelet).

8.2.2.1   A Gem in the Rough: Lafayette Parish Sheriff Reentry

In Louisiana, where robust reentry programs remain quite scarce, the Lafayette Parish Sheriff's Office (2011) has been able to replicate successful reentry models in Georgia and Minnesota and customize it for the local area. At this time, many Louisiana prisoners are slated to receive 100 hours of life skills programming, be given a 90-day prerelease packet with helpful resources, and be placed on community supervision. After screening potential Department of Corrections inmates for eligibility (risk needs screening and assessment, physical and mental health assessments, security level determination, trades and skill level assessment, and verified local area resident), the Lafayette Parish Sheriff's Office Reentry Model operates in phases.

Upon admittance to the program, an inmate gets placed at the community corrections campus—a new facility solely dedicated to reentry. A case plan is developed with a case manager and Phase I begins. Services in Phase I include manualized Moral Reconation Therapy led by trained personnel, mental health services, educational services, vocational training (forklift certification and custodial management certification are available at this time), drug and alcohol treatment, group meetings, a life skills curriculum, anger management, financial planning and employment preparation, assistance with obtaining identification, and family reunification. For higher-risk inmates, Phase II will be required after the completion of Phase I. This phase includes relapse prevention, Courage to Change, anger management, continued educational services, and more. For low-risk inmates, the transitional work program becomes available after the completion of Phase I and includes employment and educational services as well as aftercare (i.e., when these individuals are not working out in the community). Everyone at all security levels will have a 90-day prerelease program which features housing and employment assistance, financial planning, medical referrals, family reunification, and help obtaining clothing, benefits (food, disability, health care, etc.), and transportation and help create linkages to community resources. At successful completion, each inmate is transferred to community supervision and is released.

It is the hope that individuals at all risk levels receive the services they need for success. Further, the sheriff and the local area partnerships continue to explore gaps in care and better ways to ensure a continuum of care. Internal assessment shows improvement in short-term outcomes; yet, jail administration continues to look for improvements, particularly in available vocational training that links up with well-paying and needed jobs in the community.

8.2.3   Reentry Court

A concept attributed to Jeremy Travis (2000), Reentry Court is an intensive court-supervised program catering to the rehabilitation of persistently justice-involved offenders often with substance use disorders and mental health histories. Further, these individuals may exhibit symptoms stemming from complex trauma that may surmount in a post-traumatic stress disorder diagnosis or something similar (e.g., unspecified trauma and stressor-related disorder; Miller & Khey, 2017). Most reentry courts across the nation have been modeled off of the evidence base and structure of specialty courts, such as adult drug court, but not always; reentry courts refer to any programming featuring release from prison with judicial oversight. This oversight has been explained as an essential feature to ensure compliance and to prevent failure (e.g., the return to prison) by constructively using sanctions to modify behavior and to intervene when those released from prison begin to go down a wrong path or relapse. Further, court supervision gives the ability to intervene and therapeutically respond to problems that arise that may be precursors to triggers, relapse, and reoffending. In particular, a large share of focus has been spent on employment as research has uncovered that success in this domain is paramount to success in the transition back to society. In 2015, Cook and his colleagues point out:

> ...[O]ne potential limitation of previous efforts to improve the employment outcomes of re-entering prisoners is that they only start providing services after exiting from prison. It may be that post-release programs start too late to help ex-offenders deal effectively with the multiple challenges association with employment, family relations, substance abuse, and other aspects of re-entry. (p. 358)

In one of the most sophisticated analyses of a comprehensive employment-oriented prisoner reentry program located in Milwaukee, Cook and his colleagues review 236 high-risk offenders with a history of violence or gang involvement who receive services in prison, yet do not receive judicial oversight into release. Their results were less than encouraging. While they did find that the services provided in prison seemed to help with the improvement of human capital of those returning back to the community, earnings continued to be quite low on average. Bleakly, these researchers concluded that legal work continues to be unimportant "in the economic lives of released prisoners."

Currently, there are 29 reentry courts operating across the United States, 9 of which have been funded by the Department of Justice under the Second Chance Act as pilot projects with varying degrees of success and failure (Carey et al., 2017). In 2013, the National Institute of Justice commissioned the largest and most comprehensive evaluation of these funded reentry courts to date, the findings of which are beginning to emerge. Upon review, the NIJ-funded researchers discovered a wide array of differences across program, which allows for a broad review of what seems to work well and what practices may not be suitable for future investment. Preliminary findings suggest two reentry courts that show promising outcomes, two that show no gain in success relative to individuals returning to the community as they have in the past, and two that show worsened outcomes as more people are returning to prison after release than those who simply return to prison without the benefit of the program.

While these results may appear disheartening, researchers have been finding pockets of successes to draw from that can seed improvements in existing and upcoming programs. For example, the evaluation of the Harlem Parole Reentry Court initially found stagnant outcomes for participants (Ayoub & Pooler, 2015). Importantly, the evaluators on the project employed a thorough process evaluation to unveil potential sources of problems that may be restricting success. An array of modifications have since been made, and with the further aid of additional Bureau of Justice Assistance funding, these modifications are being put into practice and are being modified for potential gains in outcomes.

8.2.3.1   The 22nd Judicial District Reentry Court of Louisiana

Situated north of metropolitan New Orleans on the other side of Lake Pontchartrain (colloquially called the Northshore in Southeastern Louisiana), St. Tammany and Washington parishes comprise the 22nd Judicial District Court. This jurisdiction has been notoriable due to its incredibly high incarceration rates; in fact, some claim them to be the highest in the modern world (Galofaro, 2012). The state of Louisiana has generally led the nation in its incarceration rate, currently at 776 per 100,000 incarcerated in prison relative to 385 per 100,000 nationally (Carson & Anderson, 2016). Recent estimates of the 22nd Judicial District's recidivism are even higher, at 811 per 100,000 residents incarcerated (or 1 in 86 adults), with St. Tammany further elevated at 954 inmates per 100,000 adult residents. The punitiveness St. Tammany Parish has resulted in a local nickname—"St. Slammany"—and, at times, this moniker has been used with pride by local law enforcement and the district attorney. These times are changing.

The District's incarceration problem seems to have been fueled by a persistent drug-crime connection that has remained unabated and is destined to drive increased problems without intervention. In particular, the district also leads the state in substance abuse treatment admissions at 771 per 100,000 adult residents relative to 610 per 100,000 state residents. The moment was ripe for intervention, and one standout approach has been led by a district court judge—Judge William "Rusty" Knight— and the team he assembled to constructively address this unyielding problem. The solution is a customized reentry court that is informed by research and steeped in evidence-based programming.

The original Louisiana Reentry Court program was, in fact, established at the New Orleans criminal court in collaboration with the Louisiana Department of Public Safety and Corrections. This collaboration resulted in a new and unique partnership between local courts and state corrections. First, new sentencing legislation (LA Revised Statute 13:5401) was devised and lobbied to the state legislature to give judges more autonomy with reentry programming. Second, and more importantly, it established a comprehensive in-reach program at the Louisiana State Penitentiary at Angola. This in-reach program provides intensive programming to participants for 24 months to qualifying inmates who are sentenced under this newly devised statute. At this time, services include substance abuse education, social skills training, mentoring by trustee lifers, and substantial vocational training that leads to national and international certifications. It also features evidence-based training, such as Moral Reconation Training, and has further been outfitted with medication-assisted treatment (i.e., Vivitrol®).

The mentors are often seen as the glue of the program of the inside. Many are graduates of the New Orleans Baptist Theological Seminary Bible College housed on-site at Angola. These men offer peer-based drug education, fatherhood skills, anger management training, soft skills and personal finance education, and much more. Mentors see themselves as assisting mentees with the development or retooling of their moral compasses and as a living and breathing model of what could happen if participants cannot change their hearts and minds—spending long years (prime years) behind bars.

Intensive services continue at the moment of release through reintegration into the community with the 22nd Judicial District Reentry Court. Further, case managers and Judge Knight remain in constant contact with participants sentenced to the in-reach program, a feature that is very unique. A part of what makes this program different is his level of caring and empathy Judge Knight has for his program participants. For example, using the drug court model, each program participant is referred to as a "client" or "participant" rather than "inmate" or "justice-involved person." In fact, the judge often knows each client by name and makes it a point to hold status meetings (e.g., check-ins with District participants) on prison grounds quarterly, at minimum. The simple change in speech appears to mitigate the stigma and allow a person to overcome any a negative label. It begins a positive outlook, even before release from prison. The speech adjustment creates a thought adjustment. The clients are seen as a person rather than as a charge or a number as they are in prison. Prisoner #0947548 now becomes John, or Chris, or Tom, and is treated accordingly. He now has an identity, an opinion, and a choice in his life path. The empowerment and ownership are also extremely important for the mental health and self-esteem of a person. Upon release from prison, a person then is allowed to take back ownership for decisions in their own life and is no longer subject to those of a corrections officer, institution, or the state/federal government. On the other hand, this new-found ownership can be extremely anxiety provoking and overwhelming. Consider the amount of time a person has been incarcerated and the amount of time to change that control-less thought pattern.

This is where Reentry Court, a modified adult drug court, comes into play. The modifications made at inception were designed to accommodate men with a long history of substance use disorder (or substance abuse patterns) in addition to longer criminal histories that typically make them ineligible for drug court. Additionally, many men who qualify for Reentry Court often have charges that are eligible to be treated under the multiple offender bill in the state, which may result in substantially longer prison sentences if not for the benefit of the program. By law, this sentencing feature is kept intact as a participant progresses through the program, with the possibility of being later filed should someone fail to comply with the program and complete either the in-reach or outreach portion. This feature was designed to minimize the risk of new crimes and new victims. Before release, participants must establish employment and a housing plan (with the assistance of case management, trustee mentors, and prison staff) to ensure success on the outside. The Reentry Court outreach features a four-phase approach that span 5 years of intensive probation supervision, designed to step down services as pro-social behaviors thrive and self-sufficiency ensues. Each phase includes treatment, random drug testing, 12-step meetings, close case management, and status hearings with Judge Knight and the Reentry Court team (e.g., state attorney, defense attorney, treatment representative, and probation officer, led by the judge)—beginning with weekly status meetings, at minimum 2 drug tests per week, individualized treatment, and 2 12-step meetings per week.

To date, only 3 men of 47 have returned to prison, yielding a very promising recidivism rate. As this program continues to grow, comprehensive evaluation will be able to determine if these reductions in the return to prison are sustained. One key feature that appears to be driving the success of the program is that the vocational education is yielding meaningful and well-paying jobs for participants. In fact, the supervising probation officer of Reentry Court often jokes that the participants often get paid more than the probation officers that supervise them. Yet, it should be stressed here that this program has been able to develop a continuous continuum of treatment and programming that begins *before* entering prison, during incarceration, and through up to 5 years of intensive supervision. This level of programming seems to be extremely successful at breaking the cycle of substance use, crime participation, and antisocial behavior.

8.3 Known Gaps and Barriers

As reentry programs are shaping up across the country, literature on the known gaps preventing successful reentry are surfacing. Many of these gaps were mentioned earlier in this text and include connectivity to health care, especially Medicaid, access to evidence-based services, availability of transportation to reach these services and engage in pro-social activities like work and healthy recreation, ability to find gainful employment, and so on. This section addresses some of the less-thought of gaps and barriers to success. As Miller and Khey (2017) note:

> Even though the vast majority of individuals (95 %) sent to prison will return to their communities, the outlook for most remains bleak in that employment is often unattainable (Bushway & Apel, 2012; Stafford, 2006), personal networks are either criminogenic or broken due to incarceration (Berg & Huebner, 2011; Travis & Waul, 2003), and substance use and mental health disorders too often remain unaddressed (Binswanger et al., 2012; Mallik-Kane & Visher, 2008). Increasingly, offender reentry programs are being delivered to a wider range of targeted populations to address various combinations of offender needs and transition issues, but only a fraction include formal program evaluation. (p. 575)

The literature is growing in this area, and the following sections highlight a range of topics important in the current discussions of reentry, including promising programs with rigorous evaluations.

8.3.1 Technology as a Barrier

Technology can often create hurdles for individuals returning to the community. Smartphones, the Internet, and the state-of-the-art technology used by the modern workforce can all pose significant learning curve for someone previously incarcerated. A new version of a phone comes out each year or an upgrade to an application or program happens quickly, so keeping up, even just after a couple years, can be difficult. This, coupled with the stigma, can be intense and difficult. Practically no one wants to be judged for being out of date, particularly for embarrassing reasons.

On a positive note, an increasing amount of prisons are offering education programs within the walls of the prison. While technology can pose a significant security risk for facilities, some forward-thinking administrators are finding ways to circumvent the risk by removing the ability of inmates to access the Internet and communicate freely with the outside world while retaining the ability to learn technology and new skills effectively. These programs can be a great deterrent of negative behaviors for inmates while providing practical experience for future employment post-incarceration.

One example of the use of technology is with the Philadelphia Prison System (Rawlins, 2014). The city of Philadelphia has teamed up with two different startups to work with the prison on educating inmates. The lack of space, monitoring capacity for the technology, and funding have typically been major obstacles for adding and using technology in prisons and jails systems.

One of these startups is Chicago-based Jail Education Solutions (JES). JES, in conjunction with the city of Philadelphia, created a program to equip inmates with special, customized tablets that allow the prison to determine how they are used. These tablets "will offer everything from literacy classes and college coursework to vocational training and financial literacy seminars." JES used data from a RAND report citing, "inmates who received education while in prison were 43% less likely to become repeat offenders" (Davis, Bozick, Steele, Saunders, & Miles, 2013) The founder of JES, Ben Hill, discussed the use of the tablets, stating "If someone took the tablet and tried to use it outside the jail, it would be absolutely worthless."

As with most programs, a major issue is costs and funding. Initially, this program will allow both female and male inmates to have tablets, with the total being 100. To offset costs, the tablets will one day be rented for $2 a day since the beginning startup funds were only $30,000 provided by the city.

Reentry is major priority of the Philadelphia Prison System, "there are an average of 8,300 people in the Philadelphia Prison System—and over 50% of them return to prison within 3 years." In order to work toward successful reentry, a secondary startup, Textizen, has joined in the project. Textizen created the ability for mass text messages via a web platform. Philadelphia's Office of Reintegration Services (RISE) is hopeful for the use of the platform to better serve their caseloads of ex-offenders. The system created by Textizen will allow for better communication for all clients with such large numbers allotted to only a few case managers. The benefits of the platform span past just communication between those in the community post-incarceration with their caseworkers for check-ins but also with alerts for events and appointment reminders. Even further, program participants can use the platform to send required information like pay stubs to parole officers.

The startups involved in this pilot project were part of a competition to create adaptations and change for public safety. These are just some of the ways change can be made through technology within different areas of the criminal justice system.

8.3.2 Disenfranchisement (Felons Can't Vote)

Stigma breeds negativity in many ways for both mentally ill and incarcerated individuals (Moore, Stuewig, & Tangney, 2016). Specifically, for those involved in the criminal justice system, after receiving a felony, a person is no longer allowed to vote. While this can be a symbolic gesture, *voter disenfranchisement* is one real example of the effect of the stigmatic label "ex-felon" or "ex-convict." Under certain circumstances, the right to vote can be regained, but not always. Voting rights allow for a person to be directly connected with their community. Especially in current times, where changes to health care and potential criminal justice reform have become highly politicized, the ability to vote on these matters can be essential to the mental health of an individual. Imagine the impact on the well-being of ex-offenders to have the ability to decide (or at least have the perception of deciding) on matters that can have an impact on whether or not to eliminate mandatory sentences for drug-related crimes or to abolish the death penalty in states. Also, voting at the local level can truly change the treatment of many when there may be a proposed millage for use for local treatment services and improved reentry resources.

The other side of the voting rights argument is that by committing a crime which led to the felony, the individual violated his or her social contract with the community and deserves to have some civil rights rescinded. Although this can be true for some cases, murder being the most obvious case that most people across the political spectrum can agree upon, it may not be true, or beneficial, for all. Take, for example, a person who may have been diagnosed with an anxiety disorder and prescribed some antianxiety medications to use as needed. What if this person then becomes addicted to these same antianxiety medications? Then, the addiction progresses and self-medication ensues; to make the long story short, they then begin buying pills on the street to feed their addiction. If at some point they are arrested with non-prescribed pills, a potential felony drug conviction may be a real possibility. Think, this scenario began with a mental illness and ended in a criminal felony charge. Does that person need treatment or incarceration or both? This question is one that has been on the forefront of criminal justice and treatment professionals, as well as researchers since the turn of the millennium. Working together to form an overall outlook can be the best course of action to help those in need and potentially stop the problem before it becomes a criminal justice issue.

8.3.3 Facing Employers

There is no question that felons have trouble finding work. This book has discussed the vulnerability of the transition period both post-treatment and post-incarceration. Part of the struggle in the transition period includes money, plain and simple. How is a person supposed to rehabilitate and recover without resources? How does one acquire these resources without sufficient funds? Without the ability to obtain legal employment due to a felony charge, where does one turn? The answer is that often a person turns back to their negative habits. This is true for individuals both with or without a mental health diagnosis, as the Cook and colleagues study poignantly points out that legal work remains unimportant in the lives of those returning from prison. This desperately needs to change.

Working brings back, again, to the topic of stigma. Finding employment can be a significant barrier for those released from prison. A criminal record, disclosing said record, and stigma and shame involved can be beyond overwhelming when attempting to rehabilitate and become a productive member of society. Most job applications ask the applicant if they have been convicted of a felony in their past. Additionally, the applicant is asked to describe the charge and sentence served. Imagine discussing past mistakes and currently being judged for those mistakes even after completing the punishment attached. This can be frustrating and significantly discouraging for former inmates.

8.3.4 Facing Relationships

Relationships can also be a struggle for a person leaving prison after a significant amount of time. Resources to maintain relationships within in an institution are limited, often to only letters, phone calls, and possibly occasional in-person visits. With this in mind, it is understandable the level of difficulty in maintaining positive relationships with friends and family while incarcerated. Specifically, with regard to the type of crime committed, some friends and family may choose to no longer associate with the incarcerated person or hold a grudge. This leads to the incarcerated person mourning the loss of that relationship. Further complicated this delicate situation can be reentry of that person to society. The lost relationship may never be repaired and bring up past issues again.

After speaking with several former inmates, many have discussed struggling with family dynamics after returning home. Catching up with everyone after being away for quite some time can be a struggle. Additionally, repeating conversations regarding incarceration and prison surrounding that negative experience can hinder a person's forward progress.

8.3.5 Collateral Consequences

According to the Council of State Governments Justice Center, "collateral consequences are the legal and regulatory sanctions and restrictions that limit or prohibit people with criminal records from accessing employment, occupational licensing, housing, voting, education, and other opportunities" (Council of State Governments Justice Center, 2017). Since 2009, the Justice Center has developed and maintained an inventory of these consequences in its National Inventory of Collateral Consequences of Conviction. The inventory currently features an easy-to-use map to zero in on any jurisdiction to better understand all of the restrictions put into place by statute or ordinance. For example, selecting Louisiana reveals over 1494 legal restrictions on ex-offenders depending on triggering offense (e.g., felony, violent felony, and so on), 920 of which are listed as mandatory and automatic. Some examples of these mandatory Louisiana restrictions include the ineligibility to possess firearms (LA RS 14:95.1, any felony, crime of violence and person offenses, weapons offenses, controlled substances offenses, and sex offenses), ineligibility to serve as a chairman or vice chairman of petition for a neighborhood crime prevention and security district (LA RS 18:1300.31, any felony), ineligibility to receive a citation in lieu of arrest (LA C Cr P Art 211, any felony or misdemeanor), and even the ineligibility to wear a hood, mask, or disguise to conceal identity during Halloween, Mardi Gras, Easter, Christmas, or other holidays (LA RS 14:313, crimes of violence, including person offenses and sex offenses). Many reentry programs are building the capacity to assist individuals returning back into the community in navigating these daunting regulations to ensure compliance and, at times, appeal to the courts to receive special dispensation from the courts, if possible, to aid in successful reentry. These appeals typically revolve around barriers to work. For example, any worker who requires access to secure areas of ports, vessels, offshore facilities, and similar maritime work environments require a Transportation Worker Identification Credential (TWIC)—a felony can prevent an individual from obtaining a TWIC card. Almost always, initial applications for a TWIC are routinely denied and require appeal. This is one of many headaches facing ex-offenders as they reintegrate into society.

Additionally, a lot of "clean-up" work needs to be done simply due to the unintended consequences of being incarcerated, particularly as the incarceration period increases. While these issues may not traditionally be known as collateral consequences, they are being increasingly addressed as if they were. Imagine if you were not around to handle your affairs, such as make car payments, resolve traffic citations or parking tickets, continue mortgage or child support payments, and so on. Driver's licenses may be suspended, outstanding traffic warrants may need to be resolved, outstanding debts may need to be addressed, and even years of missing tax filings may need to be rectified before new problems steamroll those fresh from incarceration. Fortunately, many new programs and services are being created to address these issues. For example, the Internal Revenue Service (IRS) has started its own prisoner reentry program.

Get Right With Your Taxes

A series of informational publications designed to educate taxpayers about the tax impact of significant life events.

Tax Benefits and Credits

FREE HELP FILING YOUR RETURN

Volunteer Income Tax Assistance (VITA)
IRS-certified volunteers receive training to prepare basic tax returns in communities across the country. To locate a VITA site near you, go to _www.irs.gov_ and search: VITA, or call **1-800-906-9887**

Tax-Aide
Trained and certified AARP Tax-Aide volunteers help people of low-to-middle income, with special attention to those age 60 and older. To locate the nearest AARP Tax-Aide site, call **1-888-227-7669** or use the Tax-Aide Locator at _www.aarp.org_

Free File
It's fast, safe and free. Let Free File do the hard work for you with brand-name software or online Fillable Forms. You can prepare and e-file your federal return for free. Participating software companies make their products available through the IRS. Some also support state tax returns. Go to _www.irs.gov/freefile_ to get started.

TAX CREDITS

Earned Income Tax Credit (EITC)
Find out if you are eligible for this valuable credit by using the EITC Assistant at _www.irs.gov_ search: EITC. Amounts received for work performed while an inmate in a penal institution, in a work release program or while in a halfway house are not earned income when figuring this credit.

Other benefits
Information about how to learn more about the child tax credit and other credits, benefits and free services can be found in _Publication 910, IRS Guide to Free Tax Services_

TAXES AND JOBS

If you work for someone else, you can use the Withholding Calculator on www.irs.gov to help you complete Form W-4. That way, you'll avoid having too much or too little tax withheld from your pay.

If you are interested in starting your own business, the IRS has many informative videos available at www.irsvideos.gov. Select the "Small Biz Workshop" on the Small Businesses tab.

Self-employed/independent contractors gen-erally are required to file a tax return every year and pay estimated taxes. See _Publications 334, Tax Guide for Small Business_ and _505, Tax Withholding and Estimated Tax_, for more information.

TAX AVOIDANCE SCHEMES

Participating in an illegal scheme to avoid paying taxes can result in imprisonment, fines, and the repayment of taxes owed plus penalties and interest. If it sounds too good to be true, it probably is. Find more information at www.irs.gov search: tax scams.

WHAT TO DO IF YOU OWE TAXES

You should file all tax returns that are due, regardless of whether or not you can pay in full with your return. Depending on your circumstances, you may qualify for a payment plan. In many cases, filing late can result in avoidable penalties, costing you more money. If you haven't filed, go to www.irs.gov for more information about payment options or to set up a payment arrangement. You can also visit your nearest Taxpayer Assistance Center or call the IRS toll-free at **1-800-829-1040.**

Low Income Taxpayer Clinics (LITC)
Available to eligible low income or English as a second language (ESL) taxpayers seeking assistance with IRS audits, appeals and collection disputes including representation before the IRS. For specific requirements and locations in your state go to _www.irs.gov_ search: LITC assistance

Taxpayer Advocate Service (TAS)
Your voice at the IRS. Call TAS if you're having economic problems, if you need help resolving an IRS problem, or you believe an IRS system or procedure isn't working as it should. Call toll-free at **1-877-777-4778** or go to _www.TaxpayerAdvocate.irs.gov_

PRISONER RE-ENTRY EDUCATION PROGRAM

continued... ▶

8.4   How Do We Break the Cycle?

The following sections address different perspectives on how to alter the path of hyper-incarceration on which America finds itself. In particular, it discusses how everyday people can contribute to a solution. As referenced throughout this text, the

American criminal justice system has failed to provide this solution on its own, and looking beyond criminal justice seems to offer an answer. As these multifaceted solutions avail themselves across the country, it will be interesting to note whether mental health takes a prominent role as part of these solutions or if it will remain an afterthought.

8.4.1   The Role of Employers

Among employers, there exist a reluctance and oftentimes fear to hire someone with a criminal record. The risk of another criminal act, or a person leaving again due to incarceration, can be greater than most employers are willing to bear. Management also considers the potential liability of hiring someone they know to have a criminal record. For example, it may make an employer very uncomfortable hiring someone with a burglary conviction as an HVAC repair and serviceperson knowing that he or she will go into customer's homes several times per day. If something were to turn up missing and the customer were to catch wind of the employee's criminal past, is there any liability on that employer? Luckily, programs exist to help defray the costs and fears for employers, as well as explore how to mitigate this issue of liability.

For example, tax incentives exist for employers who hire justice-involved employees or individuals returning to their communities from incarceration. Progressive changes have also been made to state statutes to eliminate civil liability for employers in many circumstances should they hire an individual returning from prison. In Louisiana, recent legislative changes add that "any employer, general contractor, premises owner, or third party shall not be subject to a cause of action for negligent hiring of or failing to adequately supervise an offender *certified to be employed* due to damages or injury caused by that employee or independent contractor solely because that employee or independent contractor has been previously convicted of a criminal offense" (LA R.S. 23:291.1, emphasis added). Specifically, certain reentry program participants (who receive comprehensive programming) are eligible to receive a certification of employment from the Department of Public Safety and Corrections. These types of actions aid to address the collateral consequences of the label of "felon" and a criminal history.

Unfortunately, the stigma of mental illness, substance abuse, and incarceration do exist and prevent former inmates from being successful in their new-found futures. For example, if a person was incarcerated for a drug charge, it is often difficult for society to see that person as anything more than a "drug addict" or "drug dealer." This thought process does nothing to help someone reclaim their life and change for the better. This type of thinking only promotes an individual to return to the negative, criminal behaviors from their past. As a society, we discuss high incarceration rates, high recidivism rates, and high crime as significant negative impacts on communities, yet we do nothing to help people overcome past mistakes and regain their freedom on a permanent basis.

Luckily, in recent years, there has been an influx of opportunity for federal grant funding to create programming to help aid justice-involved individuals reenter society and remain positive and successful. This change begins inside the prison and must continue post-incarceration. Public education and awareness are essential in lessening stigma and promoting the positive welfare of these individuals. Once we accept the reality that people can change and become successful despite past convictions, things will then begin to change. This acceptance needs to come from all members of society, involved in the criminal justice system or not. Judges, lawyers, counselors, employers, loved ones, etc. can be a catalyst to change.

8.4.2   Ban the Box: Does It Work?

The Fair Chance Act aka "Ban the Box" is a law that was put into effect in New York City on October 27, 2015. The Fair Chance Act "bans job ads that say things like 'no felonies' or 'must pass background check,' bans any questions about criminal history on job applications bans any questions about criminal history during job interviews, and an employer can check your criminal record history only after a conditional job offer." Then, if a person is denied a position due to their criminal record, an explanation from the employer is required in writing to explain the denial. Further, a connection between the potential employee's criminal history to the job duties must be made and show "unreasonable risk." Finally, in order to allow for discussion between the potential employee and employer in case of an issue, the job has to be held open for 3 days. President Obama changed the federal employee job applications and "banned the box." Additionally, by December 2015, 24 states adopted the policy as well.

Keep in mind, as explained above, this law does not prevent employers from learning about a potential employee's criminal background. What the law does is allow a person to be evaluated for a position on somewhat of an even playing field. The Fair Chance Act has just a couple stories about persons whose lives have changed because of the passing of this law. In one example, a woman describes being a victim of human trafficking, and while in captive, she was arrested many times for various sexual and drug-related crimes forced by her captors. In many ways, this is an easy argument for "Ban the Box" in that her future employment should not be impacted on past crimes while being held captive.

On the other hand, there are some instances that produce controversy for the public and employers, much like any other law. The "gray area" in many situations can vary wildly from side to side and in an argument, both political and professional, not all is black or white. Unfortunately, the dark side of "Ban the Box" is that one study has shown broader discrimination occurring. According to an article in the National Bureau of Economic Research written by Jennifer L. Doleac from the University of Virginia and Benjamin Hansen from the University of Oregon (Doleac & Hansen, 2016), young Hispanic and black men are less likely to be hired due to the general discrimination of potential employers. This concern again begs the idea of ensuring education is linked to these types of policies. As with many other topics, especially those within this book, having a direct or personal experience usually lessens the negativity and stigma. For example, having a family member who was incarcerated and then released with the hopes of a better future usually helps to have a compassion and empathetic sense as a business owner or employer.

As of June 2017, Louisiana became the first state to "Ban the Box" on college applications. Louisiana governor, John Bel Edwards, signed House Bill 688 which will go into effect in fall 2017. This bill would not allow postsecondary public institutions from asking about criminal history during the admissions process. This would allow individuals with a criminal background to attend or re-enroll in a college or university with the hopes of furthering their education and leading to a better career. The law, however, does come with some exceptions in that institutions can ask about criminal history after admissions for both financial aid and housing.

8.5 Conclusion

The lack of funding and increase of incarceration have forced professionals to "think outside of the box." One brainchild has been reentry programs. These programs are changing the way society views justice-involved individuals. Additionally, these programs are helping to create a supportive environment for the success of those in need. As with any treatment, support is essential. Luckily, these programs are helping to create a safe space to begin change. The hope is that this change will lead to greater success overall. If individuals can find the means to complete programs like reentry successfully, they can become role models for others.

The other issue taking center stage in the discussion of reentry has been the collateral consequences caused by imprisonment, systemic processing, and the stigma involved with being a criminal/drug abusers/mentally ill. For everyday people, dealing with problems like having a suspended driver's license, being in arrears on child support, missing a court date, or preparing for a successful job interview may be daunting. Yet if you step into the shoes of someone with a criminal record who may be experiencing one, or most likely many of these issues all at once, visualizing and attaining success can feel like an insurmountable feat.

The vast majority of the innovations discussed in this section are yet to be fully evaluated, but some do indicate a reason to be hopeful. To be certain, we do not know if Ban the Box has been successful or if the available tax incentives offer enough of a carrot to employers to begin to hire some more perceptively "risky" individuals. However, there appears to be a push to "change the script" or rework the narrative of hiring and helping justice-involved persons. For example, Judge Rusty Knight prefers to send this message to potential employers who may hire reentry court participants: would you rather hire a perfect stranger from off of the street after reviewing his or her resume and interviewing them, or would you rather hire someone who has the full backing of a diverse array of professionals with likely better qualifications onto your team who also benefits from his judicial oversight? Who is more likely to fail a drug test? Who is more likely to be responsible? Indeed, it seems for many employers, after they experience their first success with a reentry client, they are likely to change their scripts and practices into the future.

KNOW YOUR RIGHTS!

It's illegal to be denied a job just because you have a criminal record.

A new NYC law called the **Fair Chance Act** says employers can't ask about your criminal record until offering you a job. The new law takes effect on October 27, 2015.

What does the Fair Chance Act do?
- Bans job ads that say things like "no felonies" and "must pass background check."
- Bans any questions about criminal history on *job applications.*
- Bans any questions about criminal history during *job interviews.*
- An employer *can* check your criminal record history only *after a conditional job offer*.

If you are denied a job because of your criminal record...
the employer must explain why *in writing*. The employer must also connect your criminal record history to job duties or show it creates an unreasonable risk. The employer must also hold the job open for *at least 3 days* so you have time to discuss the issue or correct any wrong info.

Which jobs does this impact?
All employers in New York City with four or more employees must obey the Fair Chance Act. And they have to follow it when hiring, promoting, demoting, or firing people. The law does not apply to some jobs, however: police and peace officers and any job where a law says that people with certain convictions cannot do that job.

Workplaces that violate the Fair Chance Act may have to pay you lost wages and other damages and be fined by the City up to $125,000. If you think your rights may have been violated, contact: Brandon Holmes, brandon@vocal-ny.org or 917-361-9865.

VOCAL
NEW YORK

References

Ayoub, L. H., & Pooler, T. (2015). *Coming Home to Harlem: A randomized controlled trial of the Harlem Parole Reentry Court*. New York: Center for Court Innovation.

Bick, J. A. (2007). Infection control in jails and prisons. *Clinical Infectious Diseases, 45*(8), 1047–1055.

Bonczar, T. P. (2003). Prevalence of imprisonment in the U.S. population, 1974-2001. *Bureau of Justice Statistics*. Retrieved July 10, 2017, from https://www.bjs.gov/content/pub/pdf/piusp01.pdf

Bureau of Justice Statistics. (2014). *Survey of state criminal history information systems, 2012*. Retrieved July 10, 2017, from https://www.ncjrs.gov/pdffiles1/bjs/grants/244563.pdf

Carey, S., Rempel, M., Lindquist, C., Cissner, A., Hassoun Ayoub, L., Kralstein, D., et al. (2017). Reentry court research: Overview of findings from the national institute of justice's multi-site evaluation (Unpublished, preliminary evaluation report). Submitted to National Institute of Justice, Office of Justice Programs, U.S. Department of Justice in February 2017.

Carson, E. A., & Anderson, E. (2016). Prisoners in 2015. *Bureau of Justice Statistics*. Retrieved July 2, 2017, from https://www.bjs.gov/content/pub/pdf/p15.pdf

Cook, P. J., Kang, S., Braga, A. A., Ludwig, J., & O'Brien, M. E. (2015). An experimental evaluation of a comprehensive employment-oriented prisoner re-entry program. *Journal of Quantitative Criminology, 31*(3), 355–382.

Council of State Governments Justice Center. (2017). *National inventory of the collateral consequences of conviction*. Retrieved July 2, 2017, from https://niccc.csgjusticecenter.org/

Davis, L. M., Bozick, R., Steele, J. L., Saunders, J., & Miles, J. N. V. (2013). Evaluating the effectiveness of correctional education: A meta-analysis of programs that provide education to incarcerated adults. *Rand Corporation*. Retrieved June 1, 2017, from http://www.rand.org/pubs/research_reports/RR266.html

Doleac, J. L., & Hansen, B. (2016). Does "Ban the Box" help low-skilled workers?: Statistical discrimination and employment outcomes when criminal histories are hidden. *Research Briefs in Economic Policy (62)*. Retrieved July 2, 2017, from https://www.cato.org/publications/research-briefs-economic-policy/does-ban-box-help-or-hurt-low-skilled-workers

Durose, M. R. Cooper, A. D., & Snyder, H. N. (2014). Recidivism of prisoners released in 30 states in 2005: Patterns from 2005 to 2010. *Bureau of Justice Statistics*. Retrieved June 1, 2017, from https://www.bjs.gov/content/pub/pdf/rprts05p0510.pdf

Galofaro, C. (2012). St. Tammany courts give parish nickname of 'St. Slammany.' *The Times Picayune*. Retrieved June 25, 2017, from http://www.nola.com/crime/index.ssf/2012/03/st_tammany_courts_give_parish.html

Hampden County Sheriff's Office. (2015). *Presentation: Special commission on substance Abuse addiction treatment in the criminal justice system*. Retrieved June 1, 2017, from http://www.mass.gov/courts/docs/specialty-courts/specialty-courts-hampden-sheriff.pdf

Johnson, R. (2002). *Hard time* (3rd ed.). Belmont, CA: Wadsworth.

Lafayette Parish Sheriff's Office. (2011). *Reentry survival manual*. Retrieved June 1, 2017, from https://www.lafayettesheriff.com/uploads/ReentrySkillsSurvivalManual62811.pdf

Lowenkamp, C. T., Latessa, E. J., & Holsinger, A. M. (2006). The risk principle in action: What have we learned from 13,676 offenders and 97 correctional programs? *Crime & Delinquency, 52*(1), 77–93.

Maruna, S. (2001). *Making good: How ex-convicts reform and rebuild their lives*. Washington, DC: American Psychological Association.

Maruna, S., & LeBel, T. P. (2003). Welcome home-examining the reentry court concept from a strengths-based perspective. *Western Criminology Review, 4*(2), 91–107.

Mellow, J., Mukamal, D. A., LoBuglio, S. F., Solomon, A. L., & Osborne, J. W. (2008). *The jail administrator's toolkit for reentry*. Washington, DC: Urban Institute.

Miller, J. M., & Khey, D. N. (2017). Fighting America's highest incarceration rates with offender programming: Process evaluation implications from the Louisiana 22nd Judicial District

Reentry Court. *American Journal of Criminal Justice, 42*(3):574–588.https://link.springer.com/article/10.1007/s12103-016-9372-4

Moore, K. E., Stuewig, J. B., & Tangney, J. P. (2016). The effect of stigma on criminal offenders' functioning: A longitudinal mediational model. *Deviant Behavior, 37*(2), 196–218.

Osher, F. C. (2006). *Integrating mental health and substance abuse services for justice-involved persons with co-occurring disorders*. Baltimore, MD: National GAINS Center.

Osher, F. C. (2007). Short-term strategies to improve reentry of jail populations: Expanding and implementing the APIC model. *American Jails, 20*, 9–18.

Pearson, F. S., & Lipton, D. S. (1999). A meta-analytic review of the effectiveness of corrections-based treatments for drug abuse. *Prison Journal, 79*(4), 384–410.

Petersilia, J. (2004). What works in prisoner reentry-reviewing and questioning the evidence. *Federal Probation, 68*(2), 4–8.

Rawlins, A. (2014). *Philadelphia's prisons are embracing technology*. Retrieved June 1, 2017, from http://money.cnn.com/2014/10/07/smallbusiness/philadelphia-technology-prison/index.html

Ryan, C. L., & Bauman, K. (2016). Educational attainment in the United States: 2015. *U.S. Census*. Retrieved June 1, 2017, from https://www.census.gov/content/dam/Census/library/publications/2016/demo/p20-578.pdf

Solomon, A. L., Osborne, J. W., LoBuglio, S. F., Mellow, J., & Mukamal, D. A. (2008). *Life after lockup: Improving reentry from jail to the community*. Washington, DC: Urban Institute.

Travis, J. (2000). *But they all come back: Rethinking prisoner reentry*. Washington, DC: US Department of Justice, Office of Justice Programs, National Institute of Justice.

Travis, J., & Visher, C. (Eds.). (2005). *Prisoner reentry and crime in America*. New York: Cambridge University Press.

Wolf, R. V. (2011). Reentry courts: Looking ahead. *Bureau of Justice Assistance*. Retrieved July 2, 2017, from https://www.bja.gov/Publications/CCI_ReentryCourts.pdf

Wolff, N., & Shi, J. (2012). Childhood and adult trauma experiences of incarcerated persons and their relationship to adult behavioral health problems and treatment. *International Journal of Environmental Research and Public Health, 9*(5), 1908–1926.

Chapter 9
Community-Based and Grassroots Programs

Mental illness, it's a bit like drugs, it doesn't give a shit who you are. And you know what's worse? The stigma doesn't give a shit who you are.—Sinead O'Connor (2017)

Community members can aid in making change in mental health awareness and improving the system of care and reentry. In fact, there appears to be substantial growth in nonprofit organizations of all sizes to affect such change, as well as the volunteer hours needed to sustain this momentum. In 2015, the Urban Institute released their annual *Nonprofit Sector in Brief*, which supports this claim (McKeever, 2015). This report reveals that the number of 501(c)(3) public charities grew 19.5% from 2003 to 2013, and 25.3% of American adults had volunteered for a nonprofit organization in 2014. While this proportion of adults who volunteer at least once per year is on a slightly downward trend, the number of total volunteer hours in any given year is at the highest ever recorded at 8.7 billion hours in 2014—valued at $179.2 billion. This volunteerism is consistently concentrated in social service and care activities, including food preparation, cleanups, food, goods, and clothing collection and delivery, direct care and/or services, teaching, mentoring, and counseling. In the cases of local mental health-care system improvements and criminal justice reform (e.g., reentry), this momentum has been buttressed by grant opportunities through the Substance Abuse and Mental Health Services Administration, the Bureau of Justice Assistance, and other Federal government funding agencies specifically tailored to support public nonprofit collaborations. For example, the Bureau of Justice Assistance Second Chance Act Comprehensive Community-Based Adult Reentry Program is specifically geared for community-based nonprofits who engage in reentry activities such as mentoring support, treatment services, legal aid, and more. These opportunities also seem to be on the rise; however, it is uncertain how the current administration will shape this trend in the upcoming years. With momentum in Congress and local governments for justice and mental health reform, it appears that the trajectory of improvements will continue to some degree. This chapter focuses on promising nonprofit activity led by icons, world leaders, and

© Springer International Publishing AG, part of Springer Nature 2018
J. Hector, D. Khey, *Criminal Justice and Mental Health*,
https://doi.org/10.1007/978-3-319-76442-9_9

everyday people to give readers some orientation of the rigorous activity that is affecting changes in mental health and justice.

9.1 Know the Role

Nonprofits have embraced the challenges facing individuals with mental illness, those who are experiencing mental health crises, and those reentering society from periods of incarceration, treatment, and hospitalization. As noted earlier, episodes of each of these can be the most volatile and difficult struggles in people's lives— and they most often occur in our communities, on our city streets, and in the countryside. The risk of overdose and relapse is assuredly higher when individuals are confronted with their triggers or being close to bars and hangouts, passing the abandoned house turned into a drug den, seeing or hearing from those acquaintances or sexual partners who engage in drug use and deviance, and so on. In the case of reentry, the stress of returning home and dealing with substance use/abuse/misuse, income and work, and family relationships can be overwhelming. Family members and loved ones may not always be supportive after a person has been incarcerated. In fact, some may be full of anger, mistrust, and spite, which may require counseling in order to heal the damage done from "losing" their loved ones to the system for acts that they may feel are the fault of the person coming back into their lives after long periods of absence.

Many people involved in the nonprofit sector in the capacity of serving mentally ill and justice-involved populations have been directly or indirectly touched by problems addressed in this text. Some are parents of a daughter or son with mental illness and/or those that have served time—or other family members. Some individuals with mental illness and/or previous justice involvement become peer supports for others who become involved with the justice system. One perfect example can be found with an even-keeled, insightful, and mild-mannered Maryland man named Eddie Ellis. In the years after his release, Mr. Ellis has been speaking about his story of incarceration after serving 22 years in prison for shooting and killing a man when he was 16 years old (Ellis, 2016). Now Mr. Ellis serves as a mentor and advocate for others with shared experiences, including being held in solitary confinement for long periods of time because of his violent conviction and not due to his prison behavior. His motivation and hard work post-release has culminated in a vibrant 501(c)(3) nonprofit organization named One by 1, which Mr. Ellis serves as Chief Executive (One by 1 Inc., 2017).

At a recent speaking event at the National Association of Drug Court Professionals, Mr. Ellis was joined by his mother to share their points of view on the effect of incarceration in their lives with justice professionals engaged in reentry work (Cherry & Ellis, 2017). Their accounts were impassioned and full of lingering signs of pain from their experiences and allowed the audience a window into the common problems returning prisoners and their families will face upon release. As the conversation progressed, Ms. Cherry voiced her concern that family members often lack support to help them process their feelings. This point in particular began a lively question and answer session about how professionals can best aid families at a vulnerable time in their lives.

Everyday people turned onto "giving back" or to be a change agent—like Mr. Ellis and Ms. Cherry—are at the heart of the grassroots effort in American communities. Peer support specialists, for example, are becoming critical—if not mandatory—for the care of individuals with mental illness, substance use disorder, and/or who are experiencing a mental health crisis. Thus, at this point, any comprehensive solution to the broken mental health system of care and justice reform almost requires grassroots, community support. The following sections highlight some of the most innovative endeavors of recent years.

9.2 Facing the Stigma Head On: Heroin Walks Like Cancer Walks

In reducing stigma and viewing mental health like physical health, changing thought processes and views about fund-raising is also important. In regard to physical health, for example, there are many activities in the month of October for Breast Cancer Awareness in most communities across the United States each year. These activities include fund raising walks, charitable donations from major corporations (think Yoplait yogurt), and even the National Football League players wearing pink accessories while they play in a dedicated week to the cause. These activities do not only raise money for different organizations that research breast cancer in hopes of a cure; they also are critical in raising awareness of the disease and need for preventative screening and regular health checks.

In this vein, mental health-related events and campaigns happen throughout the year, with peak activity during the official "Mental Health Week" (the first full week of October as recognized by Congress; not to be confused with mental health month—May—established by NAMI and its partners). For example, the local NAMI affiliates often sponsor 5 K events each year, called NAMIWalks, which raises money for each local branch. In the most recent year (2016), there are more than 80 individual communities having a walk, raising over $11 million in the United States.

In more recent times, this concept has been expanded to focus on current emerging issues, such as the opioid epidemic. In February 2017, the Addiction Prevention Coalition in Birmingham, Alabama hosted an "End Heroin Bham" walk, free to everyone, with the intent to bring awareness of the recent surge in opioid-related problems and deaths occurring in the greater Birmingham area and in the state of Alabama. Likewise, the Coalition utilized a broad array of media exposure of the event to aid in its message, even if locals did not end up attending the event. Awareness and social marketing campaigns seem to be one of the primary tools of the grassroots movement in terms of relevance and sustained funding.

9.3 Partners 4 Strong Minds (Strong 365) and One Mind Care Connect

Partners 4 Strong Minds (P4SM) was a nonprofit organization created as a result founder Chantel Garrett's long advocacy of her brother's schizophrenia diagnosis. With a background in marketing for corporations, Ms. Garrett spearheaded a modern campaign of advocacy and personal storytelling to change the way everyday people think about brain health and access to care. In particular, the organization began with a focus on creating awareness regarding the first/early onset of psychosis with the notion that addressing the psychosis early on and quickly after the first onset can aid in better results for long-term success in recovery. P4SM's use of messaging from friends, families, and loved ones often was found at the core of the organization's awareness campaigns and events, many of which were concentrated on the West Coast of the United States where P4SM was founded.

The mission of P4SM aligned with an emerging science pointing to promising results of early intervention and by being proactive. In fact, mental illness disease processes seem to be more easily managed—and possibly in some cases, symptoms can be lessened—when early intervention occurs. It often allows for the individual to live a much more productive and stable life. Further, a person can learn their triggers and be more aware of symptoms and issues before they arise, thus empowering those with mental illness.

Similarly, Shari and Garen Staglin's experiences of advocating for their son Brandon and his schizophrenia diagnosis drove them to organize and develop the One Mind Institute. Since 1995, the Staglins focused their efforts on grantsmaking in the domain of brain health research. In 2014, Ms. Garrett and the Staglins joined forces to create the One Mind Care Connect initiative: "the combined effort expands P4SM's nationwide advocacy and personal storytelling platform under the One Mind Institute brand, and complements its grassroots approach with translational research that will help us learn more about how to best evolve and scale early psychosis treatment in the United States" (One Mind Institute, 2017). One of the current programs of One Mind Care Connect is Strong 365. Strong 365 has many facets to help families in their search for help with psychosis, specifically the early stages. A treatment tracker is maintained on the Strong 365 website, which lists programs throughout the country that provide treatment after a first episode of psychosis. The information on the website makes clear that the early intervention treatment, medication management, counseling (including the whole family), brain training, and other activities are shown to aid in recovery.

9.4 Heads Together

Often, on health-related topics, a "champion" is discussed when having a celebrity or spokesperson for a campaign. As mental health emerges as a mainstream topic (again), celebrities are (re-)emerging to bring the conversation of mental health awareness to the forefront. Further, with social media, these messages are easily able to quickly reach large audiences. Some celebrities are also opening up to discuss their own personal struggles with mental illness or substance abuse (particularly with the latter). For example, Sinead O'Connor recently shared her raw feelings regarding her own mental health and suicidal thoughts with a self-shot video on her Facebook account. In her emotional 12-min clip, O'Connor explains: "I hope that this video is somehow helpful. Not to me, but the fact that I know that I am only one of millions and millions and millions of people who are just like me, actually, that don't necessarily have the resources that I have in my heart and in my purse." Often, positive messages about mental illness and treatment are used to open conversation to happen to affect change, particularly when these messages are associated with nonprofit organizations. Having these "champions" can begin to help overcome stigma and obstacles to ensure everyone receives the treatment needed.

One example of champion-led messaging comes with the Royal Foundation of the Duke and Duchess of Cambridge and Prince Harry and its project entitled Heads Together. In particular, the Heads Together project adjoins the Royal Foundation "in partnership with inspiring charities that are tackling stigma, raising awareness, and providing vital help for people with mental health challenges" (Royal Foundation, 2017). Having world leaders, such as Prince William, Duchess Kate, and Prince Harry, speak on mental health is providing legitimacy to the cause. It can further bring hope to all affected. As such, the Heads Together program is a potent awareness campaign that unites existing organizations and elevates their cause through celebrity power—partners including Best Beginnings, the Campaign Against Living Miserably, Contact (mental health coalition for the military), Mind, Place2Be, The Mix, YoungMinds, and the Anna Freud Centre. It also includes star power from across the pond in the United States with Born This Way.

9.5 Born This Way

The Born This Way Foundation founded by musician, Lady Gaga, with its slogan "empowering youth and inspiring bravery." The Foundation features different programming and advice based on research as well as tips and direct links for seeking help when needed. Lady Gaga uses her own personal experience with post-traumatic stress disorder to dispel the concept of stigma and promote a positive community.

> I have wrestled for some time about when, how and if I should reveal my diagnosis of Post-Traumatic Stress Disorder (PTSD). After five years of searching for the answers to my chronic pain and the change I have felt in my brain, I am finally well enough to tell you. There is a lot of shame attached to mental illness, but it's important that you know that there is hope and a chance for recovery. (Born This Way Foundation, 2017)

Her organization provides user-friendly information in a manner geared toward youth and helping them to create "kind communities and enhance mental wellness." Areas on the website currently focus on topics such as kindness, positive environments, mental wellness, and research and resources and further feature a Born Brave blog featuring voices and stories from across the country.

The website includes a section entitled Hack Harassment which works to combat online harassment for youth. Hack Harassment assembles its partners—Intel, Vox Media, and Recode—to work behind the scenes to find innovative ways to help keep online spaces free of harassment. Hack Harassment also includes section for users featuring an anti-harassment pledge and an application for college-aged students to become campus ambassadors at their college or university. The idea of a campus ambassador is nothing new and has used by many different organizations to promote education and information within the college campus community. Yet, the star power of Lady Gaga can further elevate campus messaging and give help to its legitimacy.

In 2017, Lady Gaga and Prince William open up to one another about their experiences with mental illness via a FaceTime call shared with the world with the hashtag #okaytosay (a Heads Together awareness tool). For Prince William, he shared personal details about his brother Harry's need to seek counseling to help with his struggles after the death of his mother.

Lady Gaga: ...The beautiful videos of the Heads Together campaign...told beautiful stories and it reminded me how much my mental health changing changed my life.

Prince William: [Most of our charitable work] seemed to stand back to mental health issues, and you know, I read your open letter you wrote the other day and I thought it was incredibly moving and very brave of you to write down such personal feelings. I wanted to ask you very much how you found speaking out and how it made you feel?

Lady Gaga: It made me very nervous at first. For me, waking up everyday and feeling sad and going on stage, is something that is something very hard to describe. There's a lot of shame attached to mental illness. You feel like something's wrong with you. And, in my life, I go "oh my goodness look at all this beautiful, wonderful things that I have. And I should be so happy." But you can't help it that if in the morning when you wake up, you are so tired, you are so sad, you are so full of anxiety and the shakes that you can barely think. But, it was like saying, this was a part of me and it was okay.

Prince William: ...for me, the little bits that I have learned about mental health so far is that it's okay to have this conversation. It's really important to have this conversation, you won't be judged. It's so important to break open that fear and taboo which is only going to lead to more problems down the line.

Lady Gaga: Yes, it can make a huge difference. I feel like we are not hiding anymore; we're starting to talk and that's what we need to do really.

Prince William: Absolutely. It's time that everyone speaks up and feels very normal about mental health. It's the same as physical. Everyone has mental health and that we shouldn't be ashamed of it. Just having a conversation with a friend or family member can make such a difference.

Lady Gaga: Even though it was hard, it was the best thing that could come out of my mental illness – was to share it with other people and let our generation as well as other generations know that if you are feeling not well in your mind, that you are not alone. And that people that you think would never have a problem do.

This collaboration will pick up again in October when Prince William plans to meet up with Lady Gaga to take the next steps in this conversation and create some action out of it. Along with this example, there are many other celebrity champions who have surfaced in recent years to bring to light issues related to mental health.

9.6 Wear Your Label

Wear Your Label is a Canadian-based clothing company created by two friends "to spark conversations about mental health" (Wear Your Label, 2017). Both of the co-founders have suffered from mental illness and wanted to let others know that "it's okay not to be okay," and the importance of self-care. Their shirts feature sayings like "stigma free" and "i am enough" and come in unisex sizing to be inclusive to all gender and gender fluid individuals. Wear Your Label has now expanding to also include jewelry with a bracelet series that not only provides awareness for different mental health diagnoses but also includes information on those disorders and where to seek help if needed.

This is one example of how individuals turn statements about mental health into mainstream society. Importantly, the success of Wear Your Label is occurring in simultaneously with other clothing labels that may have antithetical messages (e.g., cliqueish, thin-is-in, and so on). The effort of the company to advocate for mental health awareness is also echoed on its website, which includes a blog regarding mental health issues. This is one of many examples of marketing innovation that serves mental health advocacy.

9.7 Active Minds

Active Minds was created by a woman named Alison Malmon following the suicide of her older brother, Brian. As both were college students at the time, Ms. Malmon was struck by the dearth of discussion of mental health issues on her campus. After a few years of activism, she incorporated the Active Minds nonprofit in late 2003; the organization works as a student-led group on college campuses across the United States to bring awareness to mental health issues at these campuses. In almost 15 years, Active Minds has grown to over 400 chapters with thousands of student members at universities across the nation. Additionally, there is now a national conference where members of different groups can come together annually at a forum to help growth, understanding, and awareness. The organization offers many different, turnkey-style programs that can run independently at each campus (e.g., individual-led efforts) as well as group-based efforts such as Active Minds' signature Send Silence Packing® event (Active Minds, 2017).

Send Silence Packing® gives passersby a visual representation of suicide among college-aged students. To do so, a traveling tour of donated backpacks is brought to each site to be laid out in a high-traffic area on campus, like outside of the student union or main campus "quads." As a visual representation, the backpacks symbolize the number of college students who take their lives each year; signage is placed near the backpacks with statistics, ways to seek help, and other helpful information. In 2017, the Send Since Packing® campaign has reached over 15 campuses, including the University of North Alabama, Alcorn State University, the University of North Texas, The University of Denver, Colorado State University, Mt. San Jacinto College, and Occidental College.

9.8   SLIDDE, University of Louisiana at Lafayette

Further, on a direct community level, universities themselves have taken the awareness efforts on their own. One great example of programming is at the University of Louisiana at Lafayette. There, a student organization called SLIDDE, School Leaders Involved in Drinking and Drug Education, has been created. The program was started within the Counseling and Testing Center to provide education, awareness, and prevention on campus for drinking and drug use. It has now grown to be an official student-led organization and is involved in many different activities on campus throughout the academic year, such as an annual 5 K run that occurs in spring. These events are often coordinated with popular campus events to ensure wide visibility and maximum exposure. In fact, most modern colleges and universities offer such programming through a division or office of student health. Therefore, it should not be surprising to see mental health programming becoming more prominent in such messaging in some capacity. For the time being, grassroots organizations such as Active Minds are filling the voids on campuses across the country, as are campus-based NAMI organizations. Much more activity is expected in the upcoming years in this arena (University of Louisiana Counseling and Testing Center, 2017).

9.8.1   Dave's Killer Bread

Created in 2005 as part of a family bakery, Dave's Killer Bread has grown to become *the* top rated organic bread in the United States. The story of the Dahl brothers, Dave and Glenn, is a testament to community partnerships working to help solve some of the nation's struggles. Dave served 15 years in prison and was given a job by his brother to work in their family bakery after his release. Their dream was to create bread that was both organic and non-GMO, and they succeeded. Now, the company has more than 300 employees with distribution in all 50 US states and Canada (thanks to the distribution power of Flowers Foods who acquired Dave's Killer Bread; products currently reach 85% of Americans). Even further, one in three of their employees at the original bakery has a criminal background. As a company, they are working to reduce the struggles of stigma and recidivism in the United States.

Additionally, Dave's Killer Bread Foundation has been created to aid in education and implementation of Second Chance Employment. The Foundation has created a Second Chance Playbook which features all topics related to understanding how and why hiring individuals and providing them with a "second chance" is beneficial to the community and their organization. Organizations can join the community and have access to the Playbook and even attend the Second Chance Summits held across the country. The Second Chance Playbook not only provides guides but also video modules covering topics such as "risk mitigation and insurance, legal compliance and the use of criminal background checks, financial incentives for hiring Second Chance candidates, organizational culture and values, the hiring and staffing process, successful onboarding and orientation, and more" (Dave's Killer Bread Foundation, 2017).

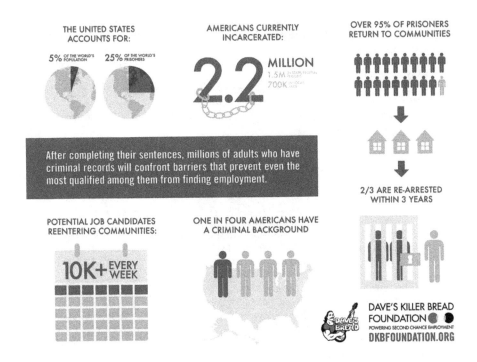

9.9   Conclusion

Many of these organizations mentioned above both reduce stigma and raise awareness about mental health and the criminal justice system. More importantly, their efforts are part of the steps in making a change for their communities and society as a whole. Support and positivity can manage to spark change in many ways. Persons suffering from mental illness that have a criminal background can also find solace in partnering with these, and many other, organizations to tell their stories. Education to the public is an essential component in success for all involved.

Part of the importance of the awareness campaigns mentioned in this chapter is to aid students and professionals to understand the normality of mental health issues in our society. If we can begin educating students and arm them with the information in these campaigns, this can drastically impact the careers of these individuals or professionals already working in these careers—which can thus have an impact on justice-involved individuals and those with mental health concerns (most likely, both).

References

Active Minds. (2017). *About us*. Retrieved October 30, 2017, from http://www.activeminds.org/about

Born This Way Foundation. (2017). *Born this way*. Retrieved October 30, 2017, from https://bornthisway.foundation/

Cherry, S., & Ellis, E. (2017). *Speaking at the national association of drug court professionals*. Washington, DC: NADCP.

Dave's Killer Bread Foundation. (2017). *About us*. Retrieved October 30, 2017, from https://www.dkbfoundation.org/about/

Ellis, E. (2016). *I am one of the success stories from D.C.'s second-chance law for young offenders*. Retrieved October 30, 2017, from https://www.washingtonpost.com/opinions/i-am-one-of-the-success-stories-from-dcs-second-chance-law-for-young-offenders/2016/12/16/f1f2c9a4-c211-11e6-8422-eac61c0ef74d_story.html?utm_term=.ae7c13f61e28

McKeever, B. (2015). *The nonprofit sector in brief 2015: Public charities, giving, and volunteering*. Retrieved October 30, 2017, from https://www.urban.org/research/publication/nonprofit-sector-brief-2015-public-charities-giving-and-volunteering

O'Connor, Sinead. (2017). *Personal Facebook post*. Retreived September 1, 2017, from https://www.facebook.com/Sin%C3%A9ad-OConnor-151509961629721/

One by 1 Inc. (2017). *Welcome to one by 1*. Retrieved October 30, 2017, from http://www.oneby-1inc.org/

One Mind Institute. (2017). *About one mind institute*. Retrieved October 30, 2017, from https://www.onemindinstitute.org/about-one-mind-institute

Royal Foundation. (2017). *About our foundation*. Retrieved October 30, 2017, from http://www.royalfoundation.com/about-our-foundation/

University of Louisiana Counseling and Testing Center. (2017). *School leaders involved in drinking and drug education (SLIDDE)*. Retrieved October 30, 2017, from https://counselingandtesting.louisiana.edu/content/slidde/school-leaders-involved-drinking-and-drug-education-slidde

Wear Your Label. (2017). *Wear your label*. Retrieved October 30, 2017, from https://wearyourlabel.com/

Chapter 10
Self-Care for Professionals

At the root of this dilemma is the way we view mental health in this country. Whether an illness affects your heart, your leg, or your brain, it's still an illness, and there should be no distinction.—Michelle Obama

The idea of burnout exists in many different professions, especially those related to both mental health and criminal justice. No matter the political stance or outlook, most would agree that the job of police officers is a difficult one. For the most part, when police are involved in an incident, it is a negative one. Police patrol for traffic stops or speeding on highways, respond to emergency calls, and escort inmates when transferred or appearing in court. Often traffic stops and speeding result in tickets, and emergency calls can result in arrests and/or involvement of medical personnel. All of these are negative, again, much of the job of police. Now, consider repeating this scenario daily for years—tough thoughts, right? This is the reality for most that serve on the "front line," yet, this sentiment can be widespread throughout the entire system coming into contact with individuals with mental illness.

10.1 What No One Talks About: Our Own Mental Health

In previous chapters, many topics were discussed as they relate to treatment for those with a mental health diagnosis as well as how those individuals interact with law enforcement, emergency medical services, and probation and parole. It is critical to take into account how these interactions impact the overall well-being of those frontline professionals. With their jobs being stressful, straining, and high intensity, there can and often will be adverse reactions. The irony is that often first responders, mental health professionals, and other law enforcement personnel spend much of their time helping others to a point where they begin neglecting themselves. Self-care for these people is not only essential for their wellness but also for their loved ones and those they are helping in the community.

© Springer International Publishing AG, part of Springer Nature 2018
J. Hector, D. Khey, *Criminal Justice and Mental Health*,
https://doi.org/10.1007/978-3-319-76442-9_10

Job strain and stress can influence anyone, both in the short and long terms. Repeating the same tasks over and over and receiving a similar result each time is frustrating no matter the context. Combining this frustration with encountering people (typically) in very negative and seemingly repetitive situations, one quickly realizes how overwhelming this can become. Stigma is also a concept that comes into play for professionals and self-care. Often, many professionals do not want to admit that they are in need of help. The idea of seeming "weak" in a profession like law enforcement can be detrimental to a career.

Burnout and compassion fatigue are two common consequences of an occupation working directly with individuals in crisis and related both to mental health and the criminal justice system. Both can touch many occupations that reach beyond first responders. Additionally, doctors, nurses, mental health professionals, case workers, and even lawyers can feel the effects of burnout and compassion fatigue. Further, the impact of burnout can vary depending on many factors. At times, a simple break or vacation can be enough to refuel and reconnect with one's work. Unfortunately, in the American work culture, taking time off or for vacation is not often celebrated. In fact, many people allow their leave time to go unused.

Many professionals benefit from attending conferences and training sessions throughout their careers. No matter the length of time in a career, there are always new and innovative techniques and programs being developed. Learning from pioneers in the industry and even peers can be valuable. Additionally, interacting with others who work in the same industry and experience a similar daily life and schedule can aid in understanding processes. Commiserating with those who lead a related professional life can often take away stress and burden. This is not unlike unwinding after a class or day of work with friends to vent. The benefits of having professional friends can be immense.

Realistically, it is impossible *not* to be impacted by the job within these occupations. The better focus and idea is to find a balance and maintain a level of positivity and happiness outside of work. Often, these occupations require long hours and days outside of the typical "9–5" and work week. Working "odd hours" can prohibit a person from finding activities and hobbies of interest to maintain a work/life balance. These challenges can be taxing on a person, no matter the nature of their occupation.

10.1.1   Burnout, Compassion Fatigue, and Vicarious Trauma: Working with People in Crisis

The literature on work burnout is continuing to become more relevant in the workplace in the twenty-first century—with mental health professionals and beyond. The concept of designing workplaces to aid in the promotion of both physical and mental wellness certainly has gained momentum, for example, the heavyweights of Silicon Valley seem to compete on designing work campuses that include such things as food courts with healthy options, gardens, creative spaces, and so on. At times, popular culture seems to highlight how some employers have taken this concept to an extreme. For example, in what has become one of the more infamous of these campuses, the Googleplex features a hair salon, on-site medical care, various cafeterias with free food, bicycles to use (free), child care (again, free), a full-service laundry room, massage therapy, and pet-friendly spaces to take advantage of the allowance of dogs on campus (Ulanoff, 2009). Mental health professionals seem to be more mindful of burnout than their colleagues in criminal justice due to the nature of their training; yet, both are at risk of two special factors that can complicate burnout—compassion fatigue and vicarious trauma (also known as secondary trauma).

Each of these terms—burnout, compassion fatigue, and secondary traumatic stress—is often conflated by various sources both professional and lay. While the three are intertwined, they are quite distinct. Burnout generally refers to feelings of exhaustion directly because of one's work. This burnout can come in the form of physical and/or emotional exhaustion and feeling drained, which can lead to low job satisfaction, interpersonal problems, sickness, substance use/misuse/abuse, and so on. For example, odds of experiencing burnout will almost always increase as one increases their work hours—if an employee consistently puts in 80, 90, or 100 h per week, burnout is almost guaranteed. While a 100-h work week may seem impossible, it can be very likely for most American medical residents as they prepare to launch into careers in medicine. The latest standards published by the Accreditation Council for Graduate Medical Education requires accredited programs to abide by the following rules: (1) "Duty hours must be limited to 80 hours per week, *averaged over a four-week period*, inclusive of all in-house call activities and all moonlighting," (2) "…up to 10% or a maximum of 88 hours to individual programs based on a sound educational rationale," and (3) "residents must be scheduled for a minimum of one day free of duty every week (when averaged over four weeks" (ACGME, 2017). Of the 1515 studies on duty-hour limits identified by Philibert, Nasca, Brigham, and Shapiro (2013), these researchers assessed 83 of the highest quality ones to review the impact of limiting the work hours of medical residents. Not surprisingly, limitations on hours had a benefit on burnout and overall mood, with some evidence to support that these limitations also improved patient safety. Note that these findings have direct consequences for the quality of mental health services, particularly in teaching hospitals (e.g., where significantly more poor and uninsured patients receive their care), as young psychiatrists push themselves to meet their work demands. Evidence bears that burnout can be problematic for the employee as well as any others impacted by their work.

To investigate burnout in depth, Maslach developed an instrument—called the Maslach Burnout Inventory (MBI)—to assess what he postulated were the three dimensions of burnout (Maslach, Jackson, & Leiter, 2006). The first dimension is emotional exhaustion caused by one's overwhelming work demands, which saps one's perceived energy. The second dimension is depersonalization and cynicism, which results in feelings of detachment from one's job. The third and last dimension is feelings of inefficacy, which one perceives themselves as ineffective, not growing or learning, and stuck in a rut. The MBI was developed in a way to gauge varying levels of burnout as Maslach felt it was not an all-or-none concept. As such, burnout is a dynamic concept that has been shown to have impacts in any vocation. It can be mitigated in various ways, such as the notorious concept of "loving what you do." However, even those who are passionate about their work can experience burnout.

Compassion fatigue is a concept developed by Charles Figley (2002), which adapts the concept of burnout to individuals who serve to care for others, such as nurses, doctors, counselors, case workers, and so on (also known as caretakers and helpers, whether professional or lay, such as in a case of an adult child taking care of their aging parent(s)). These concepts align very closely; however, the effects of compassion fatigue tend to predominately result in desensitization, depression and anxiety disorders, disconnection with family and close friends, and social isolation (Mathieu, 2012). A common popular culture example of compassion fatigue lies with adult children having to take on caretaking duties of their ailing parents. Day, Anderson, and Davis explored this issue in a 2014 article in *Issues in Mental Health Nursing* among 12 adult daughters turned caregivers of a parent with dementia. Using semi-structured interviews, these researchers discovered four overarching themes that seemed to predict risk of developing compassion fatigue in these caregivers: uncertainty (mostly over the seemingly unpredictable sickness and what the future brings), doubt (mostly that the caregivers doubted their ability to take care of their parent in a manner they deserve), attachment (noting a close attachment with the parent), and strain (due to juggling the demands of life with the added responsibilities of caregiving). The interviews in the study gave striking life to the potential results of compassion fatigue—helplessness, hopelessness, diminishing empathy, and isolation: "When [my parent walked away from the house], it's just been a constant in the back of my mind. What could happen next time?" "Not feeling that I'm able to take care of her the way I should be able to take care of her." "That kind of has my rest broken, and when I get to work the next day, I'm just no good, I'll sleep all day." "Juggling my time, taking care of the house, and my house there, and my job and friends and family. It's just hard to juggle sometimes." "I think I had reached a point where I felt resentful toward her. I used to love the weekends. I dread Fridays because that means that I don't have any relief at all. All Friday night…Saturdays… Sunday." "You can't stop" (Day, Anderson, & Davis, 2014).

Vicarious trauma layers on the potential complications that can arise in professionals or laypersons caused by caring for an individual(s) experiencing significant trauma in their lives. In a very real sense, the trauma that touches people's lives rubs off on the individuals that seek to help in the recovery process. The most salient recent examples of this lies in first responders of 9/11, the Boston Marathon bombing, Hurricane Katrina, and so on. However, horrendous images of physical trauma are certainly not necessary to trigger vicarious trauma. Professionals who aid rape victims, children in child welfare cases, and so on are certainly at risk for being exposed to vicarious trauma. If this exposure goes unabated, it may develop into clinical diagnoses, such as post-traumatic stress disorder. Specifically, the *Diagnostic and Statistical Manual V* (American Psychological Association, 2013) included new criteria for post-traumatic stress disorder (italics emphasize modifications):

A. Exposure to actual or threatened death, serious injury, or sexual violence in one (or more) of the following ways:

   1. Directly experiencing the traumatic event(s).
   2. Witnessing, in person, the event(s) as it occurred to others.
   3. Learning that the traumatic event(s) occurred to a close family member or close friend. In cases of actual or threatened death of a family member or friend, the event(s) must have been violent or accidental.
   4. *Experiencing repeated or extreme exposure to aversive details of the traumatic event(s) (e.g., first responders collecting human remains; police officers repeated exposure to details of child abuse).*

Note: Criterion A4 does not apply to exposure through electronic media, television, movies, or pictures, unless this exposure is work related.

As Levin, Kleinman, and Adler (2014) point out that no clear data exists on how the addition of A4 results in differences in PTSD incidence and prevalence or other potential impacts. Much more research needs to be done in this area. In fact, the literature on first responder physical and mental health after vicarious trauma exposure is at its nascent stage, with primary focus on line-officer police and emergency medical services personnel at this point. Further, research has yet to delve into the civilian and sworn staff who work in traumatic crime scenes (Rivera Waugh, 2016). In 2012, an extensive international search for extant literature uncovered 28 high-quality, peer-reviewed studies on PTSD prevalence among "rescue workers" through 2008 (Berger et al., 2012). On average, the "going rate" regarding prevalence of PTSD among first responders was found to be 10%. Not only is this figure alarming; Berger and his colleagues' overall search for literature did not pick up on a large array of interest in the topic before 2008, reinforcing the idea that this area is fertile ground for much needed research.

10.2 Traumatic Experiences and Fatigue: What We Know

Across occupations, especially in jobs which entail interfacing with people in difficult and traumatic situations, the symptoms of burnout are strikingly similar: emotional exhaustion, depersonalization, decreased empathy, isolation, depression, anxiety, cynicism, losing a sense of self-worth (particularly when related to job performance and ability), and so on (Walsh, Taylor, & Hastings, 2012). Research has shown that when police officers are under stress and have negative coping strategies, it can lead to problem drinking (Swatt, Gibson, & Piquero, 2007). Specifically, researchers who studied Baltimore police officers found a strong relationship between stress on the job and drinking, with problematic drinking being mediated through anxiety and depression. In other words, officers who were stressed tended to drink; yet, if they were stressed and anxious/depressed, they tended to be at higher risk to problem drink. This research echoes findings from other occupations; yet, perhaps not many other occupations experience the acute stress as do first responders.

It should not be a surprise to learn, then, that a growing array of research and treatment effort has been invested into coping skills for professionals; whereas, before the turn of the century, there was not much information to inform us (Anshel, 2000). Despite years of progress in research, there is not one particular evidence-based coping skills training program that is in regular use. Beyond just finding positive ways to cope, the development of a robust self-care program has become the best practice in public service. While the programming may not be as generous as the offerings at the Googleplex, the increasingly more prominent role of self-care programming seems to be a sustained pattern into the twenty-first century.

10.3 Self-Care: Why Is It Important

The 2016 National Survey on EMS Mental Health Services throws the importance of self-care in sharp relief (National Association of Emergency Medical Technicians, 2017). In this most recent edition of the survey, 58% of respondents (including paramedics, EMTs, EMS training coordinators, and medical and EMS directors and managers) either disagreed or strongly disagreed when asked if they are satisfied with the mental health services provided by their agency to their employees; 52% of respondents reported that their agency did not even have such mental health services (37%) or were not aware of these services if they were available (15%); only 26% of respondents claimed that their agency had programs available to help employees with substance use and dependence issues; 42% of respondents reported that their agency does not offer health and wellness services; and 41% of respondents reported that they disagree or strongly disagree when asked if they know where to go for help within their agency. The qualitative feedback is even more damning:

- Initiating mental health services through the [employee assistance program] is an invitation for mandatory competency evaluation, grounds for dismissal.
- Most of the people in my organization do not feel comfortable using any service provided by the organization for fear that the information will come back and be used against them in the future.
- [Employee assistance program] provided for three sessions per incident. I do not believe that to be adequate for someone seeking help.
- Currently, acute emotional injuries and mental health are not considered to be work-related by worker's company.
- I was seeing a mental health professional for PTSD after an ambulance accident that resulted in the death of the driver in the other. Worker's company denied my claim, leaving me stuck with the bills.

- The agency I work for sees mental health as a weakness. If you ask for help, you become verbally abused by coworkers, supervisors, and station managers. I needed help and was told, "that's why women don't belong in EMS. They're overly emotional…."
- Mental health is a joke to management. They still operate on the philosophy that if you can't handle it, you're in the wrong line of work.
- Attitude at our department is, if you can't handle it, get out, sissy.
- I strongly believe that in the workplace mental health is viewed as taboo, not to be talked about and, if found out, viewed as a weakness.
- In seeking help you are shamed, made fun of by superiors, and told to suck it up; it's part of the job.
- There is absolutely no concern for the mental or physical health of employees at my agency.
- Rural agencies that operate off monies strictly derived by billing simply cannot afford to offer these types of services to their employees.

Surveys like these are important yet are relatively uncommon among first responders. As we begin to address these issues outlined above with EMS personnel, it is important to remember that they are likely occurring with regularity among all types of first responders. Much more research is direly needed to monitor these issues, particularly as we devise ways to offer improvement in self-care among our first responders.

10.4 Examples of Self-Care Programming

At this time, there appears to be a limited array of programming tailored to meet the needs of first responders. Such programs include Addiction and Trauma Recovery Integration Model (ATRIUM), Essence of Being Real, Risking Connection®, Sanctuary Model®, Seeking Safety, Trauma, Addiction, Mental Health, and Recovery (TAMAR), Trauma Affect Regulation: Guide for Education and Therapy (TARGET), and Trauma Recovery and Empowerment Model (TREM and M-TREM). Many of these programs generally target trauma exposure and are customized to first responders by those who adopt them and/or whose creators offer some guidance on such customizations for professionals themselves. A minority of these, such as ATRIUM, Essence of Being Real, and Risking Connection®, have been formulated for specifically professionals. Regardless, the industry standard for any of these trauma-informed approaches must garner the following key principles for the best result: (1) safety (e.g., the physical setting feels safe, and human interactions promote a sense of safety), (2) trustworthiness and transparency (e.g., any decisions by the organization or leadership is transparent), (3) peer support (e.g., support involves similarly situated individuals who have been exposed to trauma), (4) collaboration and mutuality (e.g., eliminating the perception of power differences between administrators and professional staff in regard to trauma-informed

Table 10.1 Risking Connection® summary of model, program goals, and expected outcomes, adapted from the California Evidence-Based Clearinghouse for Child Welfare (2017) resources

Emphasis	Programmatic goals	Expected measurable outcomes
A framework for understanding common trauma symptoms	Utilize the proprietary risking connection framework to respond to the impact of traumatic life events	Knowledge of content and models essential to risking connection
A common inclusive language	Frame common symptoms and behaviors as adaptations to traumatic life events	Shift in beliefs favorable to trauma-informed care
Relationships as the primary agent of change	Respond to survivors of traumatic experiences from a strength-based approach	Demonstration of behaviors aligned with trauma-informed care
Respect for, and care of, both the client and the service provider (vicarious traumatization) as critical to healing	Demonstrate collaborative crisis management that reduces the risk of re-traumatization	Changes in professional quality of life including an increase in compassion satisfaction, decrease in burnout, and a decrease in secondary (or vicarious) traumatic stress
Strategies and tools to support adoption of the model in clinical, social, and organizational processes	Demonstrate increased self-awareness of their reactions to individual clients	Responses that reduce the use of restraints and seclusion at organizations
	Integrate knowledge of the impact of vicarious traumatization in the formulation of organizational and individual self-care plans	Decreases in staff turnover, staff injuries from client management, increases in staff satisfaction with job
	Create trauma-responsive cultures including policies, processes, and people systems	Increases in foster parent retention and decreases in foster placement disruptions

care/services/support), (5) empowerment, voice, and choice (e.g., ensuring the organization supports trauma-informed care throughout its organizational structure), and (6) cultural, historical, and gender issues (e.g., the organization offers services that are responsive to gender, cultural, and historical issues; SAMHSA, 2014, 2017).

For example, Risking Connection® offers organizational consulting to aid in establishing a proprietary system that equates to a turnkey solution for self-care. As with many solutions discussed throughout this book, Risking Connection® was born as a response to litigation and developed with the mitigation of litigation risk in mind. The program offers an advantage in that it is grounded in theory (constructivist self-development theory, relational psychoanalytic theory, developmental psychopathology, and cognitive schemas) and the ability for professionals to enroll in "train-the-trainer" courses to ensure sustainability within an organization after launch. See Table 10.1 for a summary of Rising Connection® to get an idea of the overall programmatic approach. Other programs named above use similar approaches to ensure that an organization develops and maintains a culture that is trauma-informed and trauma-responsive.

10.5   Conclusion

With the growth in incarcerated and justice-involved individuals, the demand on professionals has also increased. For first responders responding to a crisis, as well as those providing treatment during and after incarceration, strong anecdotal evidence documents the impact on these professionals from increasingly difficult encounters. Our system is overflowing, and those with the care and desire to help resolve it are being pushed to the limit. The importance of self-care should be evident, yet administrators of first responders have been slow to ratchet up support. Treatment is *essential* not only for the target population discussed throughout this book who seem to be in frequent contact with the criminal justice system but also for the people who spend their days helping this population. Our society needs to support and shelter those in need and ensure that all have the same access and ability to seek out and receive the treatment and care they deserve—including first responders.

For the little information that we have on the topic regarding the perceptions of mental health among first responders, coping skills, and the perception of first responder culture of being unfriendly to those who need help, there certainly is more than enough evidence to support a dire need for broader adoption of self-care programming. Remember, investing in our professionals is also investing in individuals with mental health concerns.

References

Accreditation Council for Graduate Medical Education. (2017). *Common program requirements*. Retrieved October 30, 2017, from http://www.acgme.org/Portals/0/PFAssets/ProgramRequirements/CPRs_2017-07-01.pdf

American Psychiatric Association. (2013). *Diagnostic and statistical manual of mental disorders* (5th ed.). Arlington, VA: American Psychiatric Publishing.

Anshel, M. H. (2000). A conceptual model and implications for coping with stressful events in police work. *Criminal Justice and Behavior, 27*(3), 375–400.

Berger, W., Coutinho, E. S. F., Figueira, I., Marques-Portella, C., Luz, M. P., Neylan, T. C., et al. (2012). Rescuers at risk: A systematic review and meta-regression analysis of the worldwide current prevalence and correlates of PTSD in rescue workers. *Social Psychiatry and Psychiatric Epidemiology, 47*(6), 1001–1011.

California Evidence-Based Clearinghouse for Child Welfare. (2017). *Risking Connection®*. Retrieved October 31, 2017, from http://www.cebc4cw.org/program/risking-connection/detailed

Day, J. R., Anderson, R. A., & Davis, L. L. (2014). Compassion fatigue in adult daughter caregivers of a parent with dementia. *Issues in Mental Health Nursing, 35*(10), 796–804.

Figley, C. R. (Ed.). (2002). *Treating compassion fatigue.* New York: Routledge.

Levin, A. P., Kleinman, S. B., & Adler, J. S. (2014). DSM-5 and posttraumatic stress disorder. *Journal of the American Academy of Psychiatry and the Law Online, 42*(2), 146–158.

Maslach, C., Jackson, S. E., & Leiter, M. P. (2006). *Maslach burnout inventory* (3rd ed.). Palo Alto, CA: Consulting Psychologists Press.

Mathieu, F. (2012). *The compassion fatigue workbook: Creative tools for transforming compassion fatigue and vicarious traumatization.* New York: Routledge.

National Association of Emergency Medical Technicians. (2017). *2016 National survey on EMS mental health services.* Retrieved October 30, 2017, from http://www.naemt.org/docs/default-source/ems-health-and-safety-documents/mental-health-grid/2016-naemt-mental-health-report-8-14-16.pdf?status=Temp&sfvrsn=0.9606132567905388

Philibert, I., Nasca, T., Brigham, T., & Shapiro, J. (2013). Duty-hour limits and patient care and resident outcomes: Can high-quality studies offer insight into complex relationships? *Annual Review of Medicine, 64*, 467–483.

Rivera Waugh, J. (2016). *Crime scene investigators and traumatic event-related stress: A quantitative study.* Los Angeles: SAGE.

Substance Abuse and Mental Health Services Administration. (2014). *SAMHSA's concept of trauma and guidance for a trauma-informed approach.* Retrieved October 31, 2017, from https://store.samhsa.gov/shin/content/SMA14-4884/SMA14-4884.pdf

Substance Abuse and Mental Health Services Administration. (2017). *Trauma-informed approach and trauma-specific interventions.* Retrieved October 31, 2017, from https://www.samhsa.gov/nctic/trauma-interventions

Swatt, M. L., Gibson, C. L., & Piquero, N. L. (2007). Exploring the utility of general strain theory in explaining problematic alcohol consumption by police officers. *Journal of Criminal Justice, 35*(6), 596–611.

Ulanoff, L. (2009). *The Googleplex: Everything you've heard is true.* PC Magazine. Retrieved October 30, 2017, from https://www.pcmag.com/article2/0,2817,2344010,00.asp

Walsh, M., Taylor, M., & Hastings, V. (2012). Burnout and post traumatic stress disorder in the police: Educating officers with the stilwell TRiM approach. *Policing: A Journal of Policy and Practice, 7*(2), 167–177.

Chapter 11
What Works and What's Promising

It's been a long time coming. But I know, a change is gonna come.—Sam Cooke

This book came about through the collective experience of both authors. Jada and Dave independently and together on various projects have seen a need to bring crime and mental health to the forefront of many conversations not only in the professional realm but also in working with students. As it stands today, students graduating in criminal justice will more than likely encounter justice-involved individuals with mental health concerns. It is important that those students turned professional understand the obstacles and cracks in the system that individuals face. This book is just a starting point for many conversations to come on these topics. The hope is that beginning the discussion can also begin the solution.

11.1 Looking Forward

People are slowly beginning to raise awareness on criminal justice system reform, mental health stigma, and substance abuse needs. Hopefully, these positive strides continue and bring more access to care, programming, and treatment needed for those involved in the justice system as well as preventative measures.

Prevention for mental health, substance abuse, and crime all has common ground. Programs exist at the federal, state, and local levels to implement prevention framework for behavioral health and public health topics. Integration with these programs is essential for individuals in need, specifically within substance abuse and criminal justice.

Prevention thought processes can be important for changing stigma and being proactive about concerns within society. For example, proactive preventative measures can inform the public about risks and potential problems a person can experience. Even further, being part of a certain group can increase those risks. Whether it be a specific racial or ethnic group, gender, socioeconomic status, or even just a

© Springer International Publishing AG, part of Springer Nature 2018
J. Hector, D. Khey, *Criminal Justice and Mental Health*,
https://doi.org/10.1007/978-3-319-76442-9_11

specific neighborhood can affect the risk of someone's potential to experience negative impact. Education and awareness about crime risks, drug addiction risks, and mental health symptoms can help to create an informed individual. Additionally, this also lessens the stigma associated with each and creates an open dialogue to begin discussing these topics in a healthy manner.

Continuing to have conversations regarding mental health and overall behavioral health is important to keep the topic relevant. These conversations allow for education and information to be exchanged. As with any important topic, positive message creates positive outlooks.

11.1.1   Legislative Progress

State legislatures often address bills related to both mental health and criminal justice, especially when there is a change in administration. These bills can themselves be solely about addressing issues within either of these areas, or there may be amendments hidden within another bill related to a completely different topic.

Each year, NAMI provides a report titled State Mental Health Legislation: Trends, Themes and Effective Practices. This report helps to shed light on both positive approaches states are taking in mental health, as well as those that are lacking in improvements. Additionally, the report breaks down information by subjects including criminal justice, suicide prevention, and inpatient and crisis care. Each section provides a summary of the bill as well as links to the state-related bills within that area of focus. This report serves as a yearly guide to how mental health legislation is changing in each state.

In Utah, the state legislature introduced a bill to work toward positive criminal justice reform, including mental health initiatives. The 2015 bill HB 348 entitled Criminal Justice Programs "amends Utah Code provisions regarding corrections, sentencing, probation and parole, controlled substance offenses, substance abuse and mental health treatment, vehicle offenses, and related provisions to modify penalties and sentencing guidelines, treatment programs for persons in the criminal justice system, and probation and parole compliance and violations to address recidivism."

Highlights of Utah's HB 348 incorporate the state's Division of Mental Health and Department of Corrections to work together to establish performance goals and outcome measures for treatment programs. Then, these departments are to collect data and evaluate those performance goals and outcome measures and supply the results to the public. These policies are to not only increase awareness for the populous of Utah but also begin the process of working toward treating those in need and reducing recidivism. Further, HB 348 requires the Department of Corrections of Utah to establish and implement standards for treatment programs in county jails as well.

This bill is one of many in the steps toward positive change for both persons with a mental illness in the criminal justice system. Other positive notes in the 2015 NAMI State Mental Health Legislation report surround topics previously discussed in this book. For example, CIT or Crisis Intervention Training for Law Enforcement

Table 11.1 Summary of findings from the NAMI State Mental Health Legislation Report

State	2013	2014	2015	State	2013	2014	2015
Alabama	*Maintain*	Increase	*Maintain*	Montana	Increase	*Maintain*	Increase
Alaska	*Decrease*	*Decrease*	*Decrease*	Nebraska	*Decrease*	*Decrease*	Increase
Arizona	Increase	Increase	Increase	Nevada	Increase	*Maintain*	*Decrease*
Arkansas	Increase	*Decrease*	*Decrease*	New Hampshire	Increase	Increase	Increase
California	Increase	Increase	*Maintain*	New Jersey	Increase	Increase	Increase
Colorado	Increase	Increase	Increase	New Mexico	*Maintain*	Increase	Increase
Connecticut	Increase	Increase	Increase	New York	*Maintain*	Increase	Increase
Delaware	Increase	Increase	Increase	North Carolina	*Decrease*	*Decrease*	*Decrease*
District of Columbia	Increase	Increase	*Decrease*	North Dakota	*Maintain*	*Maintain*	*Decrease*
Florida	*Maintain*	Increase	Increase	Ohio	Increase	Increase	*Decrease*
Georgia	Increase	*Maintain*	Increase	Oklahoma	Increase	Increase	*Maintain*
Hawaii	Increase	*Decrease*	*Maintain*	Oregon	Increase	*Maintain*	Increase
Idaho	Increase	Increase	Increase	Pennsylvania	*Maintain*	Increase	Pending
Illinois	Increase	*Maintain*	Pending	Rhode Island	Increase	*Decrease*	*Maintain*
Indiana	*Maintain*	*Maintain*	Increase	South Carolina	Increase	Increase	Increase
Iowa	Increase	Increase	*Decrease*	South Dakota	Increase	Increase	Increase
Kansas	Increase	Increase	*Decrease*	Tennessee	Increase	*Maintain*	*Maintain*
Kentucky	Increase	*Decrease*	*Decrease*	Texas	Increase	*Maintain*	Increase
Louisiana	*Decrease*	*Decrease*	*Maintain*	Utah	Increase	Increase	*Maintain*
Maine	*Decrease*	Increase	Increase	Vermont	Increase	Increase	*Maintain*
Maryland	Increase	Increase	*Maintain*	Virginia	Increase	Increase	Increase
Massachusetts	Increase	*Maintain*	Increase	Washington	Increase	Increase	Increase
Michigan	Increase	*Decrease*	*Maintain*	West Virginia	*Maintain*	Increase	Increase
Minnesota	Increase	Increase	Increase	Wisconsin	Increase	Increase	*Maintain*
Mississippi	Increase	*Maintain*	*Maintain*	Wyoming	*Decrease*	*Decrease*	*Decrease*
Missouri	Increase	Increase	*Maintain*				

has been added in different ways to Indiana, Illinois, and Maryland. Illinois is requiring a standard certified training program, while similarly, Maryland is mandating a program for Baltimore City and county police officers. Additionally, Indiana is creating a CIT Technical Assistance Center (TAC) to create an advisory committee to oversee all CIT-related activities within the state.

States are also looking into creating other specialty courts as well. South Carolina and Arizona have put bills in place to create mental health courts. These are just the changes within 2015 and not inclusive of the past successes of other states (Table 11.1).

As a society, working together, change can be done to better the health of everyone. Using history and current data, there appears to be hope in small organizations or movements to work toward positive, health change.

11.2 Change Is Taking Place Slowly

Often, when changes are attempted in states and local communities, mental health is shot down because of misinformation, lack of education, and stigma. Health departments are making cuts due to losses in federal funding. Those cuts often come from mental health programming since other areas are viewed as more urgent needs as it relates to health.

A quick Google search of any combination of the words "mental illness," "jail" or "prison," and "death" will bring forth some truly eye-opening results. Change can begin with a conversation, continued awareness campaigns, and increasing collaborations where they previously did not exist. It appears that some of the most successful changes are occurring at the local level with partnerships that span from the courts to professionals to persons of faith to laypersons.

11.3 Change Agents

A positive resource for many partnerships and the organization they represent can be grant writing. Grants can range from thousands of dollars to millions and cover varying aspects of topics related to both crime and mental health. These grants can be offered from both private organizations and the federal government. For example, in some instances, the specialty courts mentioned in previous chapters were initially funded by a federal grant.

Organizations like SAMHSA and BJA offer grants on a yearly cycle. State and local governments and nonprofit organizations can submit an application to receive the funding. These grant opportunities allow communities that would not otherwise have the funding available to show proof of concept for their ideas, implement them, evaluate their results, and refine their knowledge of the problems they are attempting to solve. If these awards can provide proof of success with evidence and support, the hope would be continued funding to allow for the sustainability of these programs to continue positive change (and to replicate these models elsewhere throughout the country).

As highlighted throughout this book, the change agents involve partnerships among mental health and criminal justice professionals, lawyers, faith leaders, congregants, employers, researchers, legislators and policymakers, nonprofits, and community resource liaisons, among many others. Many of these grant opportunities force the issue of having these key stakeholders come together to be eligible for funding. It matters less on what brings these players together rather than the outcomes they can create when they get on the same page. These changes are occurring throughout the country thanks to federal leadership on mental health and criminal justice reinvestment and reform over the two decades (Table 11.2).

Table 11.2 Recent grant programs targeting mental health, substance use disorder, and reentry issues (2017)

Grant program	Program description
Adult Drug Court Discretionary Grant Program (BJA)	Supports specialty courts and their key partnerships; current categories include implementation (e.g., startup capital), expansion (e.g., offer broader treatment modalities, expand to target special populations, etc.), and statewide enhancement
Second Chance Act Reentry Program for Adults with Co-Occurring Substance Use and Mental Disorders (BJA)	Targets adults with co-occurring disorders as they return to communities after a period of incarceration; supports units of government or tribal government
Justice and Mental Health Collaboration Program (BJA)	Supports broad collaboration to improve outcomes for individuals with mental illness and co-occurring disorders; geared for county and parish governmental units to take lead on collaborative partnerships with its key stakeholders in the community *or* law enforcement agencies to serve as lead partner in this type of project
Grants to Expand Substance Abuse Treatment Capacity in Adult Treatment Drug Courts and Adult Tribal Healing to Wellness Courts	Supports specialty courts needing to beef up their evidence-based treatment provisioning, particularly medication-assisted treatment

11.4   Theoretical Considerations

Many theorists have opined on the critical nature of theory to structure our understanding of human behavior. As such, pouring over theory and testing their hypotheses and practicality in the real world can give us insight on how to intervene on behalf of those who are suffering from mental illness and/or substance use disorder. For example, if we know that selecting and prioritizing social relationships with individuals who like to use drugs and get themselves into criminal trouble increase the risk one engages in the same behavior, we can act to disconnect those ties as best as we can. Perhaps, more likely, if we assist in helping someone connect with pro-social ties and assist in making these relationships a priority for this same individual, the risk of getting into trouble is greatly diminished even if bad influences remain in the background (Akers, 1990). Theory can help vet practical solutions, test these ideas, refine them, and provide a scientific process on solving the problems facing us.

11.4.1   Restorative Justice and Relevant Theory

According to classic labeling theory, societies are hardwired to use social control to regulate behavior—particularly to correct behavior that breaks social norms (Klein, 1986; Schur, 1969). An easy example of this process can be found in the concept of the "outlaw" in the American Old West. Outlaws were the worst of men, formally casted off from good society with a complete loss of legal rights. Labels exist in many forms: criminal, bad, bandit, robber, druggie, and so on; these also serve to reify those on the normative side and reinforce good behavior ("don't be like 'them'"). According to theory, these efforts of social control routinely backfire. In other words, efforts to punish bad or wrong behavior may drive vulnerable people, particularly the young and impressionable, toward a criminal lifestyle or deeper into mental illness.

This idea originated with Frank Tannenbaum (1938) who observed that official reactions to social behavior (e.g., by the criminal justice system or its parts or by the mental health-care system) can change a person's self-concept (e.g., their identity) in two ways. First, when a label such as "criminal," "convict," "delinquent," "incorrigible," "insane," or "mentally ill" is applied to a person by the system, these individuals are often subsequently immersed into an environment (jails/prisons) rich with learning opportunities from others who have been similarly labeled. Second, labeled individuals are frequently subjected to social admonishment by everyday people ("informal" sources, such as family, school, potential employers, etc.), which erects barriers to any hope of getting on the "right" path—a crime-free or healthy life. This second effect of a label is called secondary deviance (Lemert, 1951, 1972). At some point in the lives of labeled people, the labels are gradually accepted until they "stick." Over time, these individuals align their lifestyles and their behaviors to suit their altered "primary status"—a concept called "the self-fulfilling prophesy."

These twentieth-century concepts witnessed a renaissance in criminology and criminal justice when the restorative justice movement came about, yet have remained relevant in circles of mental health researchers for their obvious ties to the effects of stigma on individuals (Center for Justice and Reconciliation, 2012; Tyler, 2006). For newcomer theorists in the restorative justice movement, there was a missing element in older renditions of labeling when applying it to crime. In some cases, these theorists saw shame as *good*, and healthy, for offenders and victims alike. When done in a certain way, shame can bring reconciliation and healing. John Braithwaite calls this reintegrative shaming; the theory of reintegrative shaming focuses on *the manner* by which the formal system applies shame by punishment and admonishment. Namely, if the system can correct behavior holistically, it can be rehabilitative—shame must be accompanied by general forgiveness, acceptance, and reintegration to be transformative (Ahmed & Braithwait, 2012; Ahmed, Harris, Braithwaite, & Braithwaite, 2001; Braithwaite, 2002; Braithwaite, Ahmed, & Braithwaite, 2008).

Shame is normal and natural. It is a reaction to social behaviors that fall outside of social and/or legal norms. For example, a disapproving mother may react to a son's bad attitude and signs of disrespect. This condemnation could be reinforced by others close by, for example, neighbors, family members, or church members, depending on localized cultural values. Shame works primarily to elicit feelings of remorse and drive recompense. A kid caught stealing an expensive graphing calculator at school may be admonished by a teacher and disciplined by the principal. Quickly thereafter, the principal may call the child's family, starting this cycle of shaming at home. According to reintegrative shaming, the goal would be to make sure the student quickly reconnects with pro-social ties at school, at home, and even in the community through apology, forgiveness, and acceptance. The calculator goes back to the victim, the victim makes peace with the offender, and surrounding players help to heal everyone accordingly. Braithwaite (1989) warns that shaming can be stigmatizing, and this can possibly amplify deviance—as seen with traditional labeling theory. If this calculator-stealing kid was sent to detention with all the other bad kids, kicked out of Advanced Placement Calculus, and left to pick up the pieces, his shame may put him on a darker future path.

Each modern society seems to have its own brand of shaming. For example, Japanese culture has promulgated a pure type of reintegrative shaming in each generation for many centuries. In fact, Japanese offenders are expected to enter a ritual that begins with an apology to which the victim is compelled to help bring the offender back into the fold. If either offender or victim violates these cultural mores, it can bring shame and scrutiny. Any observer of American culture can note the departure this Japanese ritual has with similar interactions in the United States. Thus, reintegrative shaming can be considered a paradigm shift—much like what is going on with criminal justice reform at this time.

11.4.2 Reintegrative Shaming in Action

According to a stream of new literature, the concept of reintegrative shaming can easily guide the practices of a model mental health court for optimal results—at least theoretically. In fact, sociologists Ray, Dollar, and Thames (2011) picked up on this notion and attempted to determine whether observed court proceedings of model mental health courts promulgated feelings of respect and forgiveness while tamping down feelings of disapproval when compared to traditional court proceedings. To scientifically accomplish this task, Ray, Dollar, and Thames used an observation instrument that was designed to measure these constructs in action, called the Global Observational Ratings Instrument. Specifically, this instrument taps into the following:

- How much reintegrative shaming was expressed?
- How much stigmatizing shaming was expressed?
- How much support was the offender given during the court proceedings?
- How much approval of the offender as a person was expressed?
- How much respect for the offender was expressed?
- How much disappointment in the offender was expressed?
- To what extent was the offender treated as a criminal?
- How often were stigmatizing names and labels used to describe the offender?
- How much disapproval of the offender as a person was expressed?
- How clearly was it communicated to the offender that they could put their actions behind them?
- How much forgiveness of the offender was expressed?

To ensure to minimize any bias in applying a score to each of the items to be observed above, the study uses three observers to ensure interrater reliability. If mental health courts operate as intended, the researchers should find substantial differences between the mental health court process and the traditional court process in these domains—and this research supports this hypothesis (Hiday & Ray, 2010). Yet, while these findings are hopeful (pun intended), they did not seem to translate into reductions in recidivism. In this vein, the researchers did not holistically observe the fidelity of the observed mental health courts to other important components required for the optimal success of these programs (Miller & Khey, 2017). In other words, while court proceedings could elicit feelings of reintegrative shaming and forgiveness, adequate treatment protocols may have not been followed or, if followed, may not have employed evidence-based practices proven to work within this target population. In a recent follow-up study, Dollar and Ray (2015) strengthen their original work by continuing to follow the court for 3 years. In all, the conclusions remain the same—client's disapproval by the judge and mental health court personnel was done in a way that was respectful, relationships among participants and court personnel showed evidence of respect and caring, disapproval tended to focus on the behavior and not on any individual, everyone on the mental health court team avoided stigmatizing words and labels, and so on.

By now, it should be easy to see how theory can inform practice; yet, in this case, and for this target population, reintegrative shaming does not offer a complete solution. It certainly optimizes the chances for success and eliminates significant barriers (if not *the* most significant barrier—stigma) that prevent ultimate success. Importantly, the fundamentals of evidence-based mental health treatment are paramount. These findings certainly inform future research and evaluations of the mental health court model. In particular, it underscores the importance of process evaluations. In other words, it is important to not only ensure that the mental health court process is working as intended, and as guided by the principles of reintegrative shaming, evaluations also need to probe the treatment protocols to determine if these are modeled after practices are already proven to work in the field (Miller & Khey, 2017).

11.4.3   The Future of Reintegrative Shaming in Research

The interest in the practicality of reintegrative shaming in the United States has waned since a peak of interest in the late 1990s and early 2000s (as determined by federal funding specifically to explore reintegrative shaming in theory as well as in practice). Mental health courts seem to be the exception. In fact, funding for these programs continues to grow as well as the interest in establishing new courts across the country. Further, interest in the topic remains strong in academia and in research organizations—the online library of the Centre for Justice and Reconciliation holds over 12,800 citations and abstracts for scholarly work and technical "white papers" on restorative justice. In fact, the Centre continues to add about 1000 entries in each year (Khey, 2014). Even with all of this positive activity, some of these entries warn proponents of the impediments that exist to stymie future development of programming based on restorative justice principles (e.g., Dollar & Ray, 2015). Reintegrative shaming may not be *the* solution, but certainly holds promise of optimizing the results of evidence-based programming discussed throughout this book.

One of the missing pieces of current research seems to align with one of the greatest barriers to justice reinvestment—being able to specify a target population known to respond to particular treatment to result in crime reduction. Over the years, researchers have found success in changing offenders' perceptions after being exposed to reintegrative shaming processes. As a whole, research shows that these differences translate into reductions in recidivism for only some individuals, not a majority or all (e.g., Hipple, Gruenewald, & McGarrell, 2012; Sherman, Strang, & Woods, 2000; Strang, Sherman, Woods, & Barnes, 2011). Future research will need to give better clarity as to why this is occurring. This research should also consider blending in the literature of the reentry and criminal justice reform movements—again, reintegrative shaming may help optimize the power of programming that has come about. Programs that offer aftercare to help people returning back to their communities that connect them to employment, mental health and substance abuse treatment, counseling, housing, transportation, education, and vocational training may need to seek out opportunities to apply reintegrative shaming techniques. This appears to be the advantage of reentry court relative to other programs of the sort; just like we have seen with mental health court in providing the structure for reintegrative shaming to occur, reentry court offers the same potential. Future research will need to explore whether this reintegrative shaming is complete in reentry courts in that it can translate into tangible things like gainful employment, family reunification, and pro-social relationships.

With the growth spurt of both mental health and reentry courts, it appears that the reintegrative shaming principles will continue to flourish and guide continued success of criminal justice reform programming. Much more research needs to be done—for example, at what point must reintegrative shaming principles be applied to work properly in the reentry process? Is it possible to start this process before release? If so, does it help? In the community, what is the earliest point criminal justice professionals can apply these principles in the sequential intercept model? Essentially, all of these questions seem to ask, at what point in time is it reasonable to start the healing process and welcome offenders back into the fold.

11.5 Concluding Remarks

Treatment for mental illness can help in many ways, particularly with reducing the chances of individuals to not become justice-involved or—more likely—reduce the chances of not returning to the criminal justice system. Data suggests that there is, on average, an 8-year delay from the onset of mental health symptomatology to first indications of treatment. This delay is due to a complex array of barriers to treatment, of which stigma tends to be the most potent. All too often, the criminal justice system becomes an entry point to mental health services. This is not to say that jails and prisons are illegitimate entry points; yet, these institutions have long been beleaguered with the lack of resources to engage this target population with the care they need. Likely, jail and prison administrators and their staff are unaware of specific mental health diagnoses among their inmates as there are far too many gaps in even the detection of these issues in incarcerated populations.

The aging data on mental health—and, generally speaking, the lack of data in many areas—inhibits progress, particularly among justice-involved populations. It is also important to invest in broader epidemiological surveillance systems as we do with other diseases and conditions. Doing so will allow for professionals to better monitor progress, change incidence of new and emerging issues, and so on. As the Twenty-First Century Cures Act begins to shape the infrastructure of change, it is important for professionals to understand their role in mental health awareness and how the organizations they belong can fill a gap of information that is all too common in this domain.

This book is not meant to be negative in nature, but rather bring to light the issues surrounding crime and mental health—particularly on how crime and mental health intersect all too often. The first steps to change involved acknowledging and understanding the issues at hand. As a society and community, the cracks in the system need to be viewed, reviewed, assessed, and reassessed in order to move forward with solutions. This will take some time and effort, but it can be done.

References

Ahmed, E., & Braithwaite, V. (2012). Learning to manage shame in school bullying: Lessons for restorative justice interventions. *Critical Criminology, 20*(1), 79–97.

Ahmed, E., Harris, N., Braithwaite, J., & Braithwaite, V. (2001). *Shame management through reintegration*. New York: Cambridge University Press.

Akers, R. L. (1990). Rational choice, deterrence, and social learning theory in criminology: The path not taken. *Journal of Criminal Law & Criminology, 81*(3), 653–676.

Braithwaite, J. (1989). *Crime, shame, and reintegration*. Cambridge, UK: Cambridge University Press.

Braithwaite, J. (2002). *Restorative justice and responsive regulation*. New York: Oxford University Press.

Braithwaite, V., Ahmed, E., & Braithwaite, J. (2008). Workplace bullying and victimization: The influence of organizational context, shame and pride. *International Journal of Organisational Behavior, 13*(2), 71–94.

Center for Justice and Reconciliation. (2012). Retrieved May 16, 2012, from http://www.restorativejustice.org

Dollar, C. B., & Ray, B. (2015). The practice of reintegrative shaming in mental health court. *Criminal Justice Policy Review, 26*(1), 29–44.

Hiday, V. A., & Ray, B. (2010). Arrests two years after exiting a well-established mental health court. *Psychiatric Services, 61*(5), 463–468.

Hipple, N. K., Gruenewald, J., & McGarrell, E. F. (2012). Restorative, procedural justice, and defiance as predictors of reoffending of participants in family group conferences. *Crime &*

Delinquency. (OnlineFirst version) Retrieved May 16, 2012, from http://cad.sagepub.com/content/early/2011/11/16/0011128711428556

Khey, D.N. (2014). Reintegrative shaming. In J.M. Miller (ed.) *The Encyclopedia of Theorethical Criminology.* Malden, MA: Wiley Blackwell.

Klein, M. (1986). Labeling theory and delinquency policy: An empirical test. *Criminal Justice and Behavior, 13,* 47–79.

Lemert, E. M. (1951). *Social pathology: A systematic approach to the theory of sociopathic behavior.* New York: The Free Press.

Lemert, E. M. (1972). *Human deviance, social problems, and social control* (2nd ed.). Englewood Cliffs, NJ: Prentice Hall.

Miller, J.M. & Khey, D.N. (2017). *Am J Crim Just, 42,* 574. https://doi.org/10.1007/s12103-016-9372-4

Ray, B., Dollar, C. B., & Thames, K. M. (2011). Observations of reintegrative shaming in a mental court. *International Journal of Law and Psychiatry, 34*(1), 49–55.

Schur, E. M. (1969). Reactions to deviance: A critical assessment. *American Journal of Sociology, 75,* 309–322.

Sherman, L. W., Strang, H., & Woods, D. (2000). *Recidivism patterns in the Canberra Reintegrative Shaming Experiments (RISE).* Center for Restorative Justice. Research School of Social Sciences. Australian National University. Retrieved May 16, 2012, from http://www.aic.gov.au/criminal_justice_system/rjustice/rise/recidivism.aspx

Strang, H., Sherman, L. W., Woods, D., & Barnes, G. (2011). *Experiments in restorative policing: Final report on the Canberra Reintegrative Shaming Experiments (RISE).* Retrieved May 16, 2012, from http://www.aic.gov.au/en/criminal_justice_system/rjustice/rise/final.aspx

Tannenbaum, F. (1938). *Crime and the community.* New York: Columbia University Press.

Tyler, T. R. (2006). Restorative justice and procedural justice: Dealing with rule breaking. *Journal of Social Issues, 62*(2), 307–326.

Index

© Springer International Publishing AG, part of Springer Nature 2018
J. Hector, D. Khey, *Criminal Justice and Mental Health*,
https://doi.org/10.1007/978-3-319-76442-9

Printed in the USA
CPSIA information can be obtained
at www.ICGtesting.com
LVHW010938190823
755703LV00005B/70